OFFICIAL PORTRAITS

The Executive Heads of State of the 191 member states
of the United Nations Organisation

trolley

Editorial note

When we started to collect the images shown in this book from embassies, governmental press offices or permanent missions of each of the 191 United Nations Organization member states the responses varied.

Although most countries supplied images by e-mail, some countries sent us posters, some countries sent us books, others took the portrait of their Head of State in the embassy off the wall and sent it to be scanned or suggested to photograph the picture in their offices.

There was however no identifiable pattern to the range of replies we received. Neither the country's size, geographical location, type of government or state of economic development determined the kind of response or the availability of the official portrait.

The decision who constitutes the Head of State in executive power was left to each country. Even if we disagreed with the assessment we have printed their selection.

The countries whose official portrait did not meet our print requirements are in a separate section at the end of the book.

All Heads of State shown were in power on September 13th 2004.

BERLIN PRESS

Fax

Dear Mr. ████████,

Berlin Press is currently preparing the book Official Portraits.
The official portrait of each executive Head of State of the
191 UN member states will be included. Our aim is to show
the diversity in official photography of worldwide leaders.

For this purpose, I ask you to please send a copy of the official
portrait of your head of state in executive power.
(We are looking for the head of state who actually "runs" the country,
e.g. in France it is the President and not the Prime Minister, in Germany
it is the Chancellor and not the President, in Great Britain it is the
Prime Minister and not the Queen.)

Please include their full name and title and the full name of state.
If possible please also include the name of the photographer
so they can be credited.

This image must be a "tiff" or "jpeg" file with a minimum resolution of
300dpi if formatted at 15cm x 20 cm sent by e-mail. (Please note that
we are unable to print your Official Portrait in a lower resolution.)
If you do not have a digital image, a normal photographic print is suitable.

Berlin Press is a publishing company based in Berlin specializing in art and
photography. We will publish a visual record only, no text will be included in
this publication, simply the photograph of each head of state and their
full name and title.

In order for our book to be as up to date as possible we have a fast
approching deadline. The portrait needs to reach us by the
10th of September.

It would be a great disappointment to us if we were unable to
include a state due to not having received the necessary image.
We would greatly appreciate your help and look forward to
hearing from you.

If you have any questions please do not hesitate to contact us.

Yours sincerely

David Brown
(Project Manager)
Berlin Press
London Office
Tel. +44 207 253 0881
Fax.+44 207 336 0800
portraits@berlinpress.net

BERLIN PRESS

Götz und Zwangsleitner Verlagsgesellschaft mbH & Co. KG
Kreuzbergstraße 71   D-10965 Berlin   Deutschland

17-19 Lever Street   EC1V 3QU London UK
T + 44 - 20 - **7253 0881**
F + 44 - 20 - 7336 0800
E info@berlinpress.net

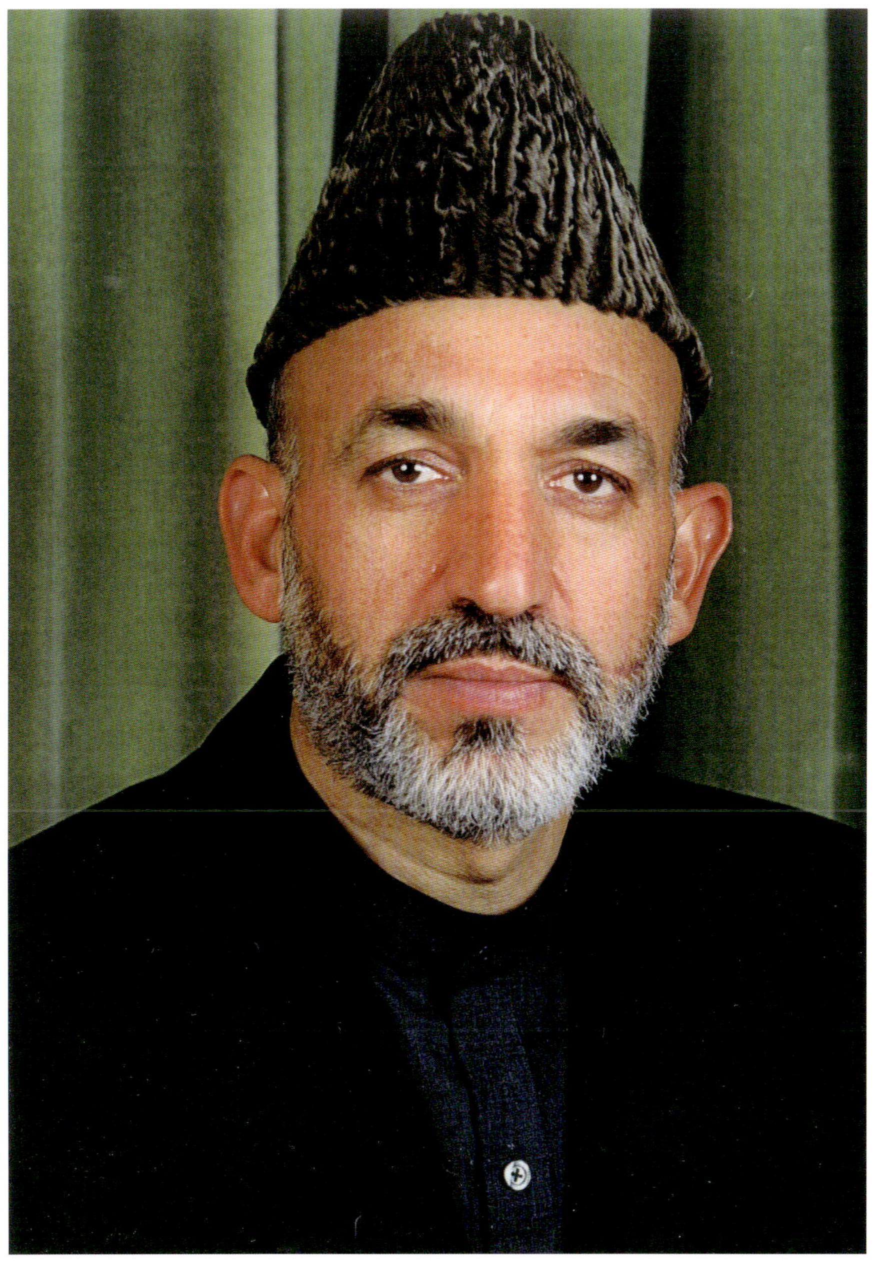

Islamic State of Afghanistan – President Hamid Karzai

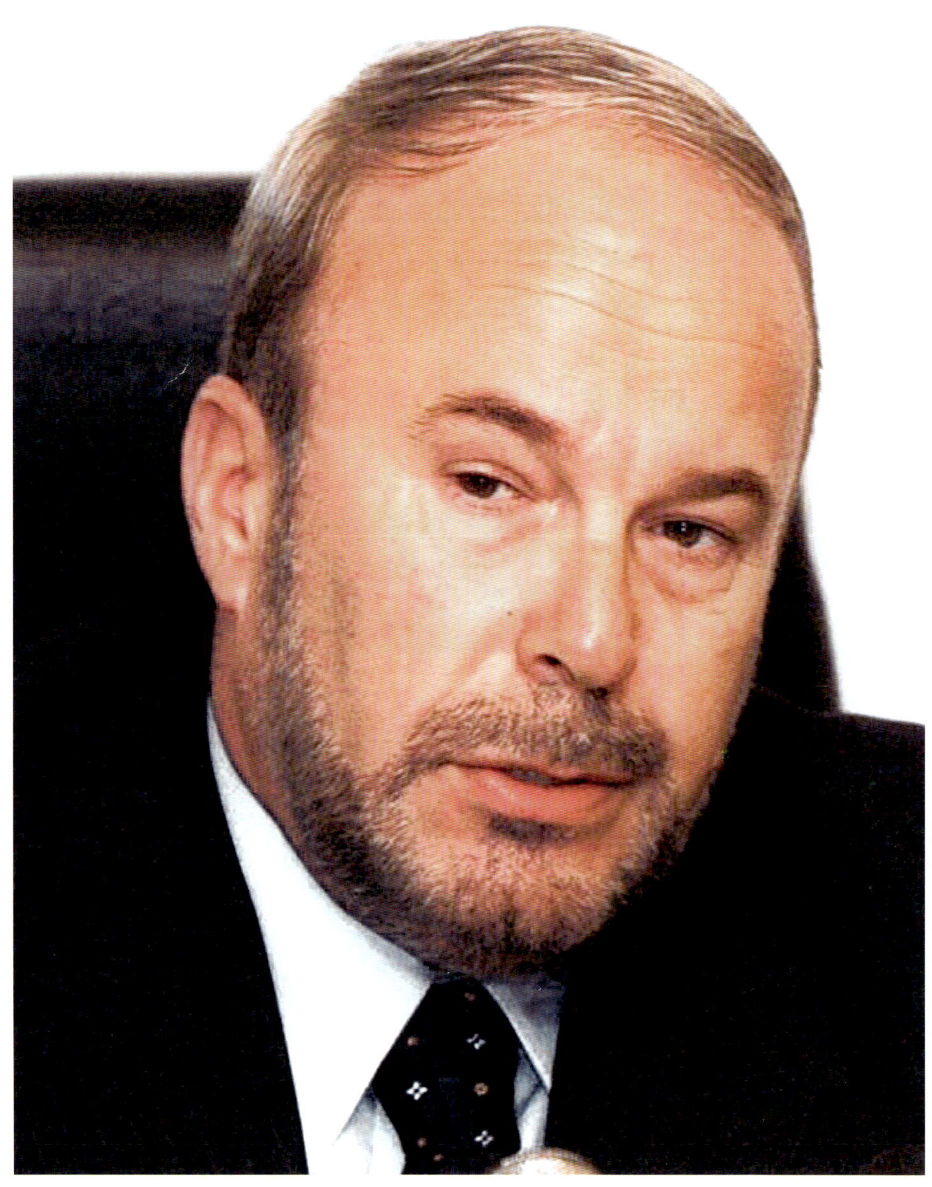

Republic of Albania – Prime Minister Fatos Nano

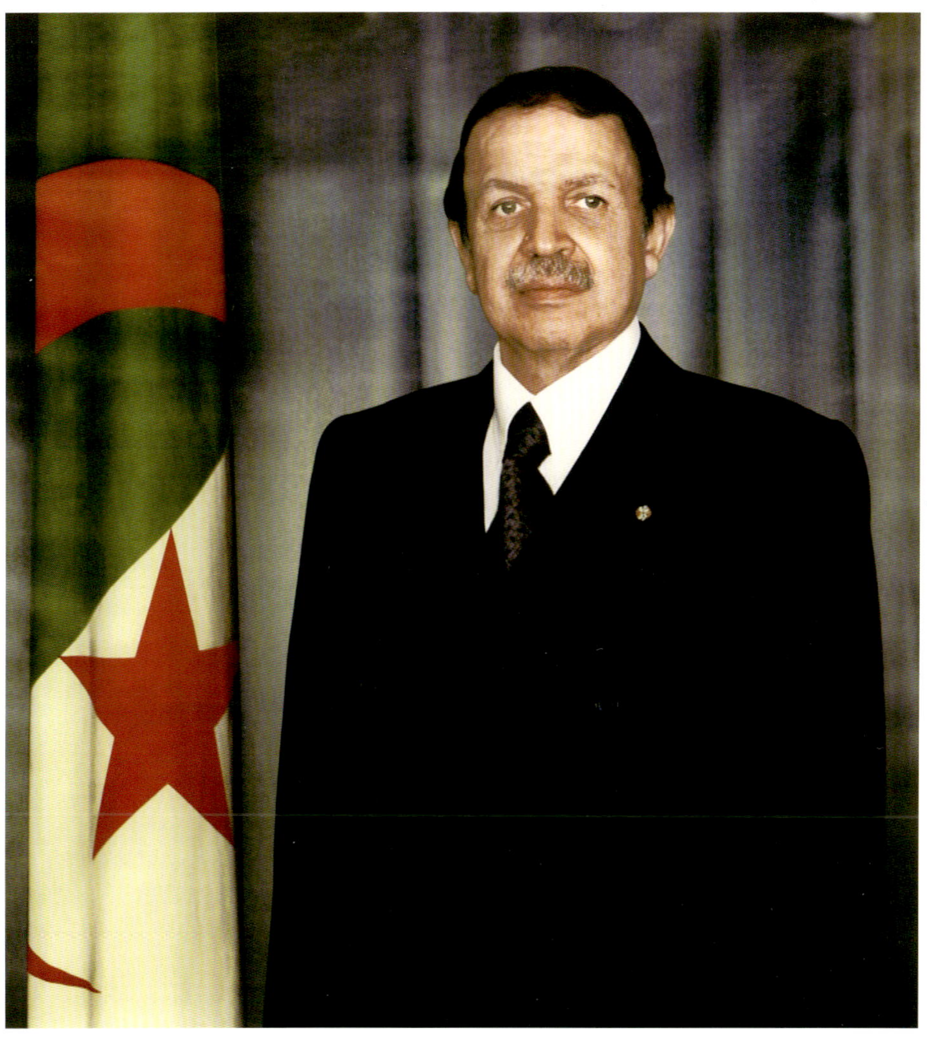

People's Democratic Republic of Algeria – President Abdelaziz Bouteflika

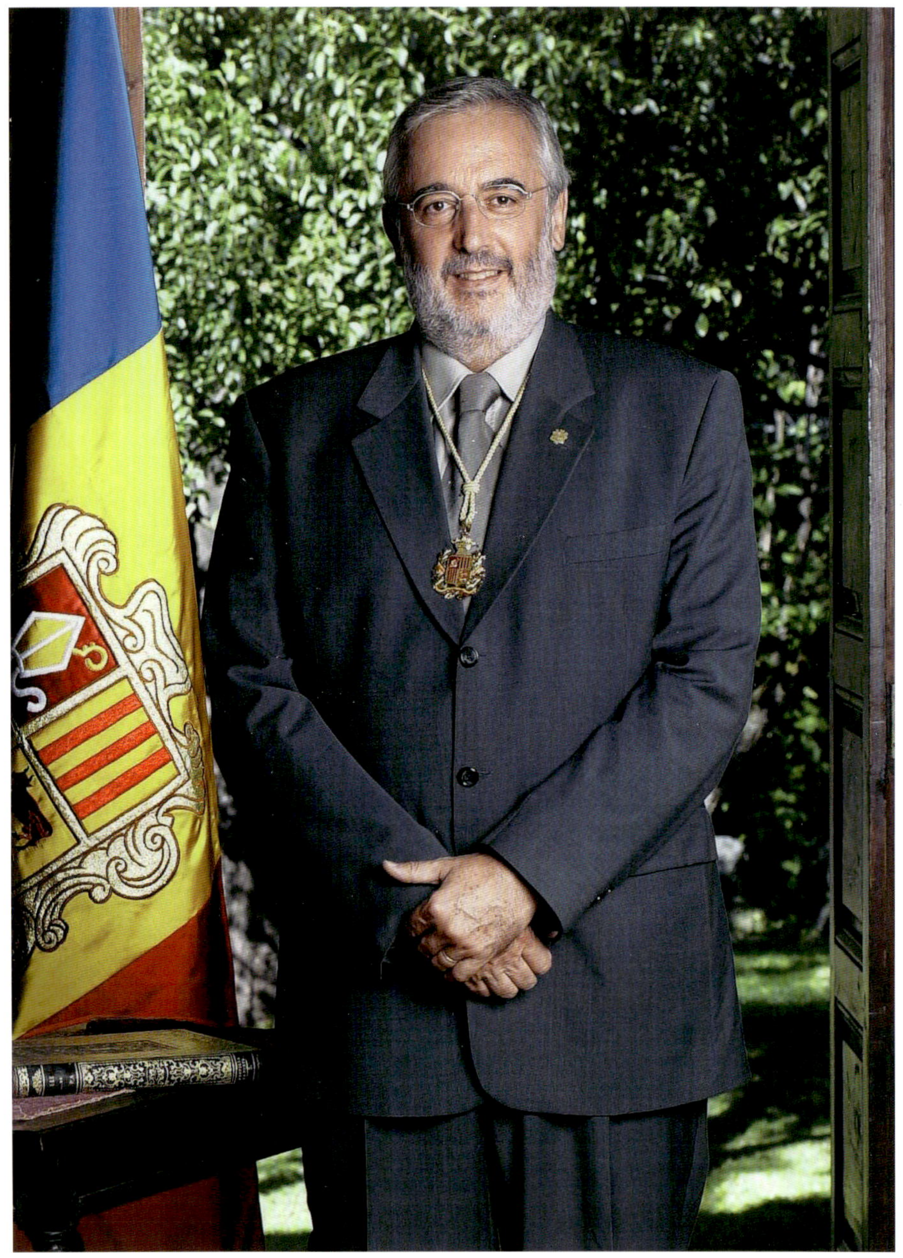

Principality of Andorra – Prime Minister Marc Forné Molné

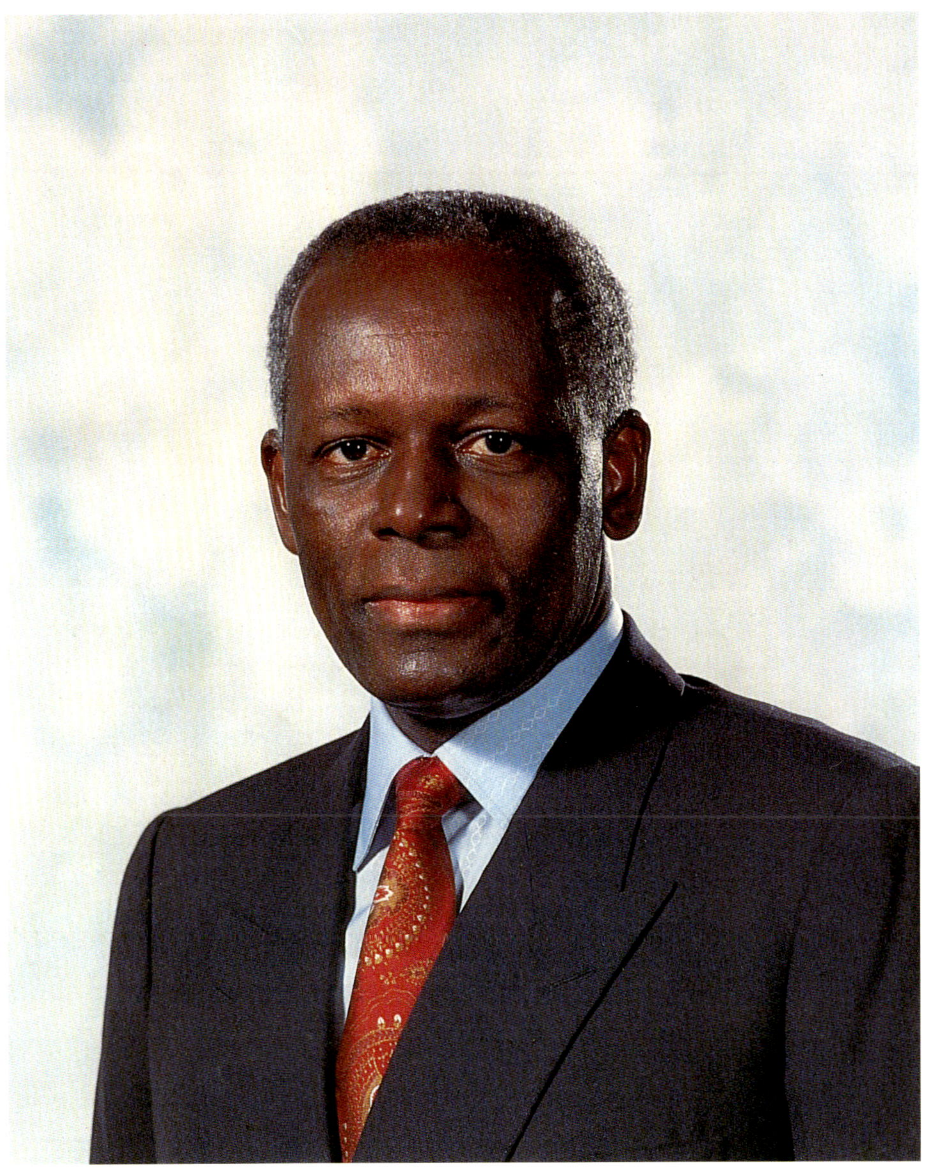

Republic of Angola – President José Eduardo dos Santos

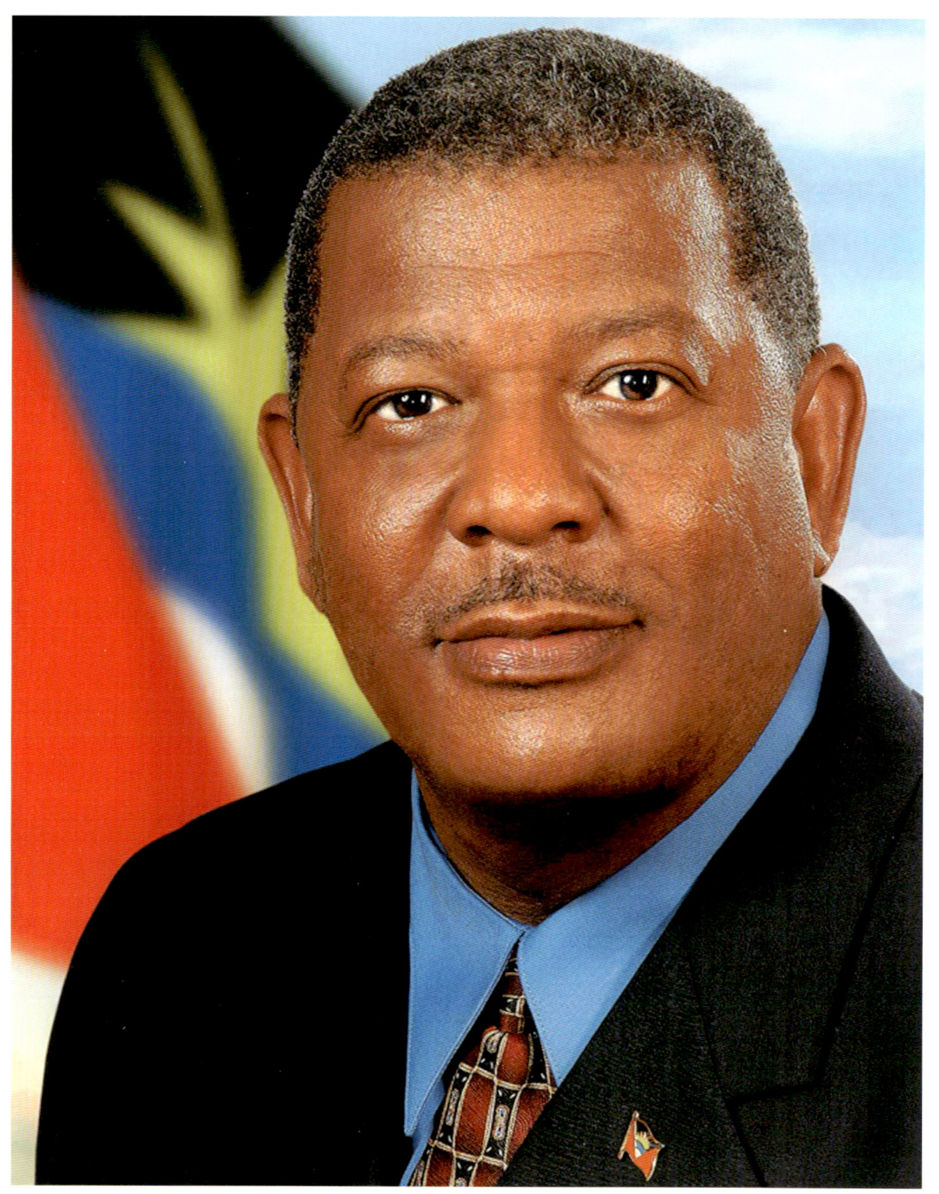

Antigua & Barbuda – Prime Minister Baldwin Spencer

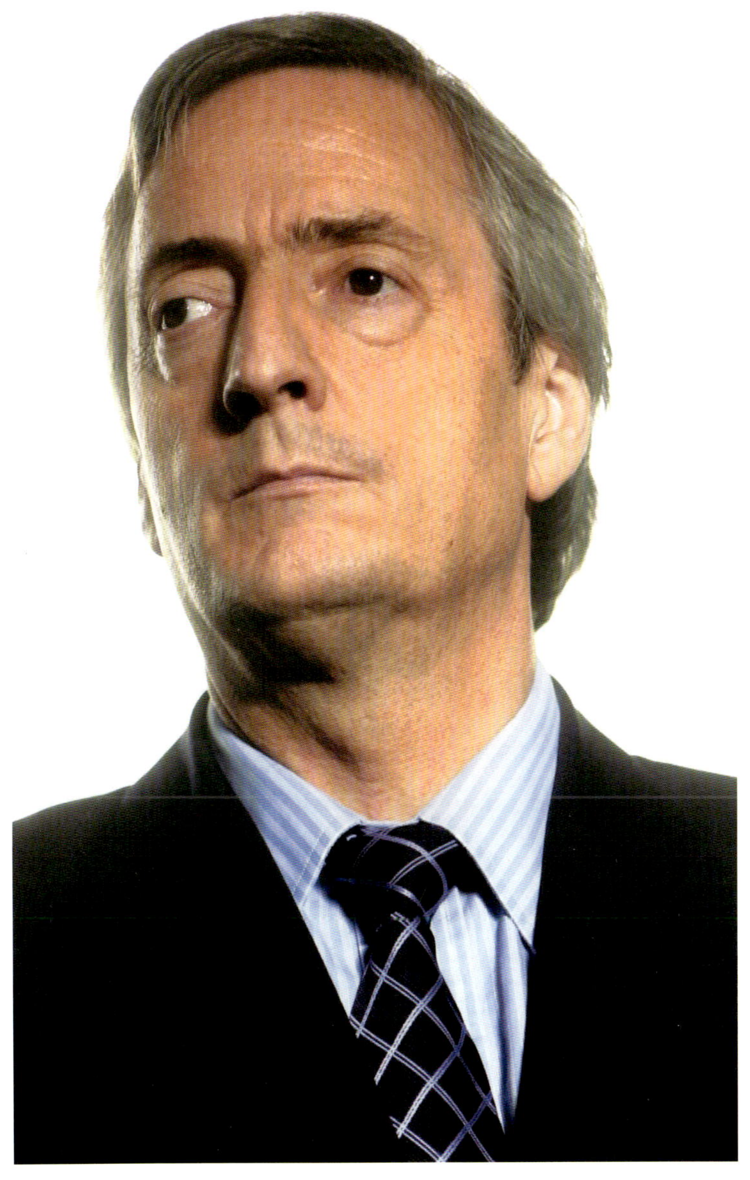

Argentine Republic – President D. Néstor Carlos Kirchner

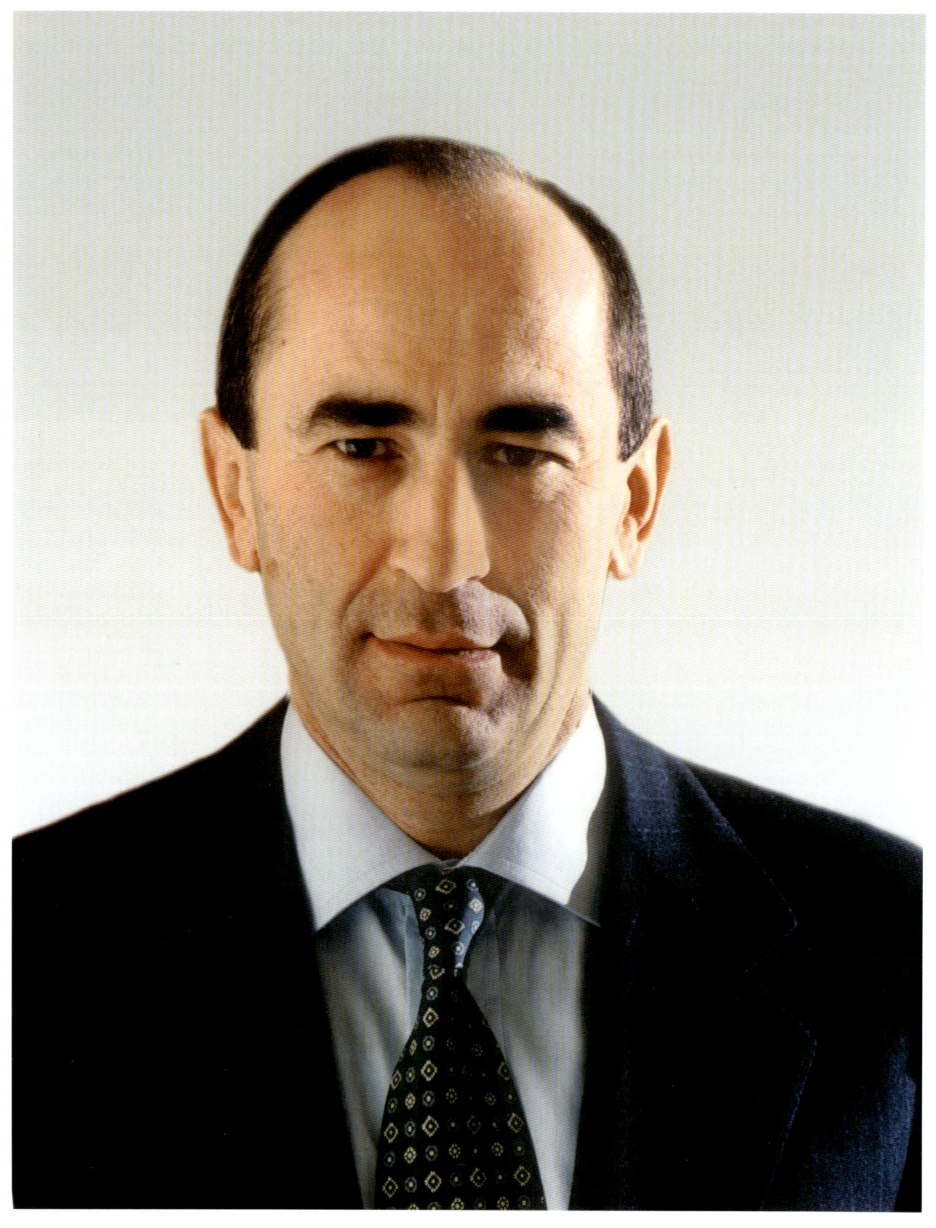

Republic of Armenia – President Robert Kocharian

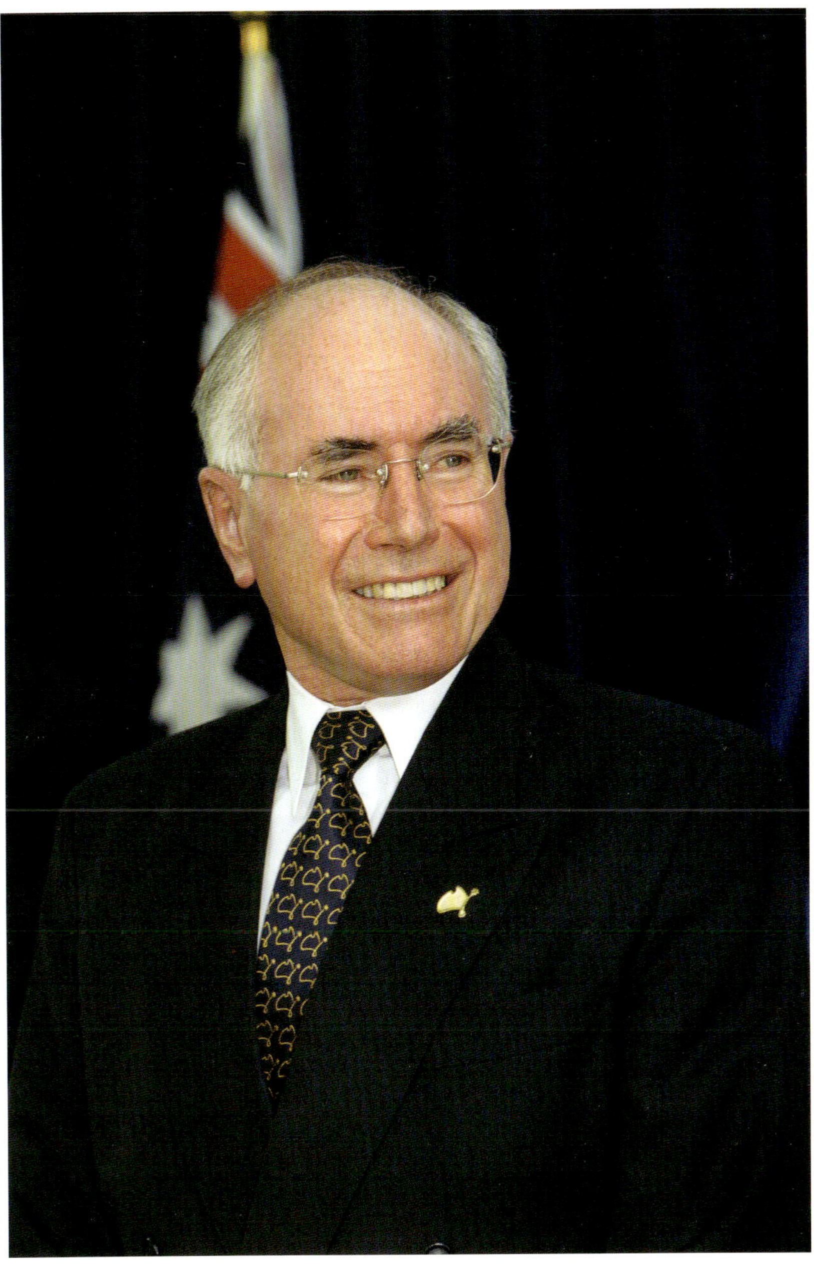

Commonwealth of Australia – Prime Minister John Howard

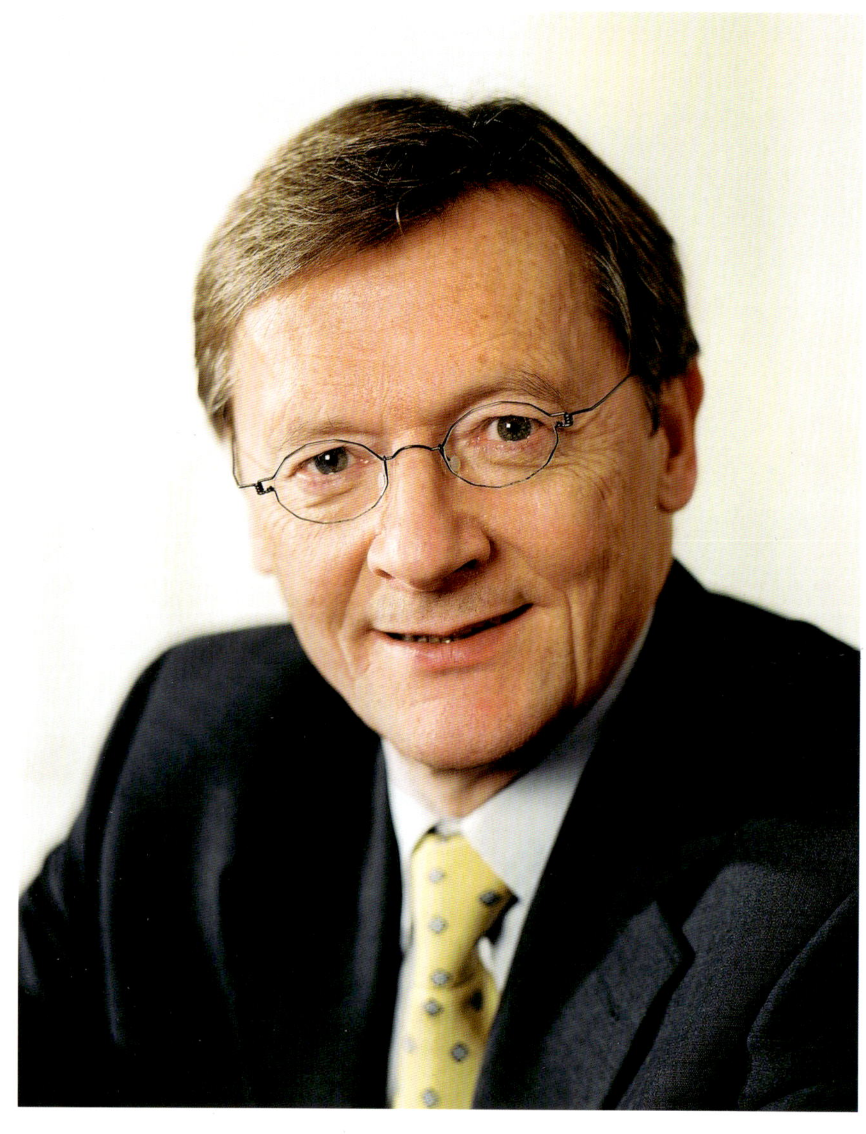

Republic of Austria – Chancellor Wolfgang Schüssel

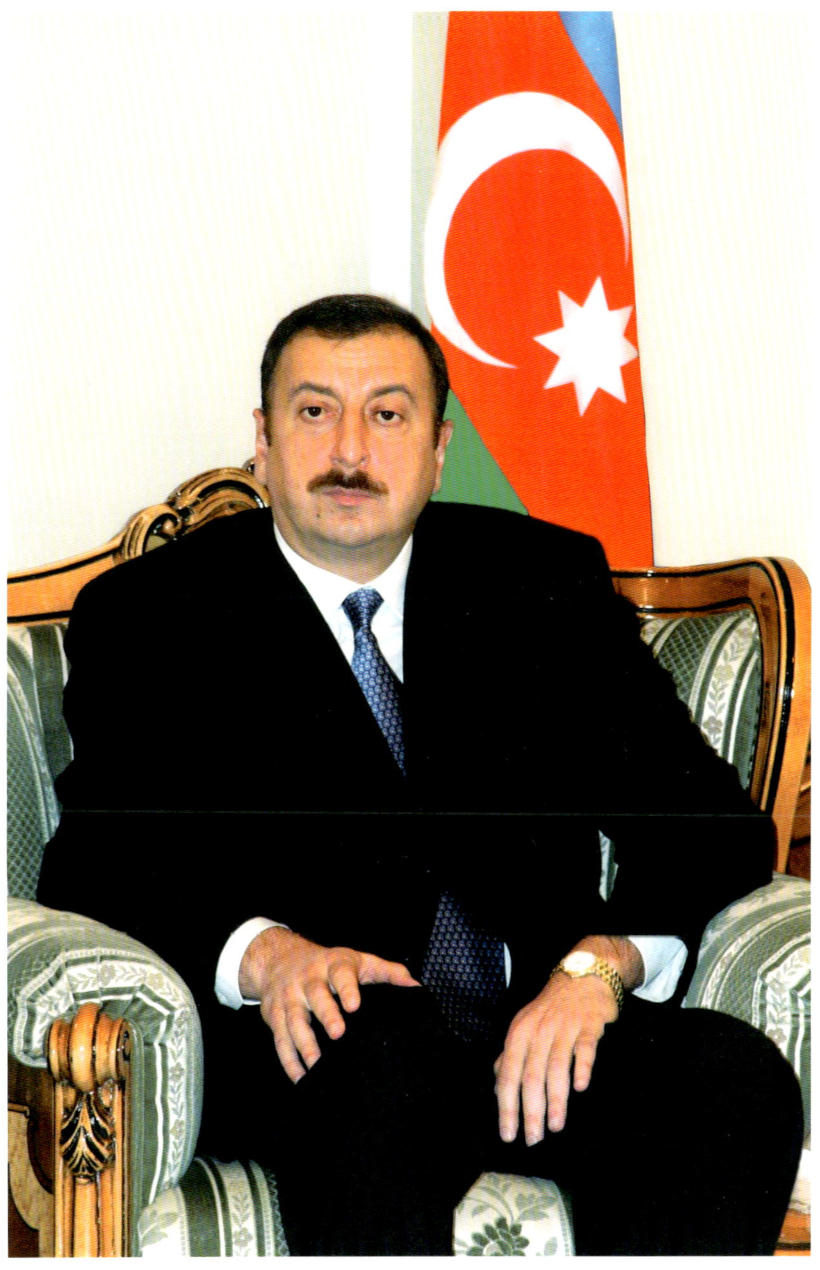

Republic of Azerbaijan – President Ilham Heydar oglu Aliyev

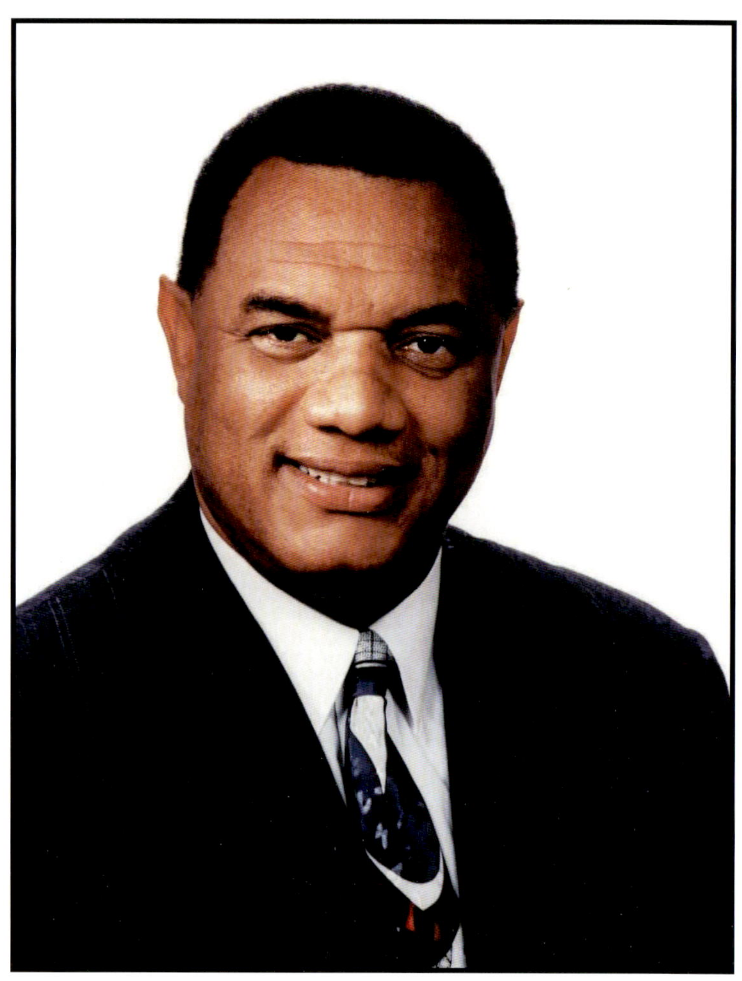

Commonwealth of The Bahamas – Prime Minister Perry G. Christie

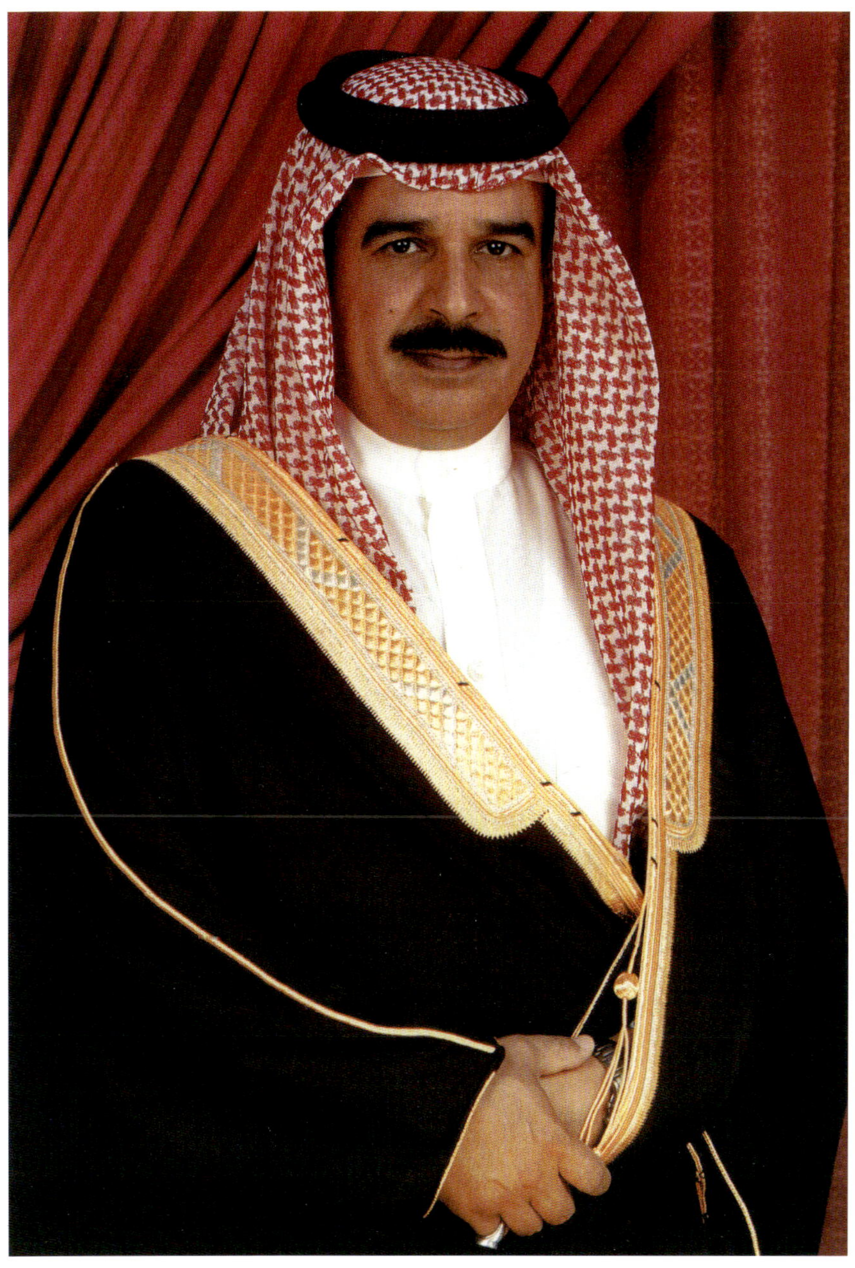

Kingdom of Bahrain – King Hamad Bin Isa Al-Khalifa

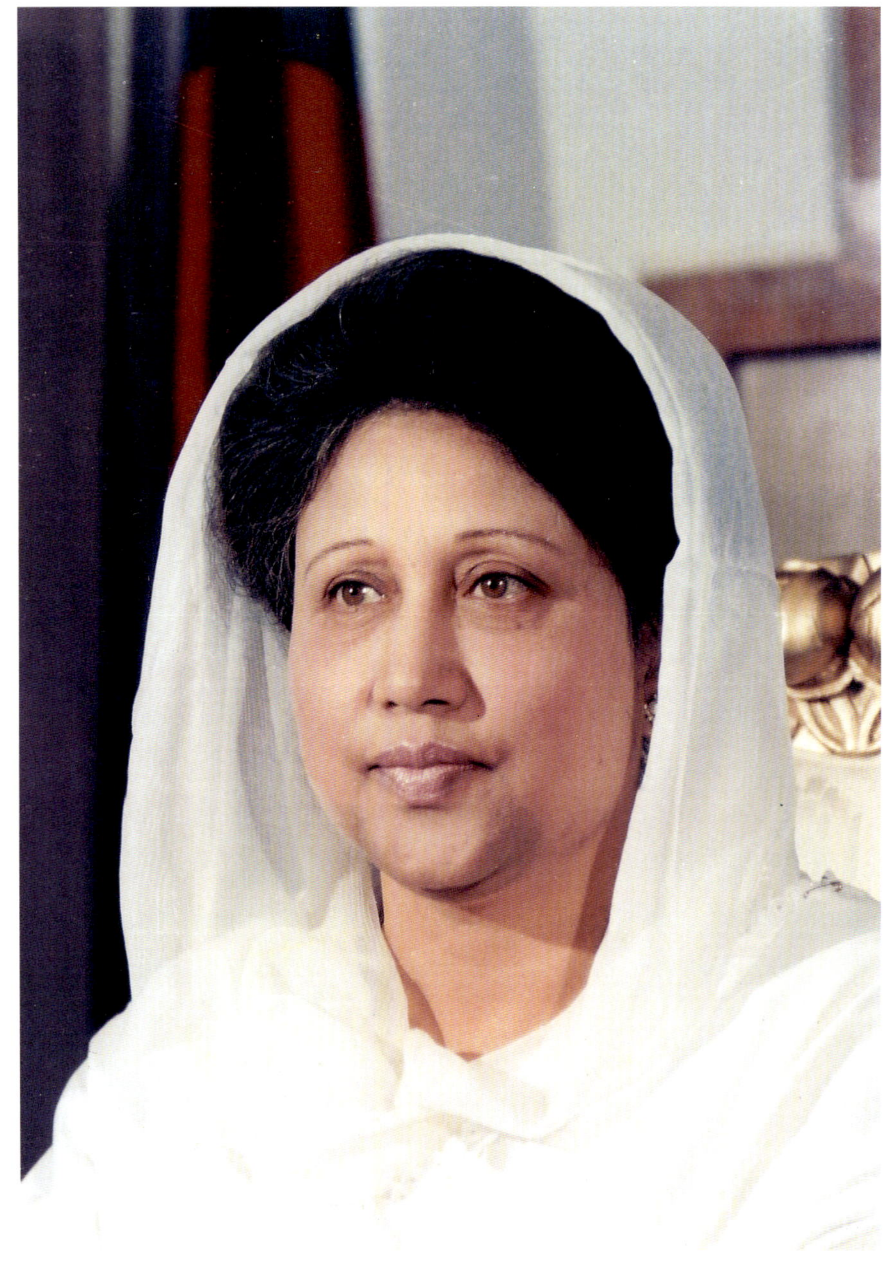

The People's Republic of Bangladesh – Prime Minister Begum Khaleda Zia

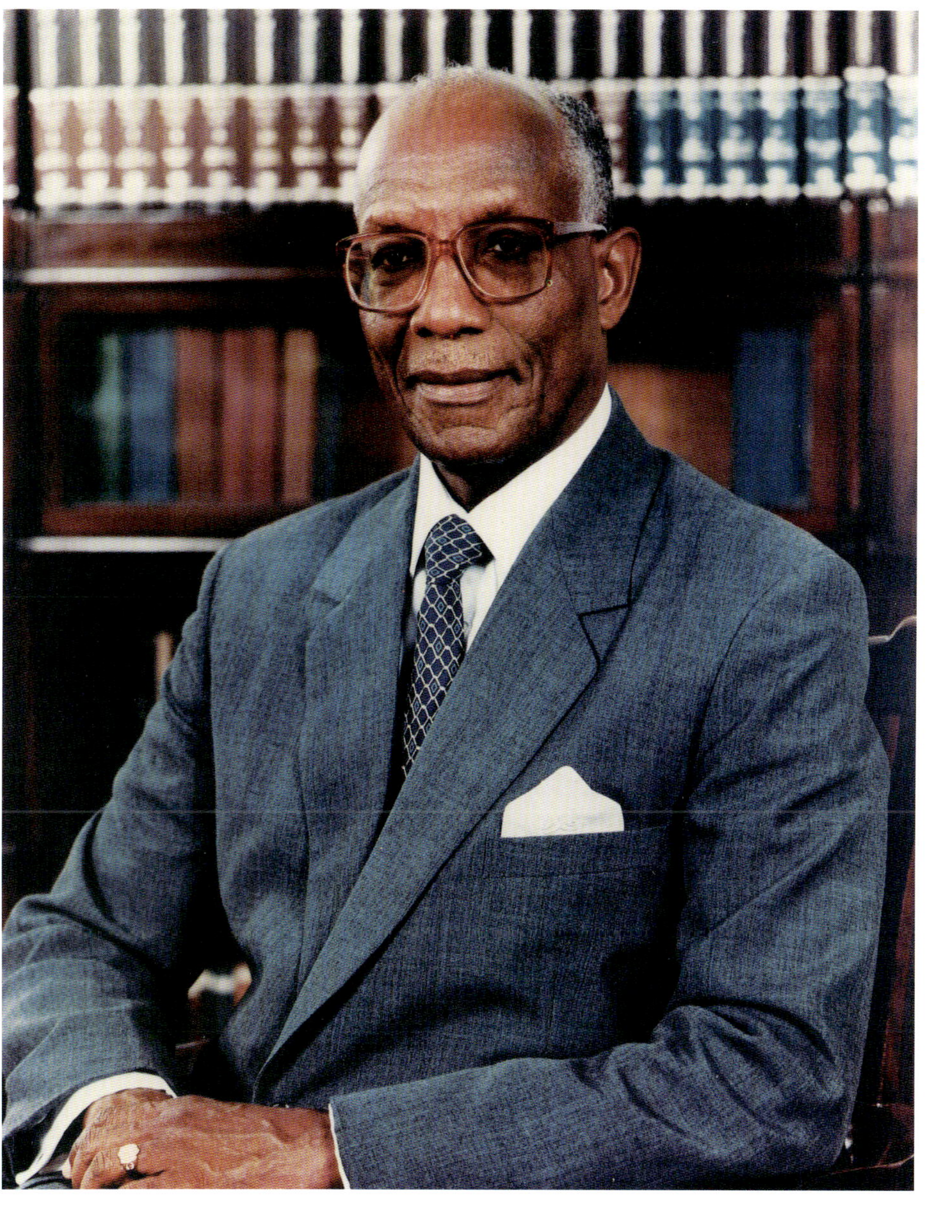

Barbados – Governor General Sir Clifford Straughn Husbands

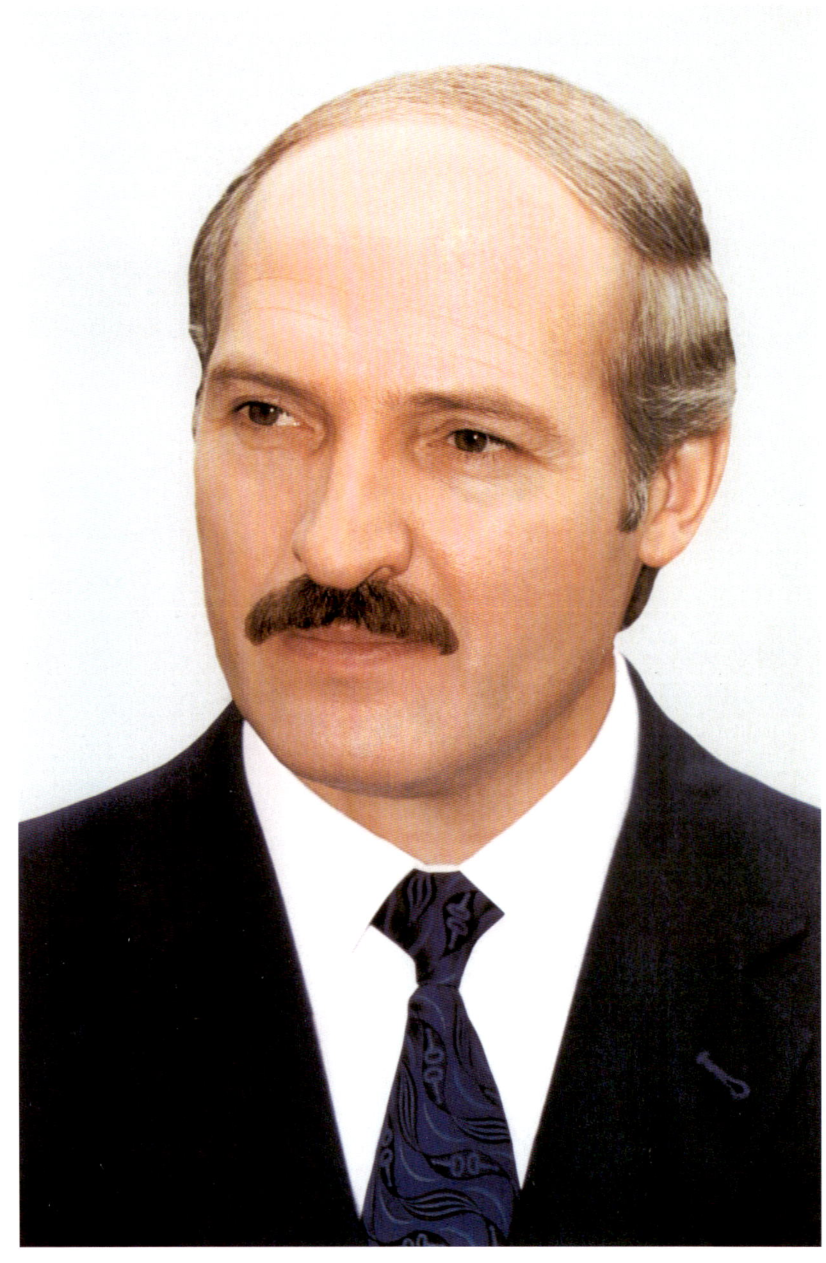

Republic of Belarus – President Alexander Lukashenko

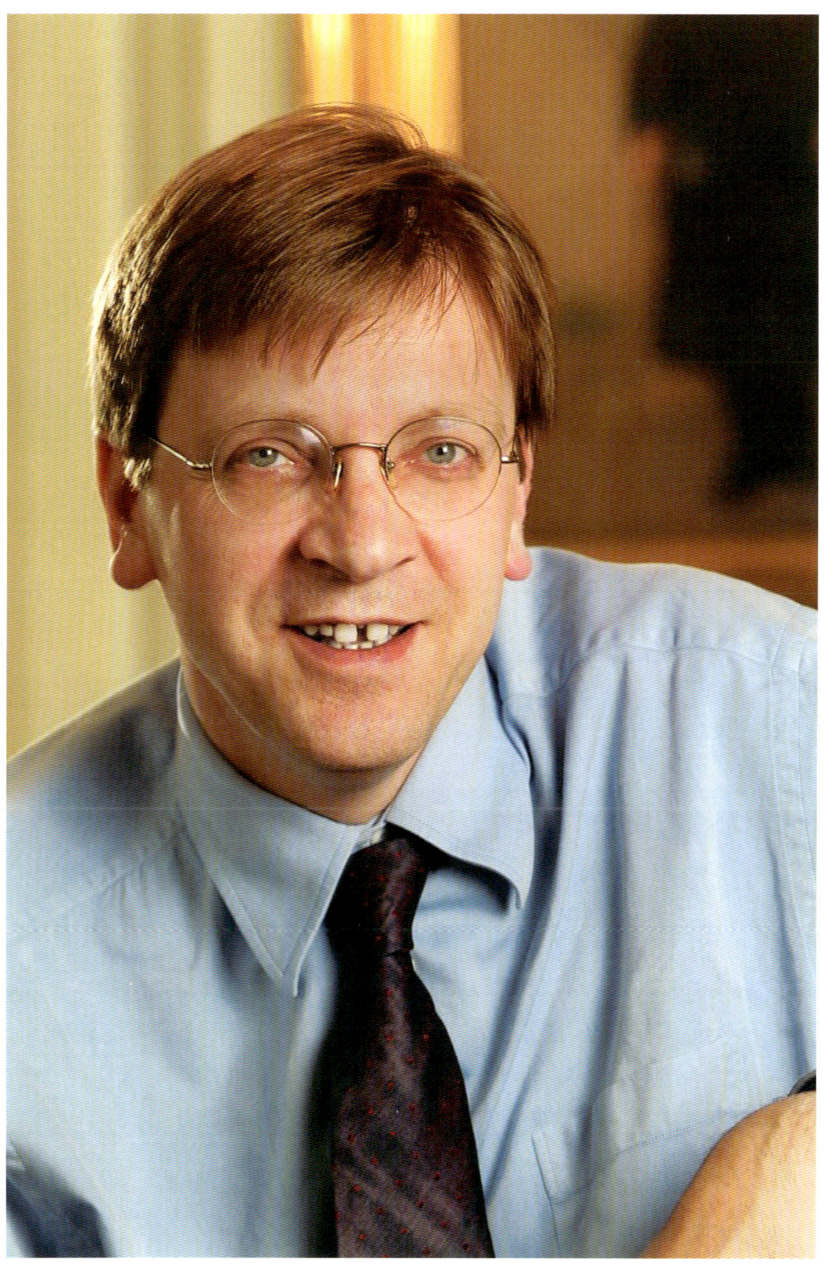

Kingdom of Belgium – Prime Minister Guy Verhofstadt

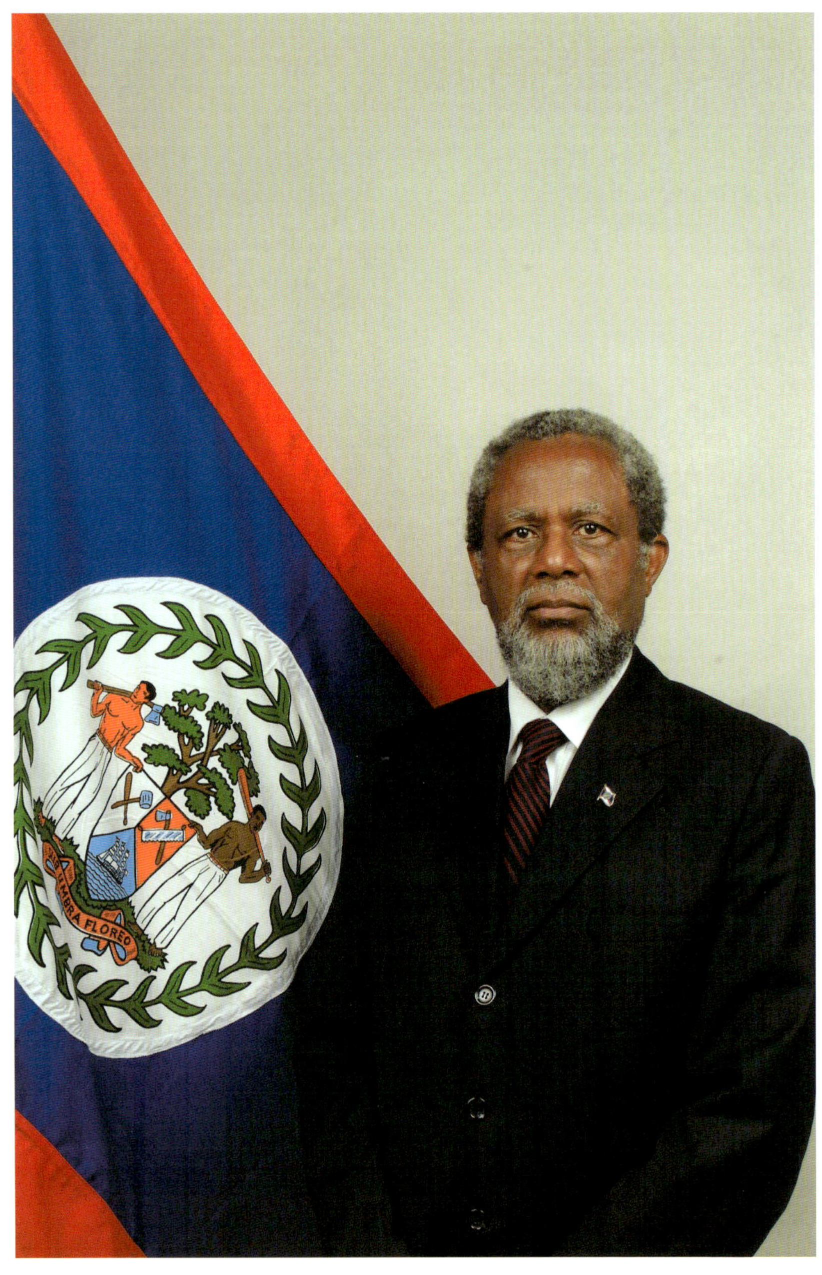

Belize – Governor General Sir Colville Young, Sr.

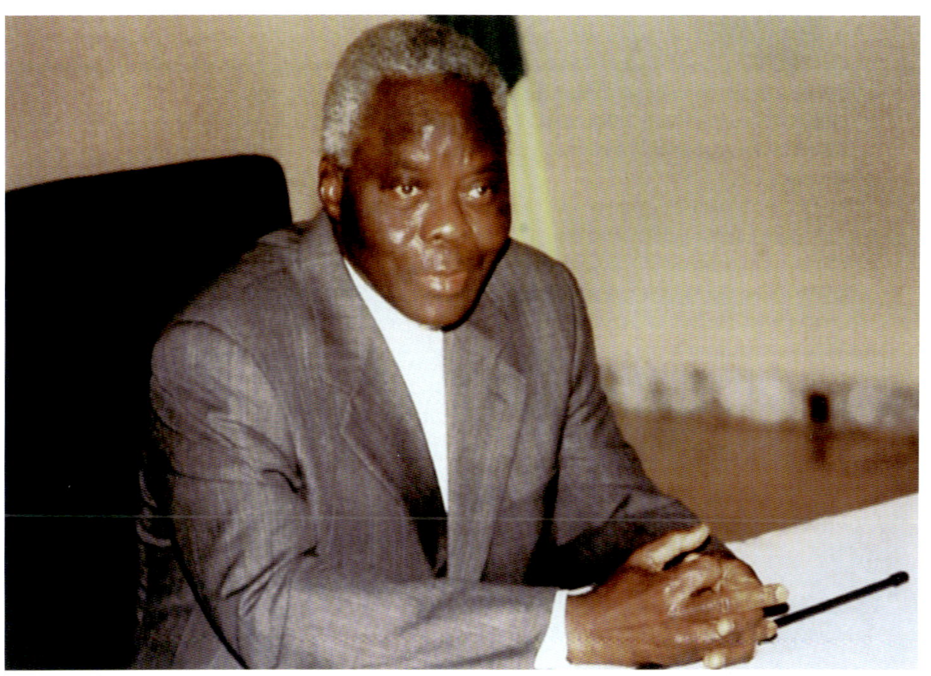

Republic of Benin – President Mathieu Kérékou

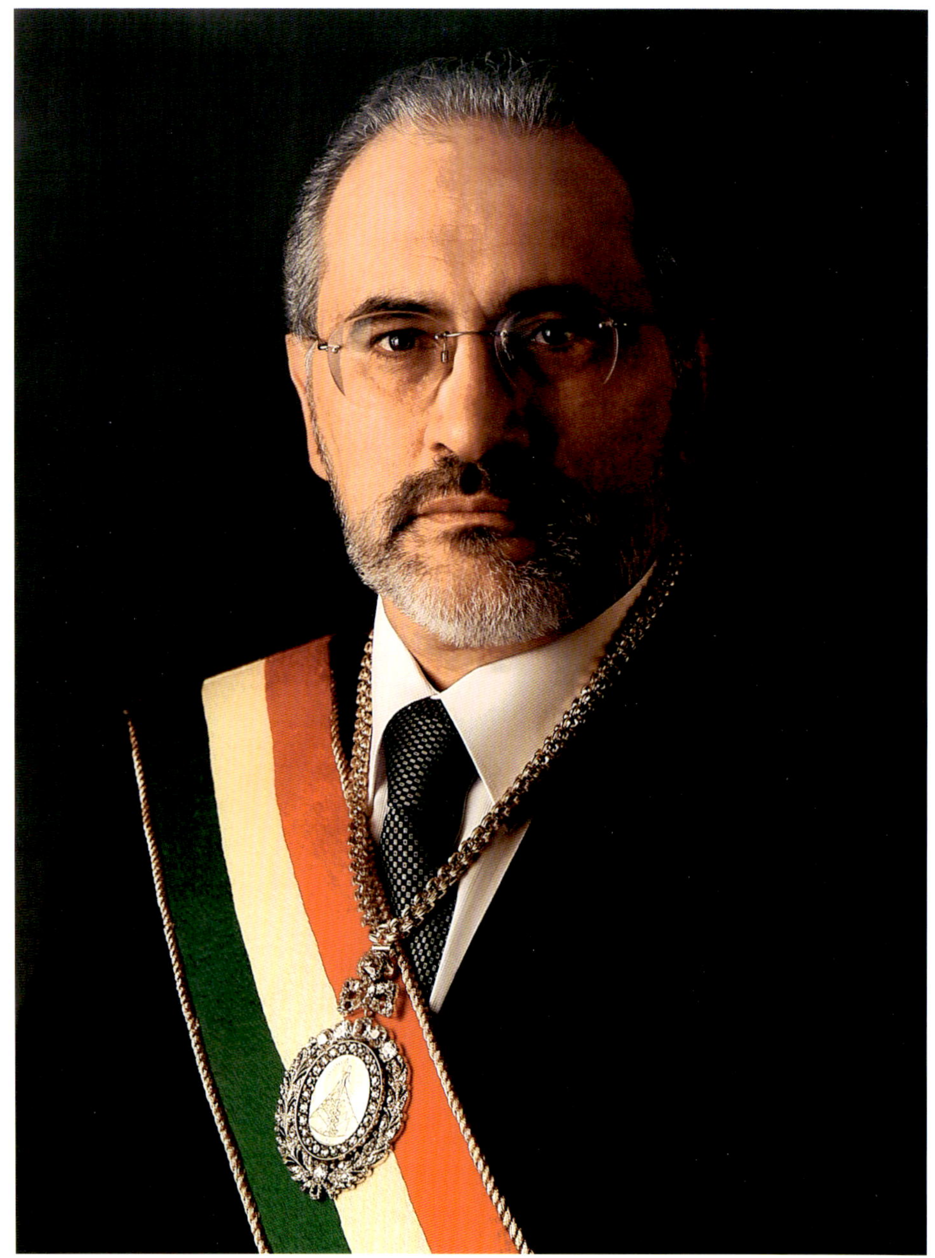

Republic of Bolivia – President Carlos D. Mesa Gisbert

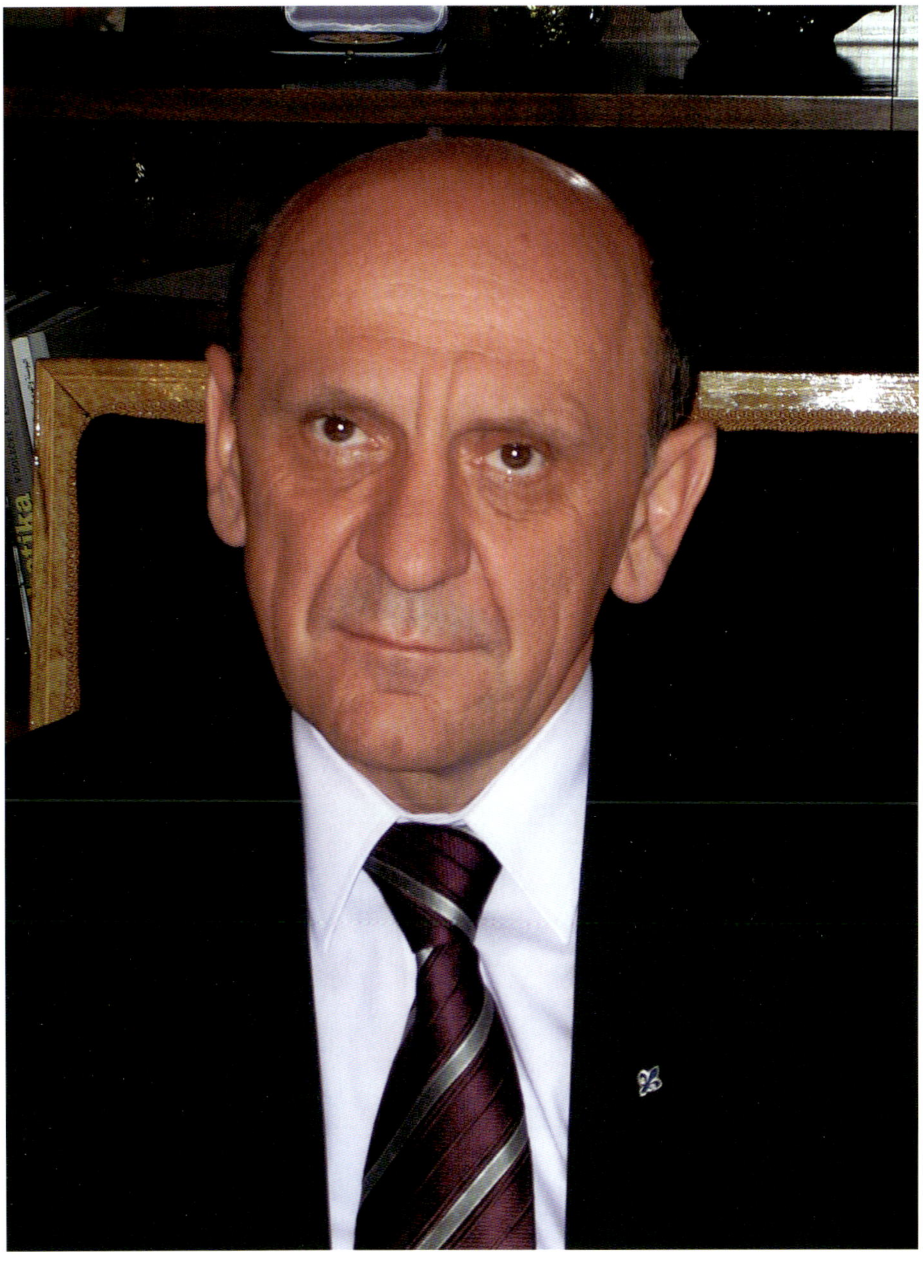

Bosnia & Herzegovina – Chairman of the Presidency Sulejman Tihić

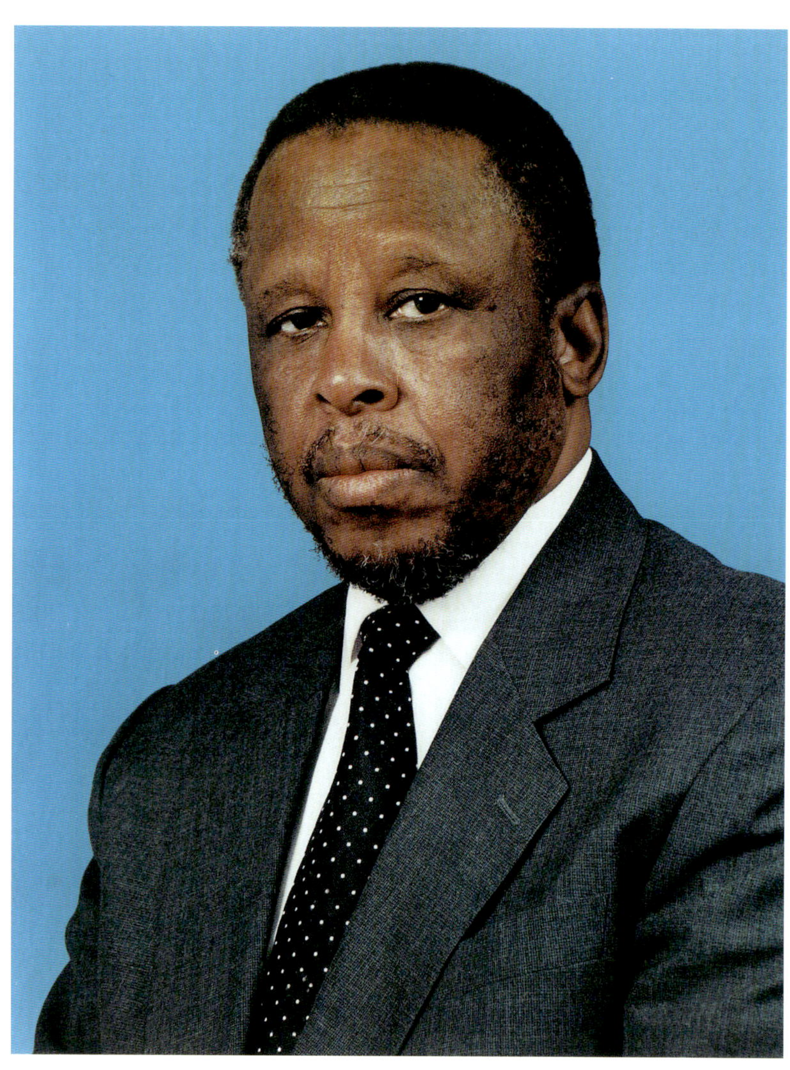

Republic of Botswana – President Festus Gontebanye Mogae

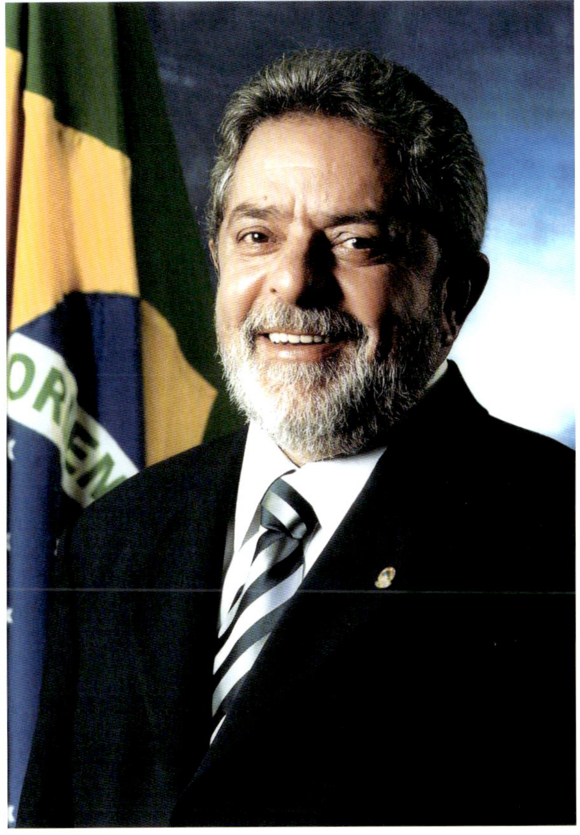

Federative Republic of Brazil – President Luiz Inácio 'Lula' da Silva

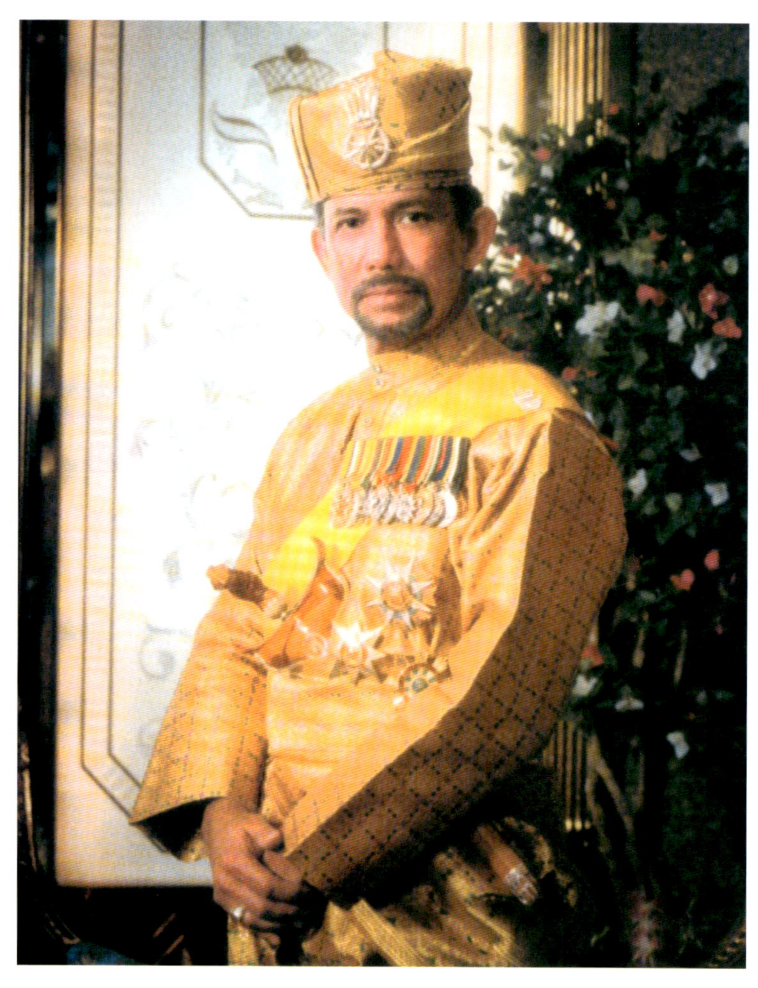

Brunei – Sultan Haji Hassanal Bolkiah Mu'izzaddin Waddaulah,
Sultan and Yang Di Pertuan of Brunei Darussalam

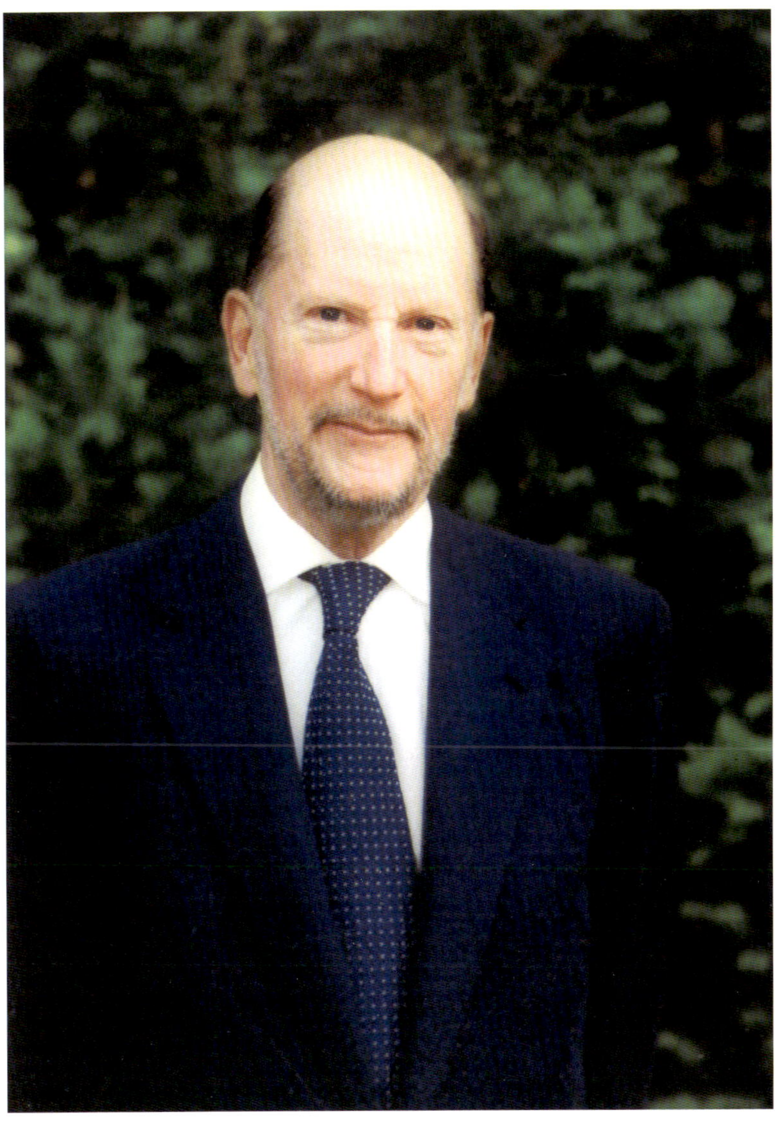

Republic of Bulgaria – Prime Minister Simeon Saxe-Coburg

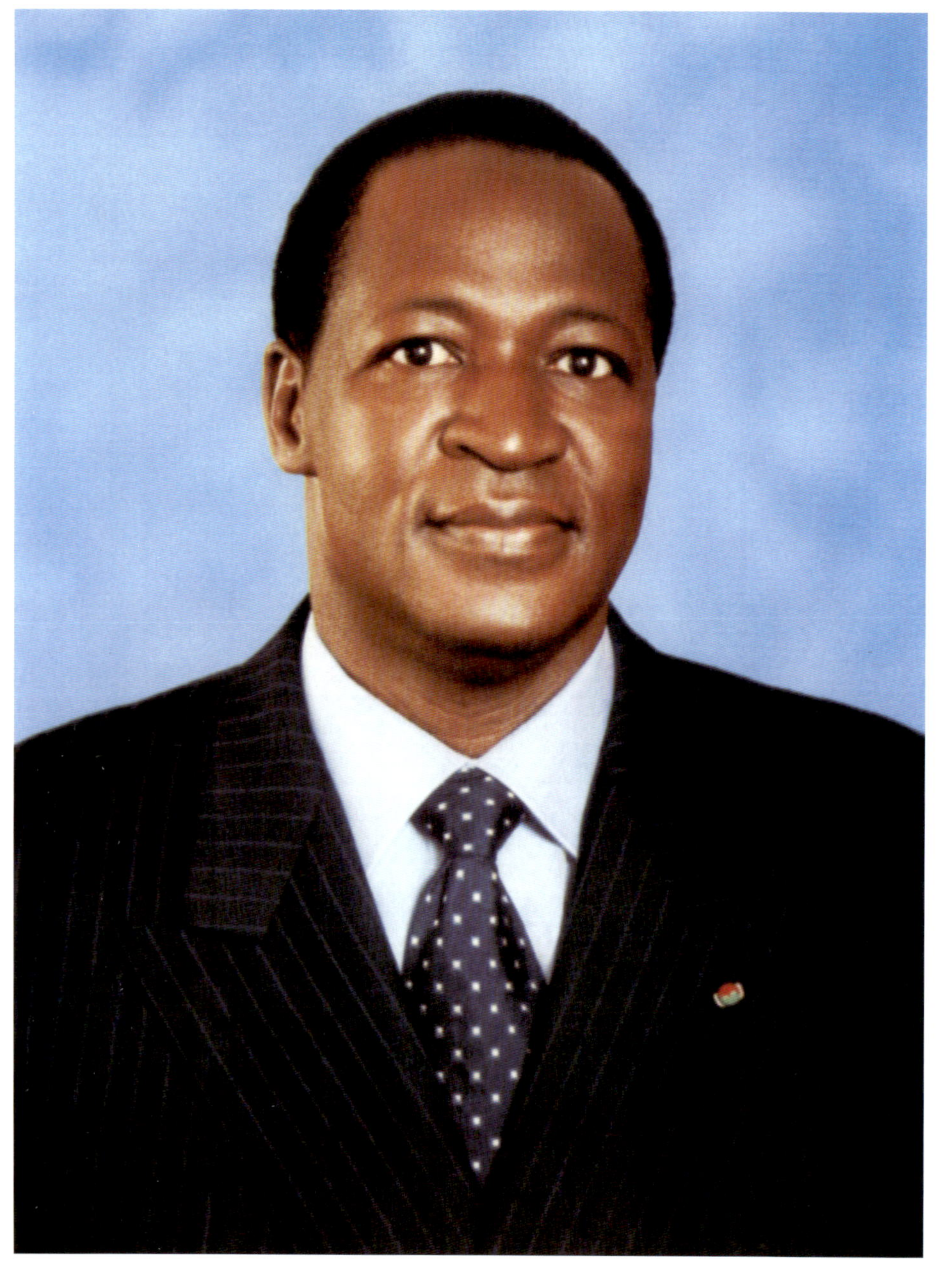

Burkina Faso – President Blaise Compaoré

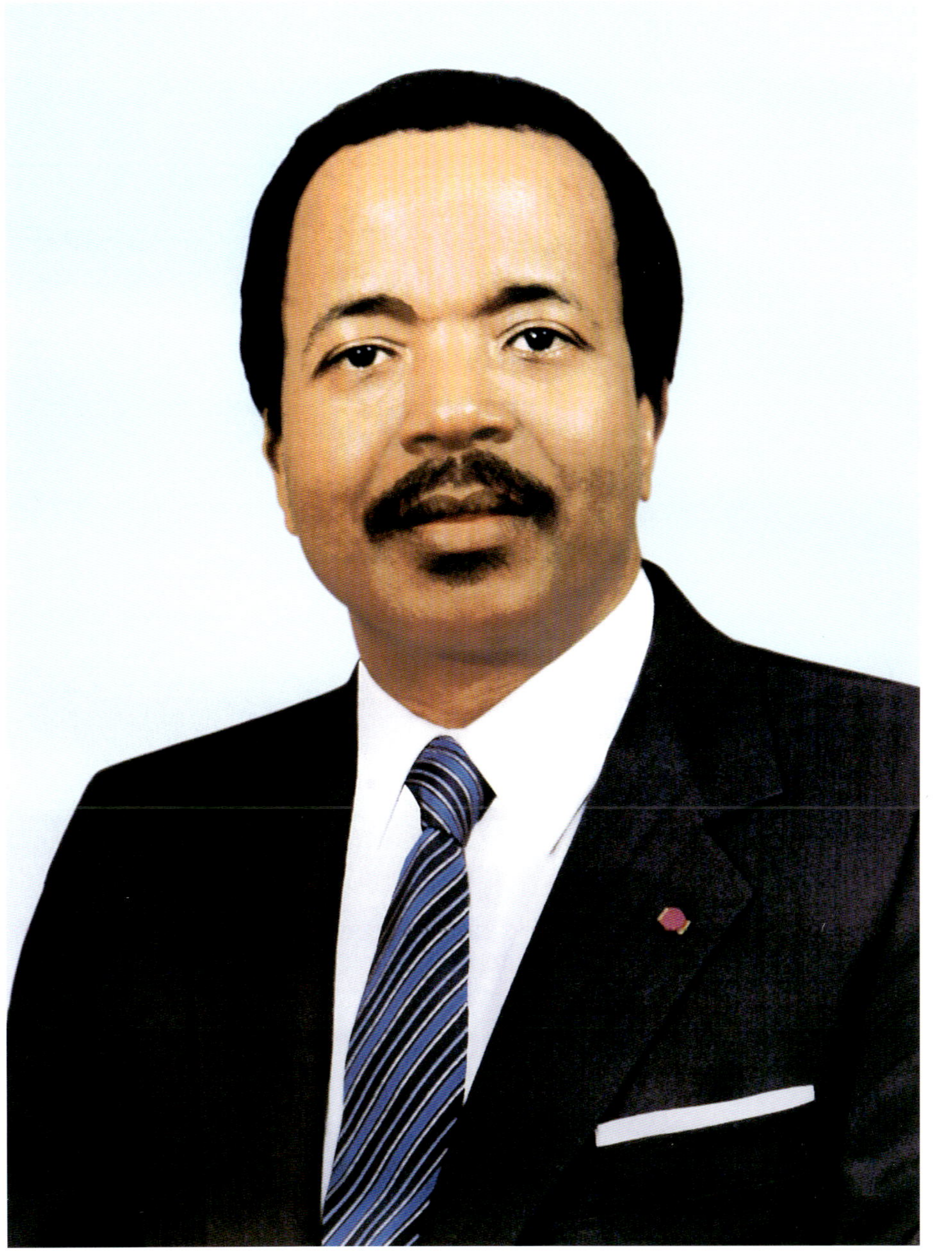

Republic of Cameroon – President Paul Biya

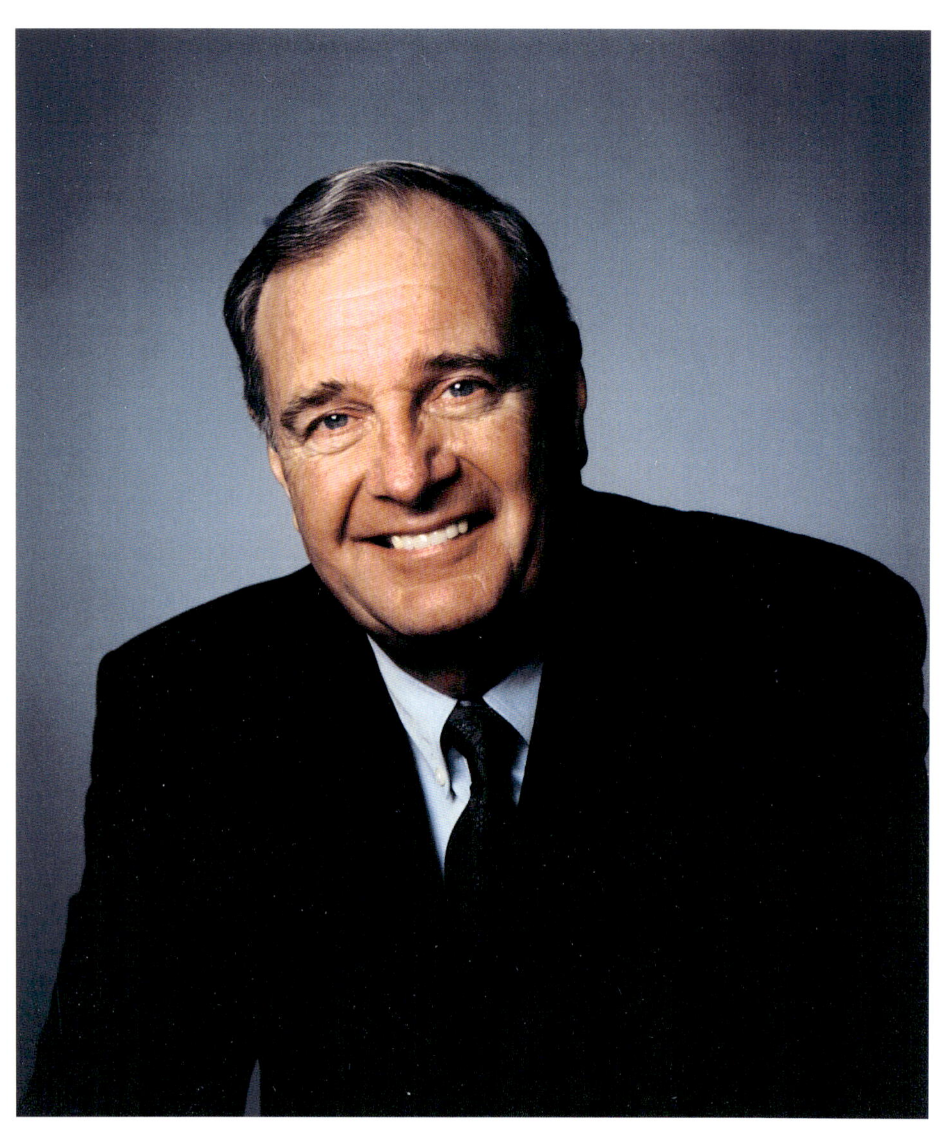

Canada – Prime Minister Paul Martin

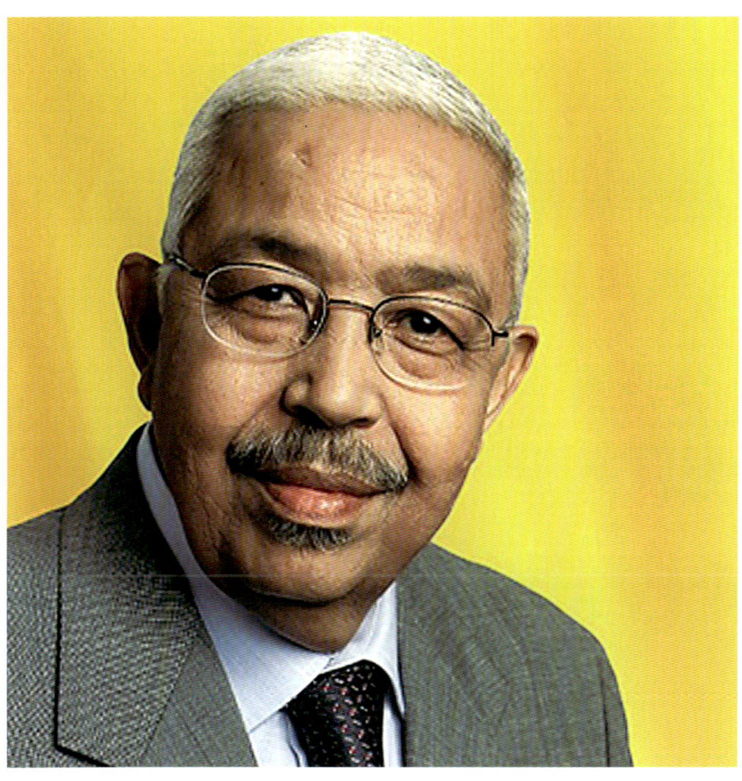

Republic of Cape Verde – President Pedro Pires

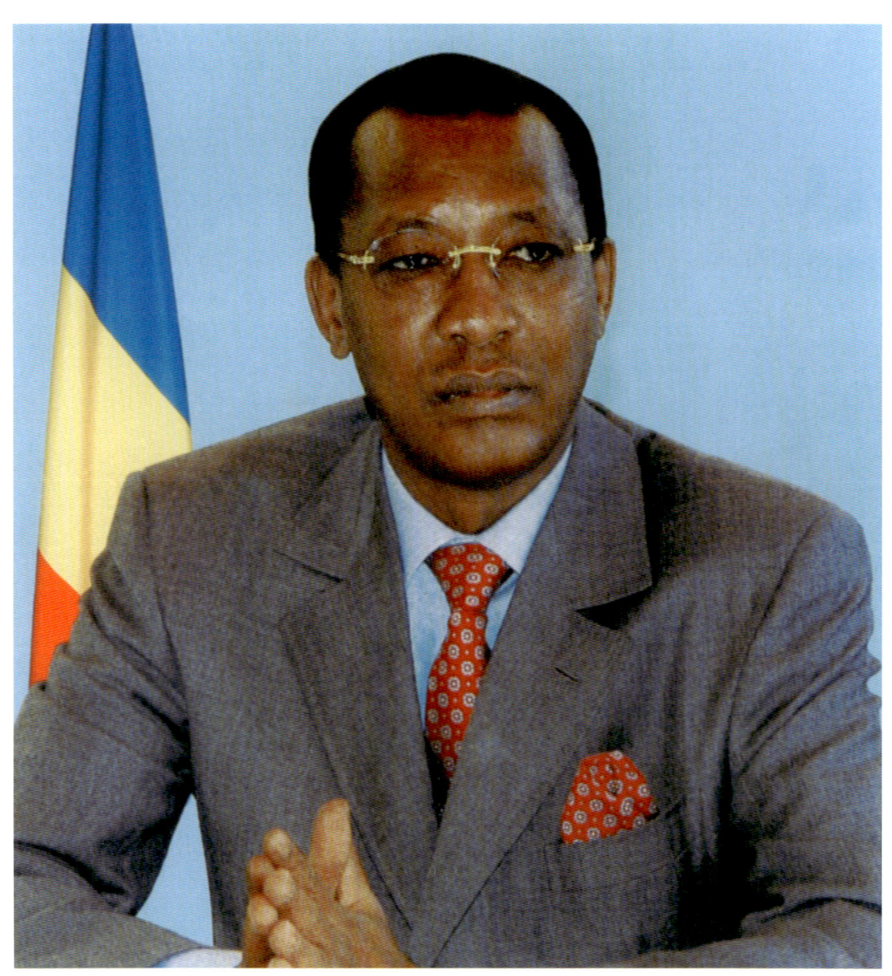

Republic of Chad – President Idriss Déby

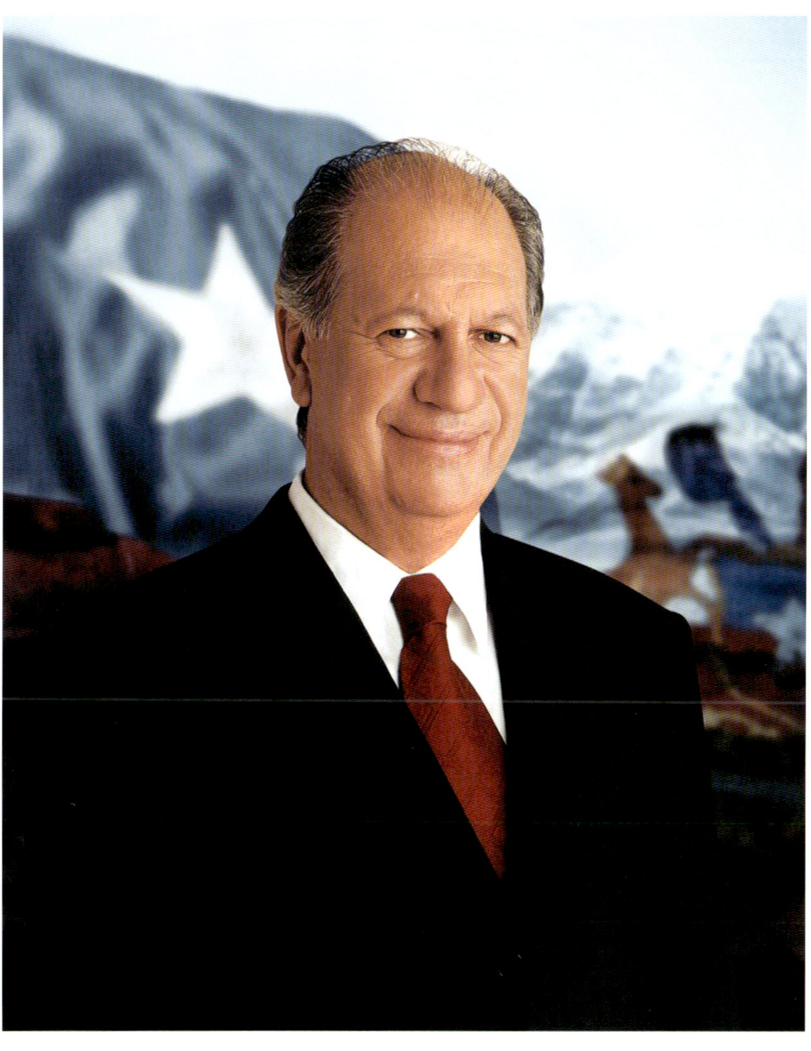

Republic of Chile – President Ricardo Lagos

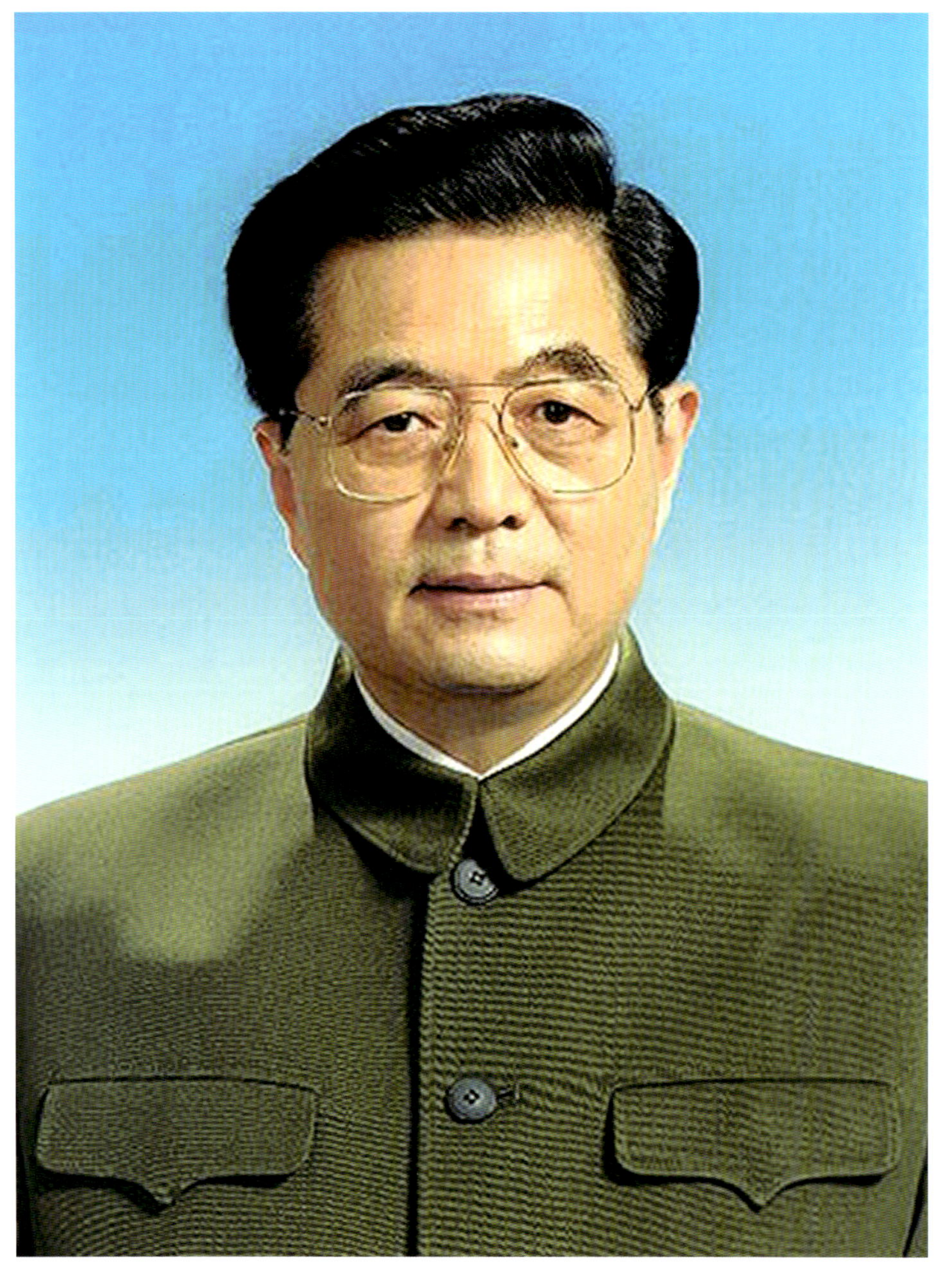

People's Republic of China – President Hu Jintao

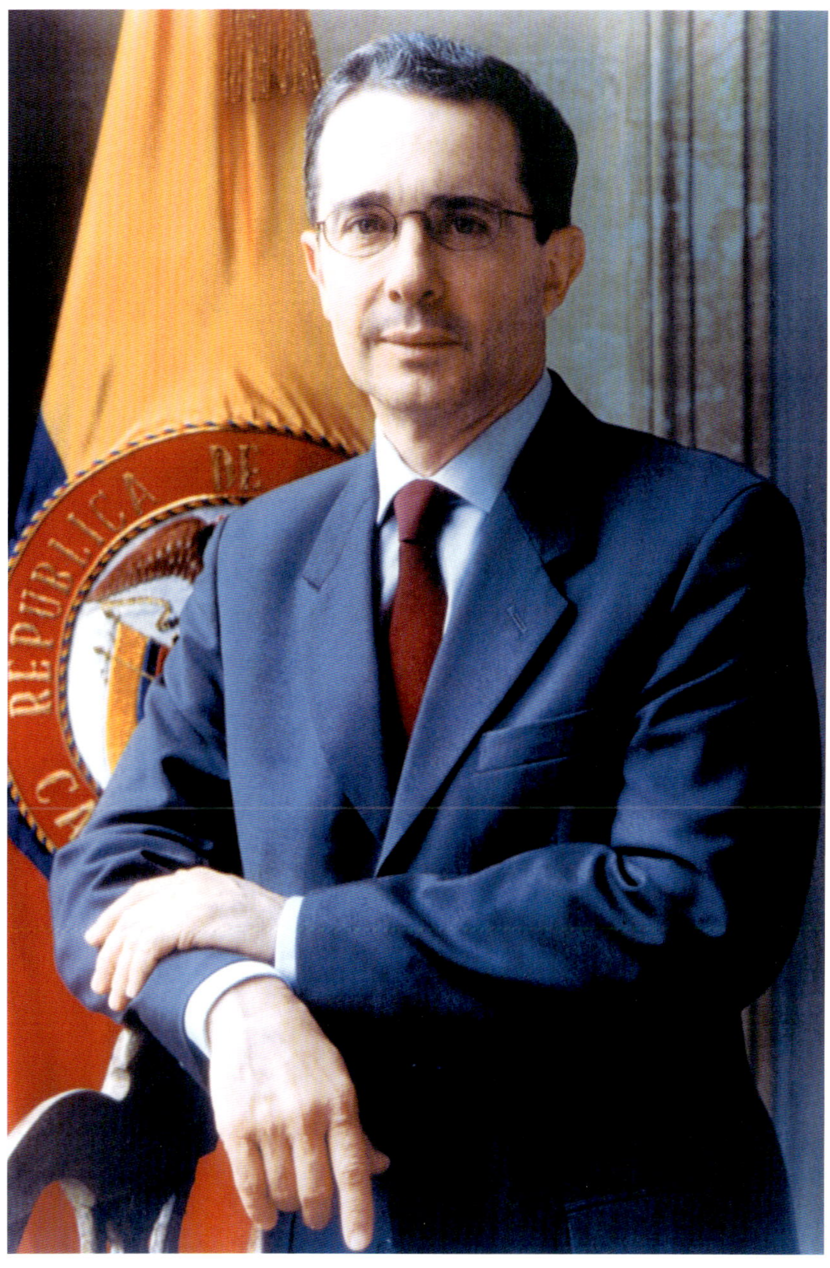

Republic of Colombia – President Alvaro Uribe Vélez

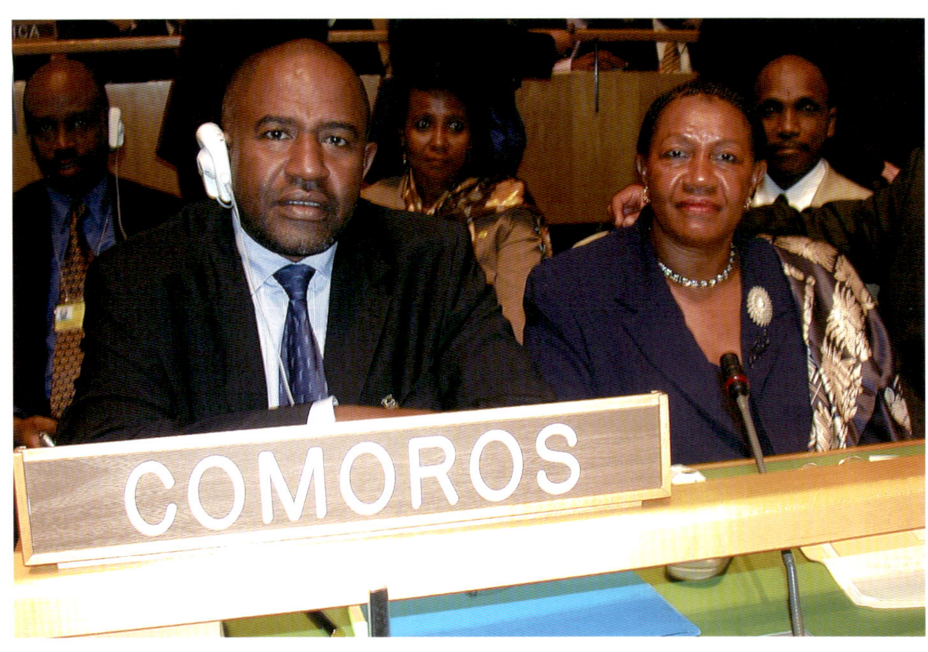

Federal and Islamic Republic of the Comoros – President Azali

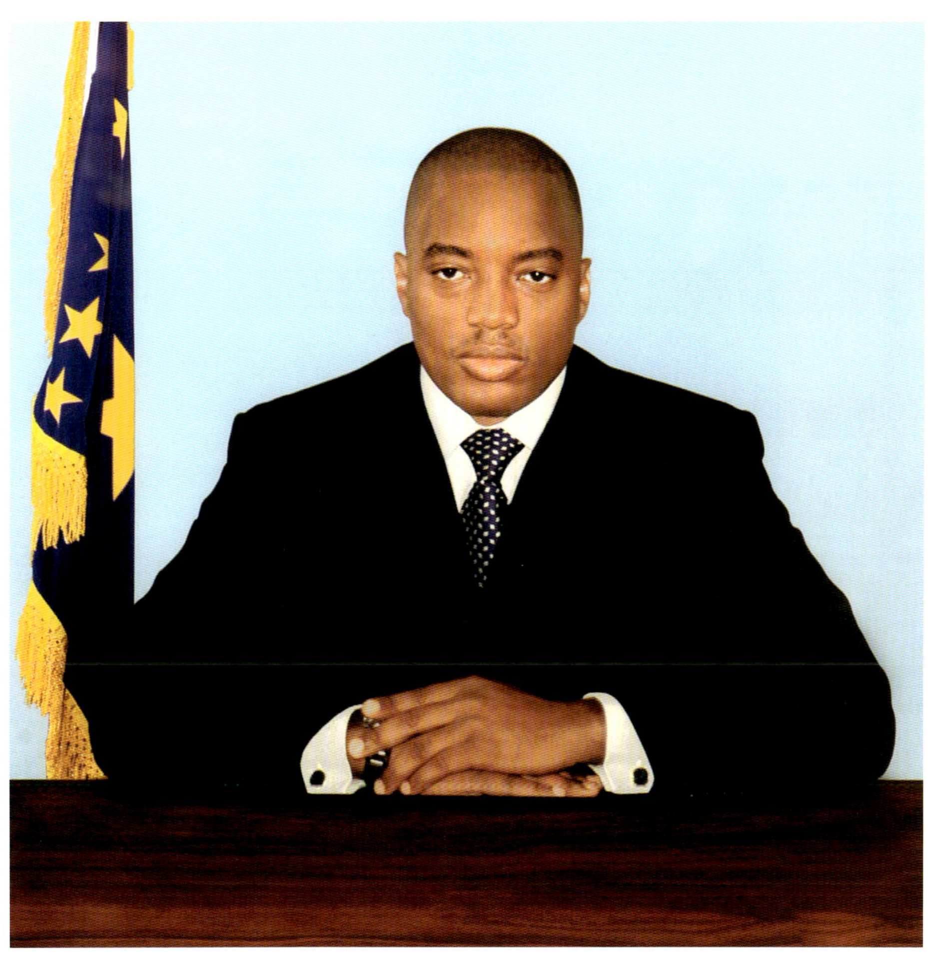

Democratic Republic of the Congo – President Joseph Kabila

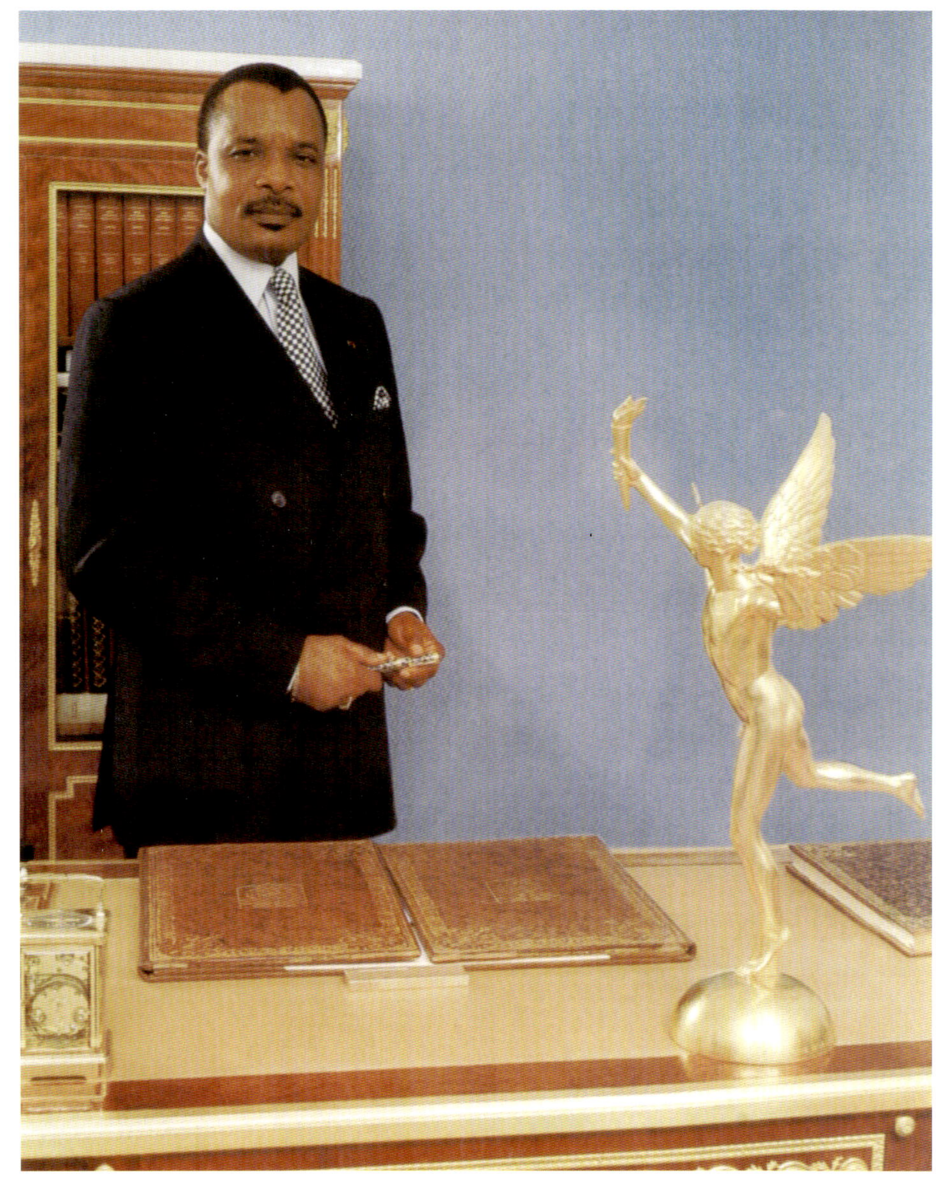

Republic of Congo – President Denis Sassou-N'Guesso

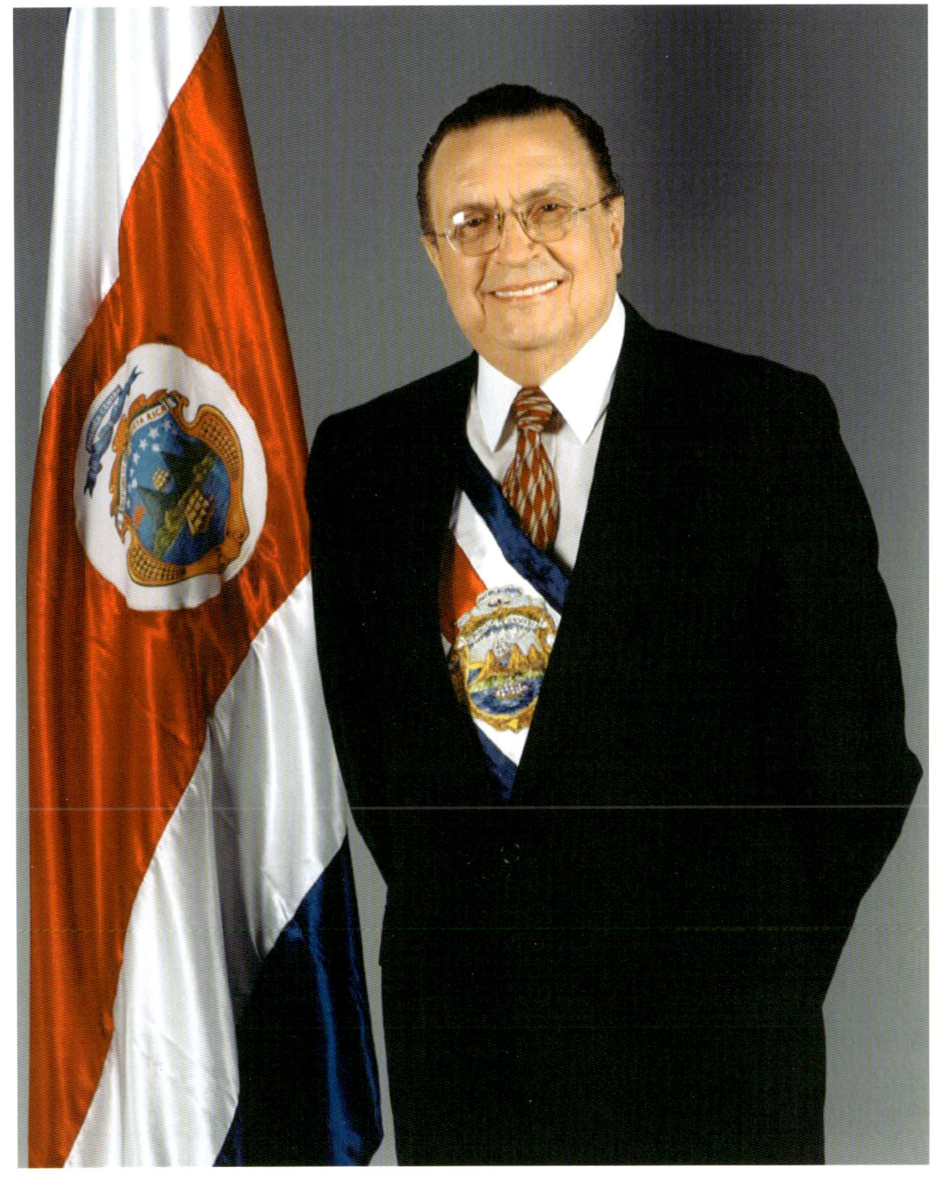

Republic of Costa Rica – President Abel Pacheco

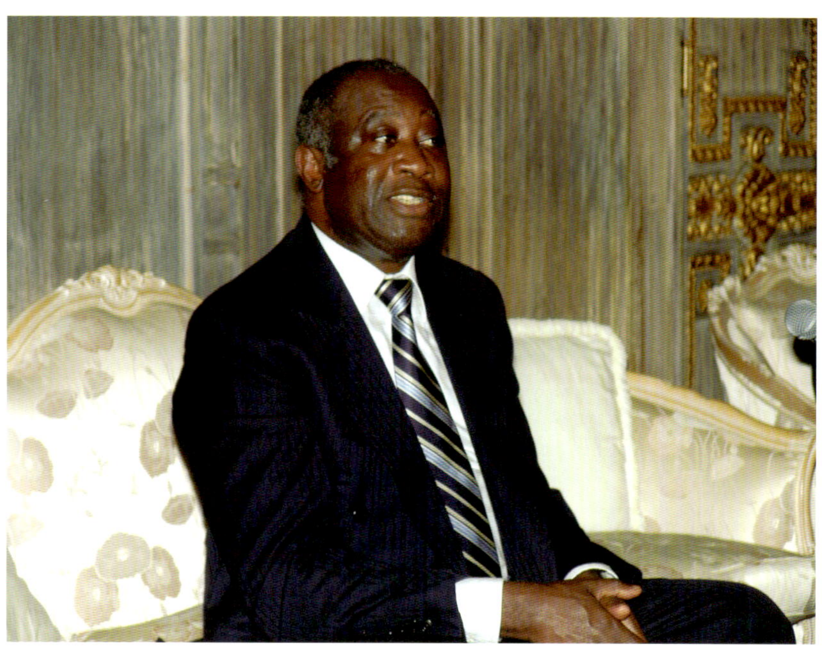

Republic of Côte d'Ivoire – President Laurent Gbagbo

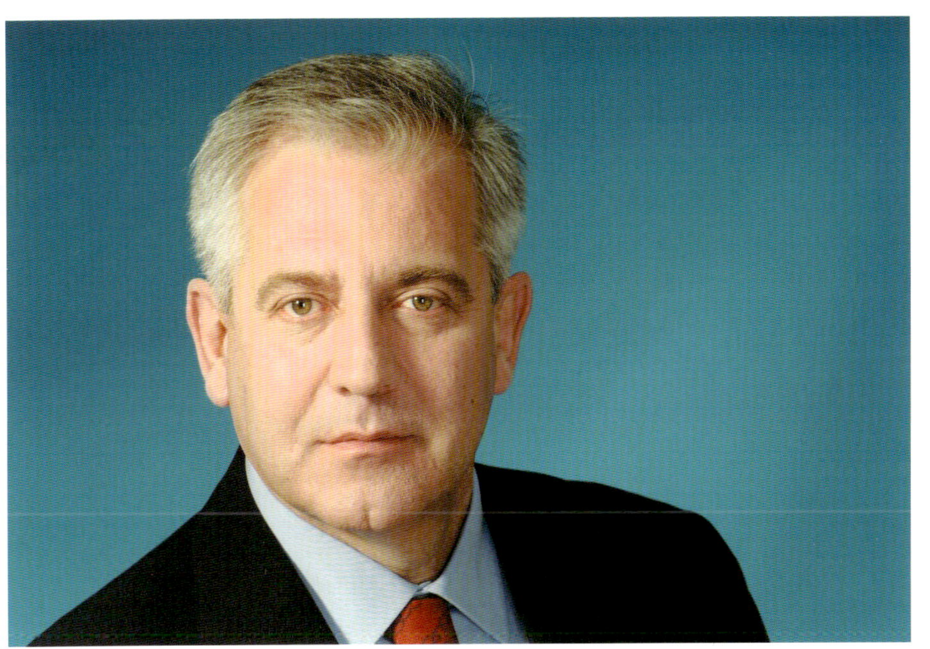

Republic of Croatia – Prime Minister Ivo Sanader

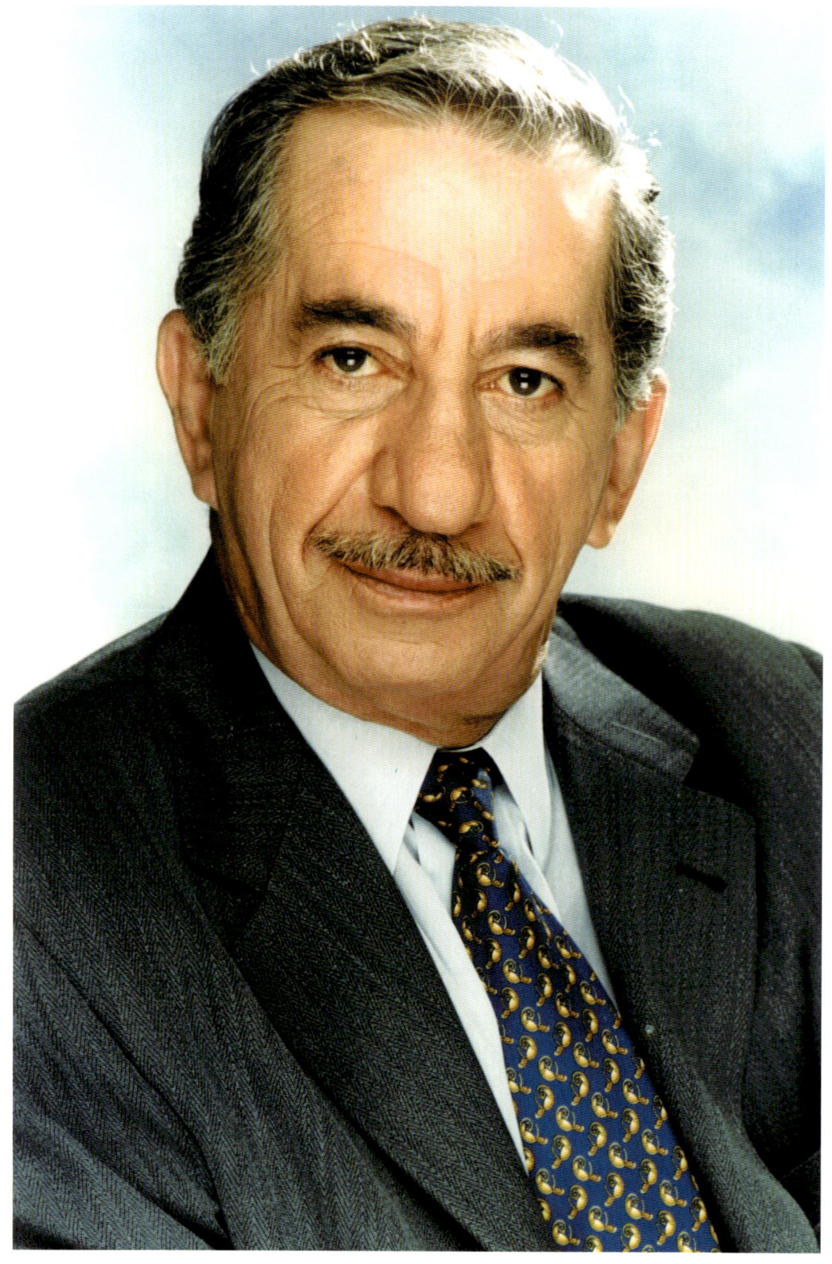

Republic of Cyprus – President Tassos Papadopoulos

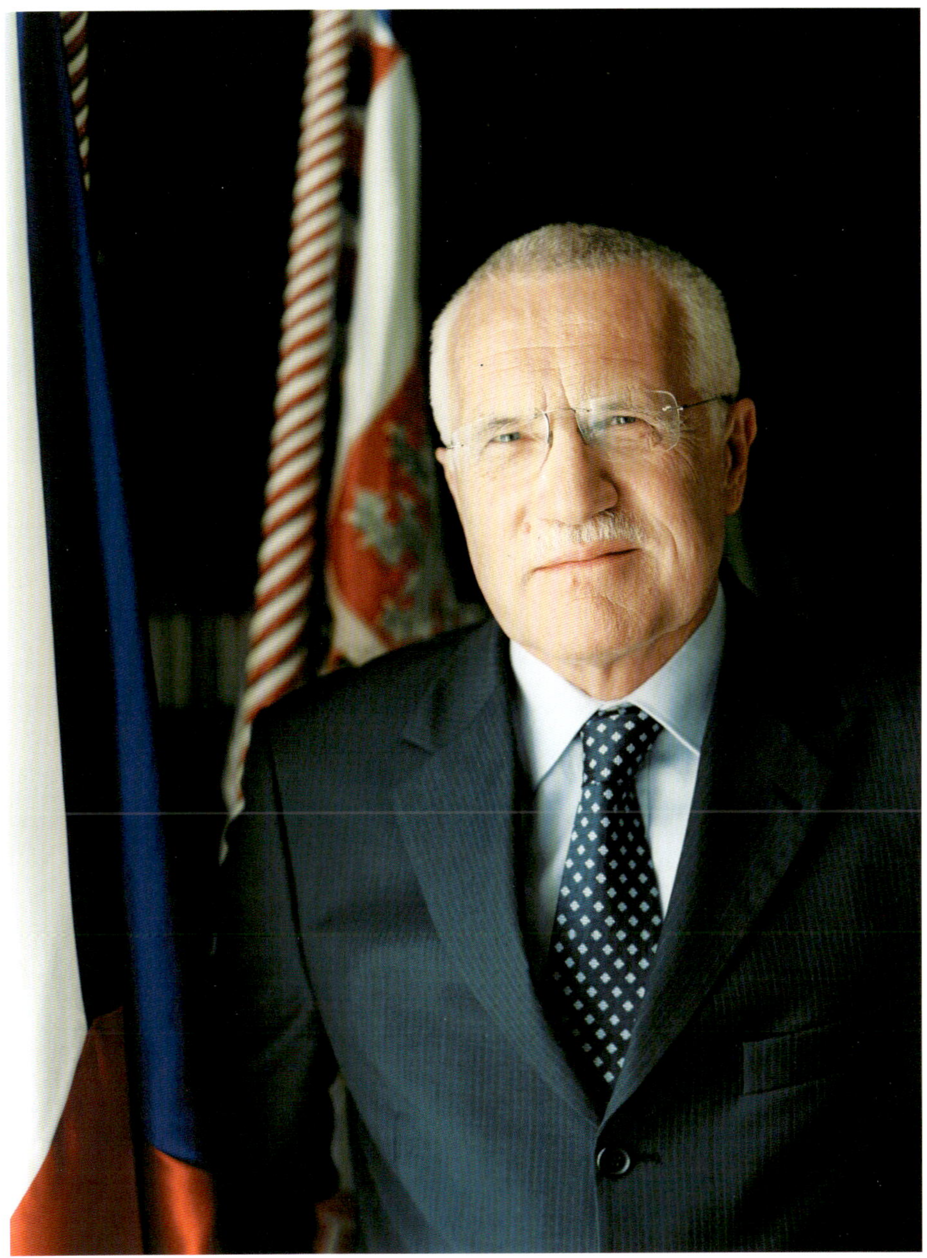

Czech Republic – President Vaclav Klaus

45

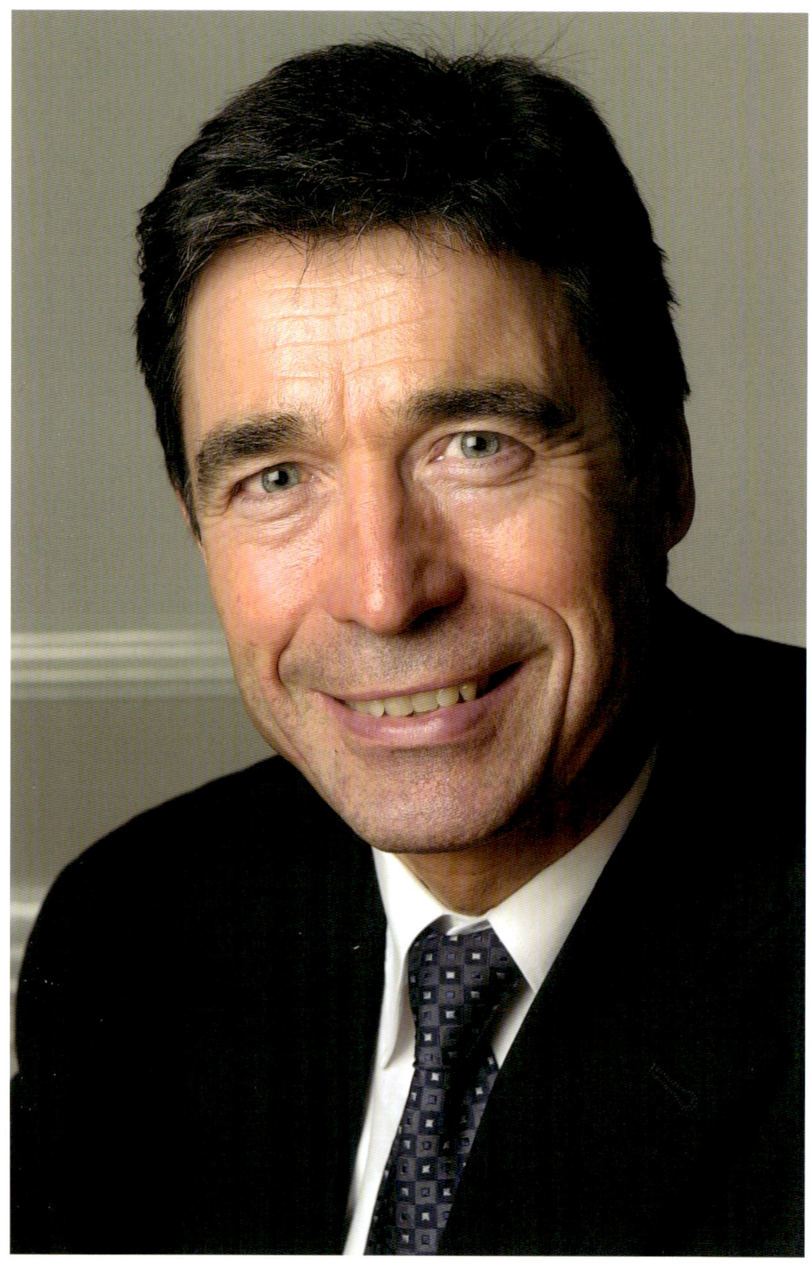

Kingdom of Denmark – Prime Minister Anders Fogh Rasmussen

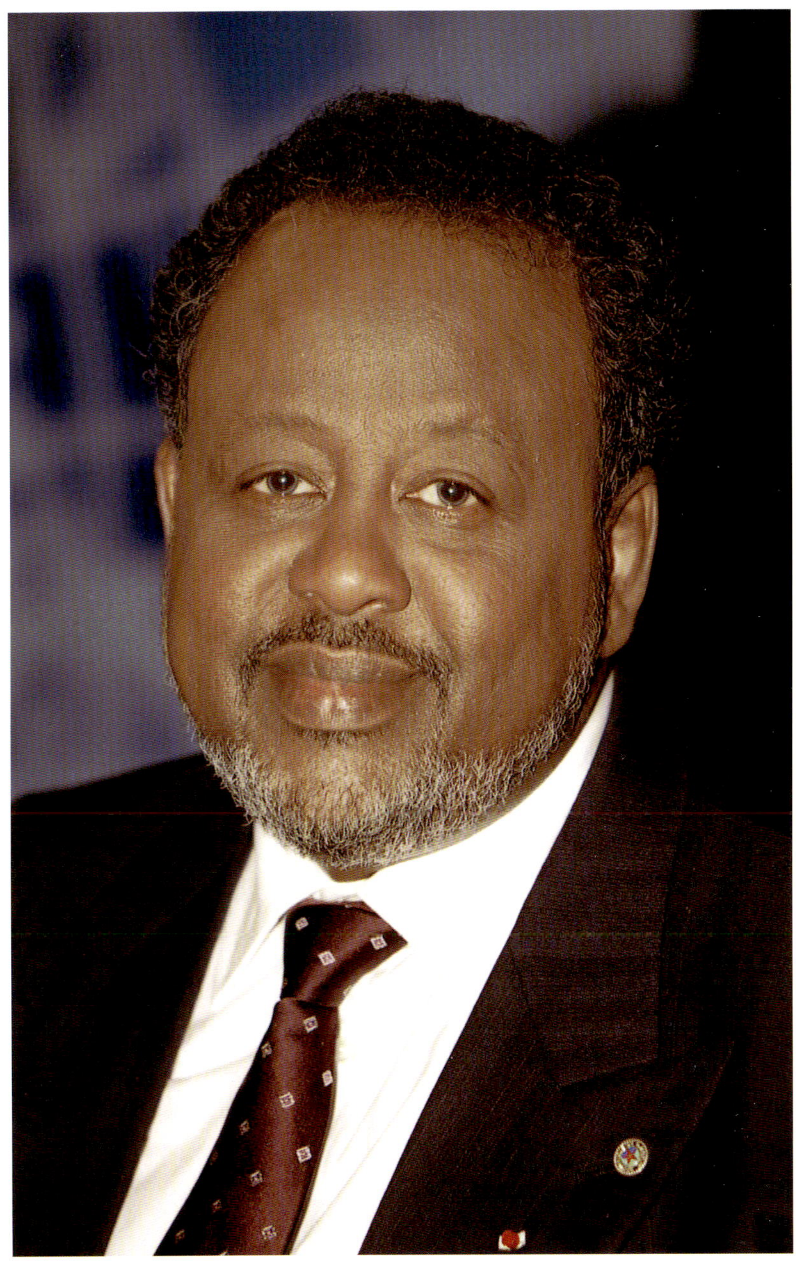

Republic of Djibouti – President Ismaïl Omar Guelleh

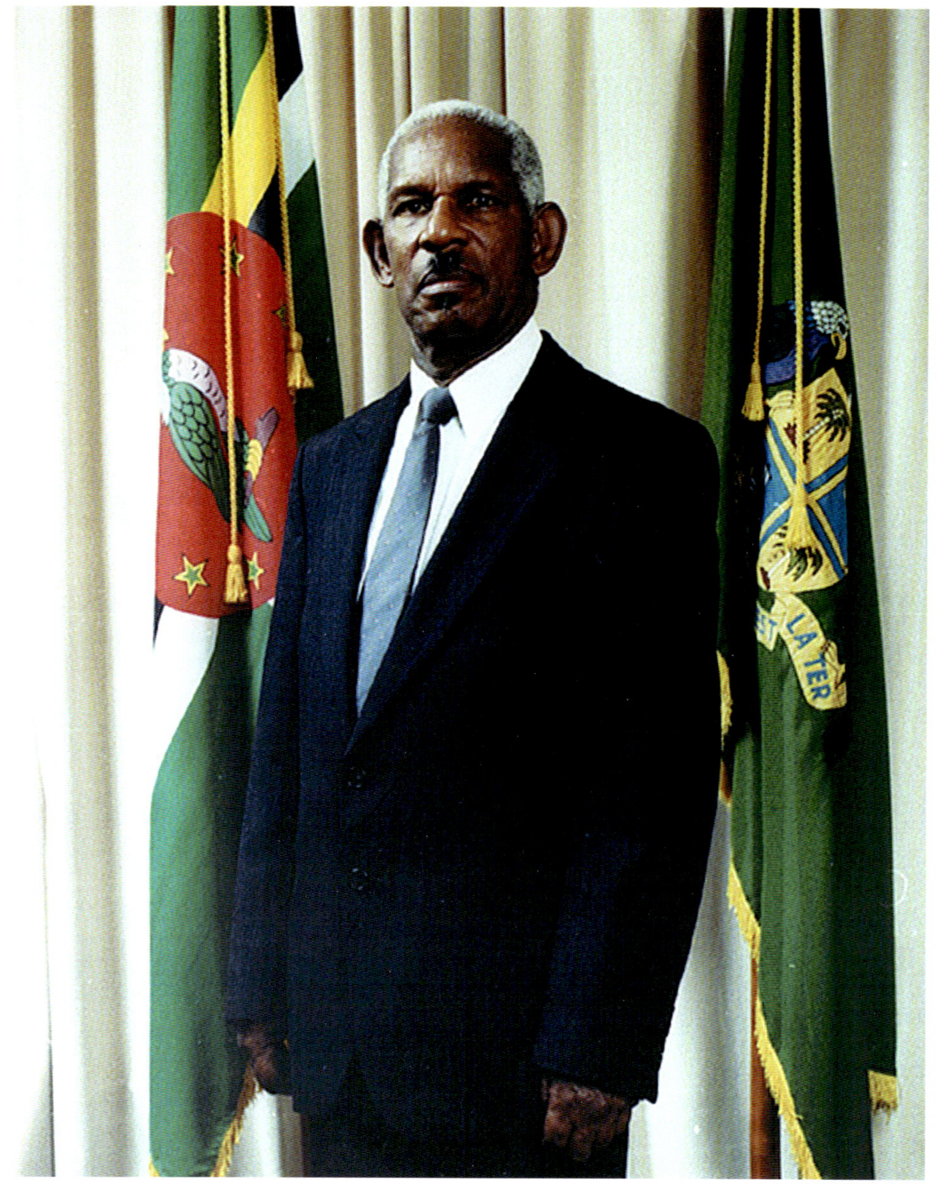

Commonwealth of Dominica – President Vernon Lorden Shaw

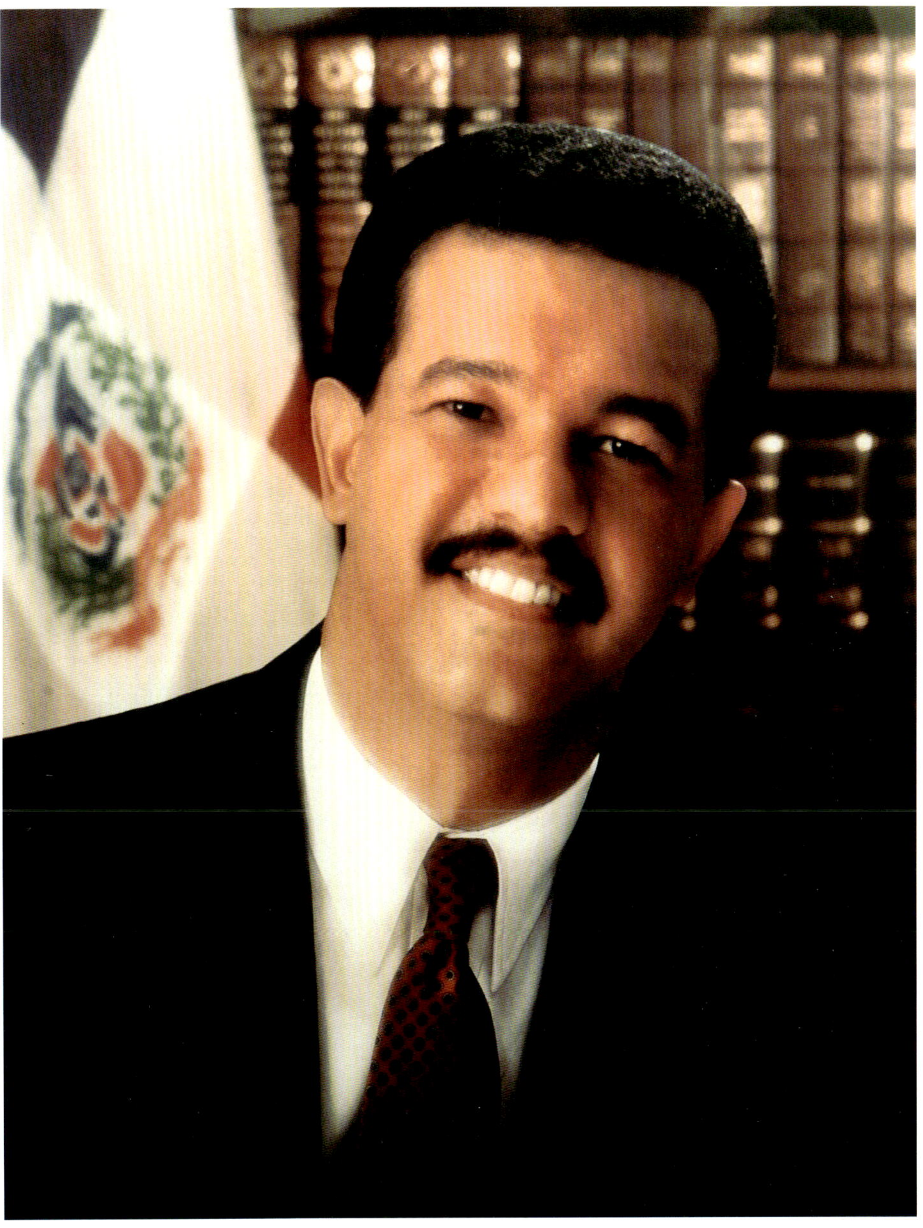

Dominican Republic – President Leonel Fernandéz

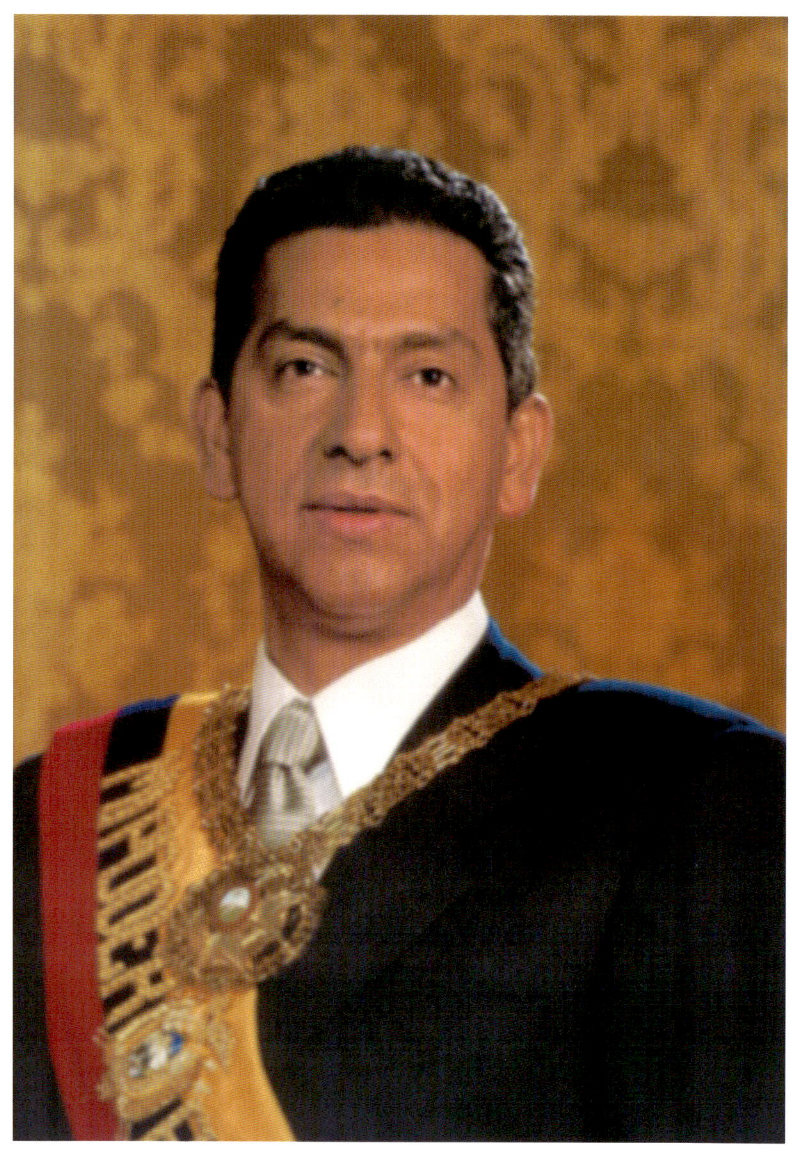

Republic of Ecuador – President Lucio Gutierrez Borbua

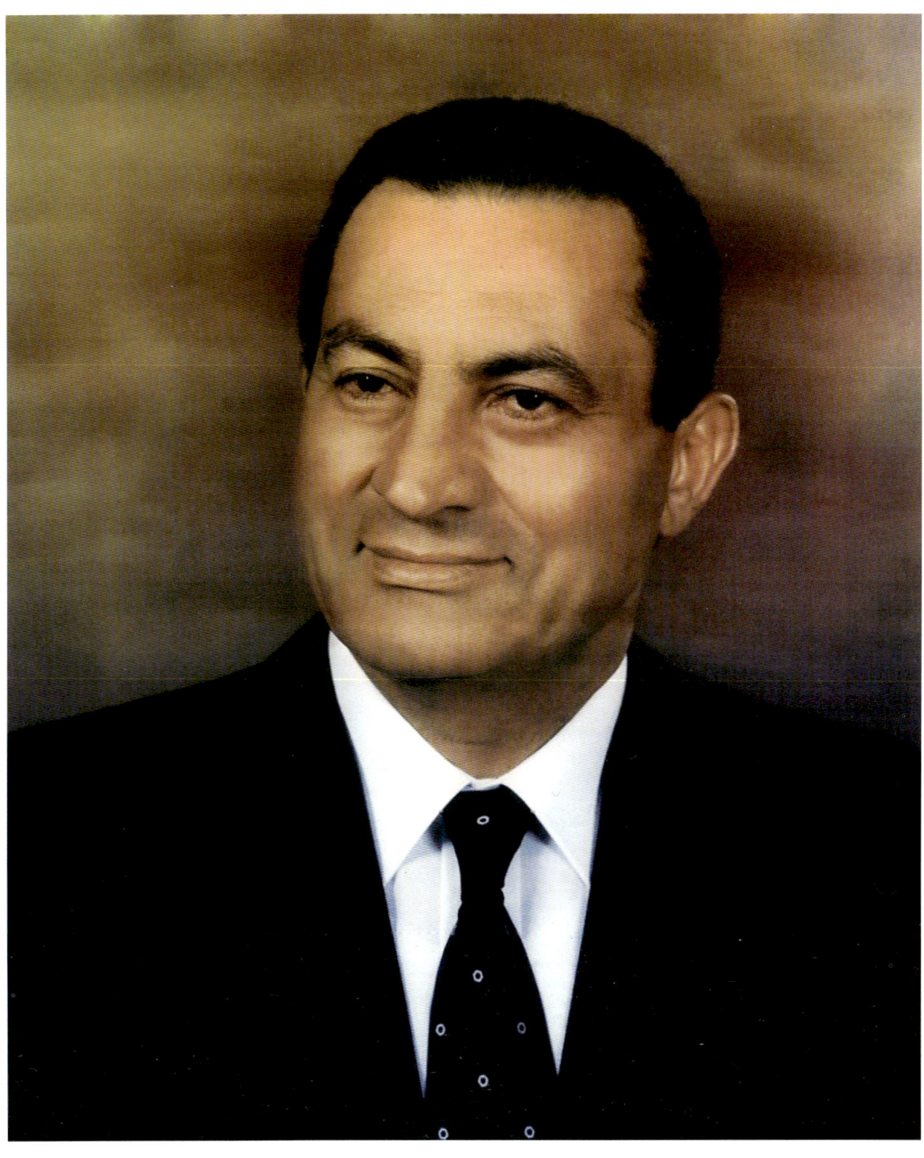

The Arabic Republic of Egypt – President Mohamed Hosni Mubarak

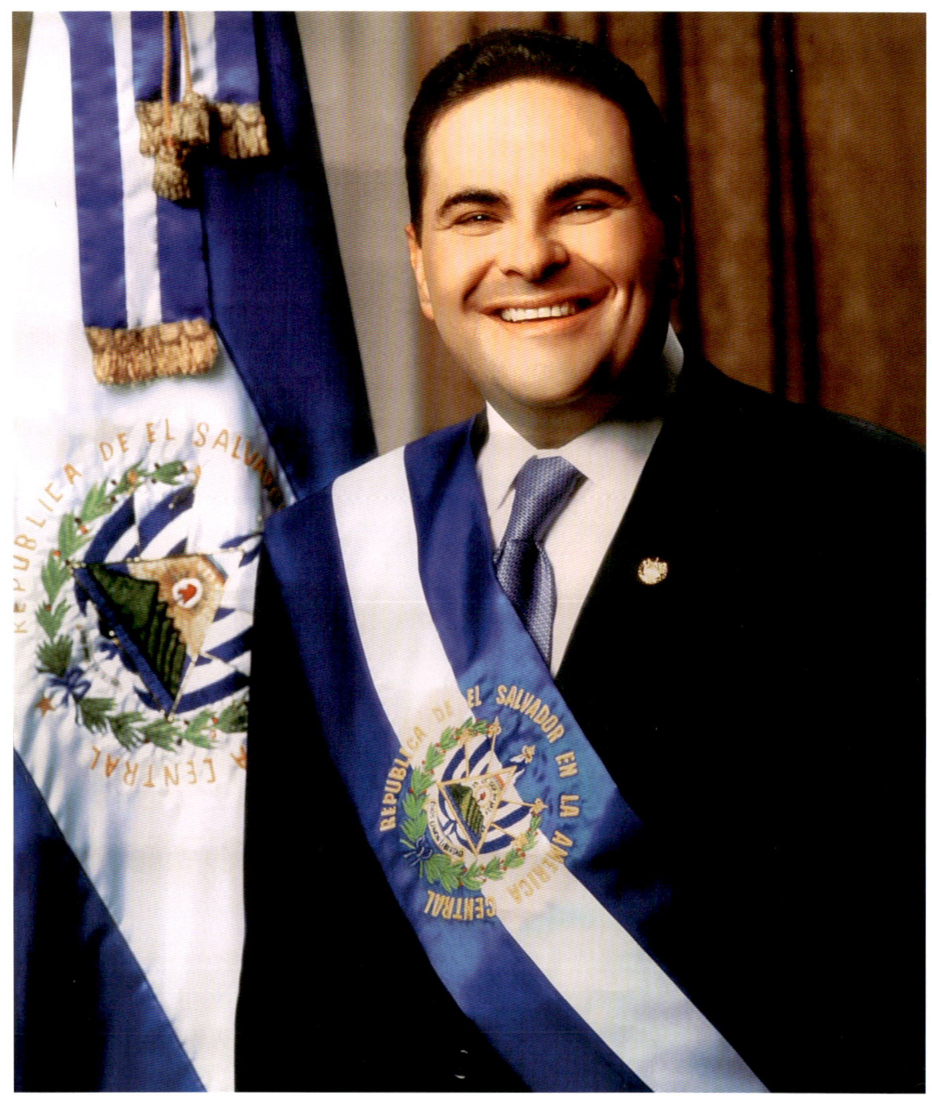

Republic of El Salvador – President Elías Antonio Saca González

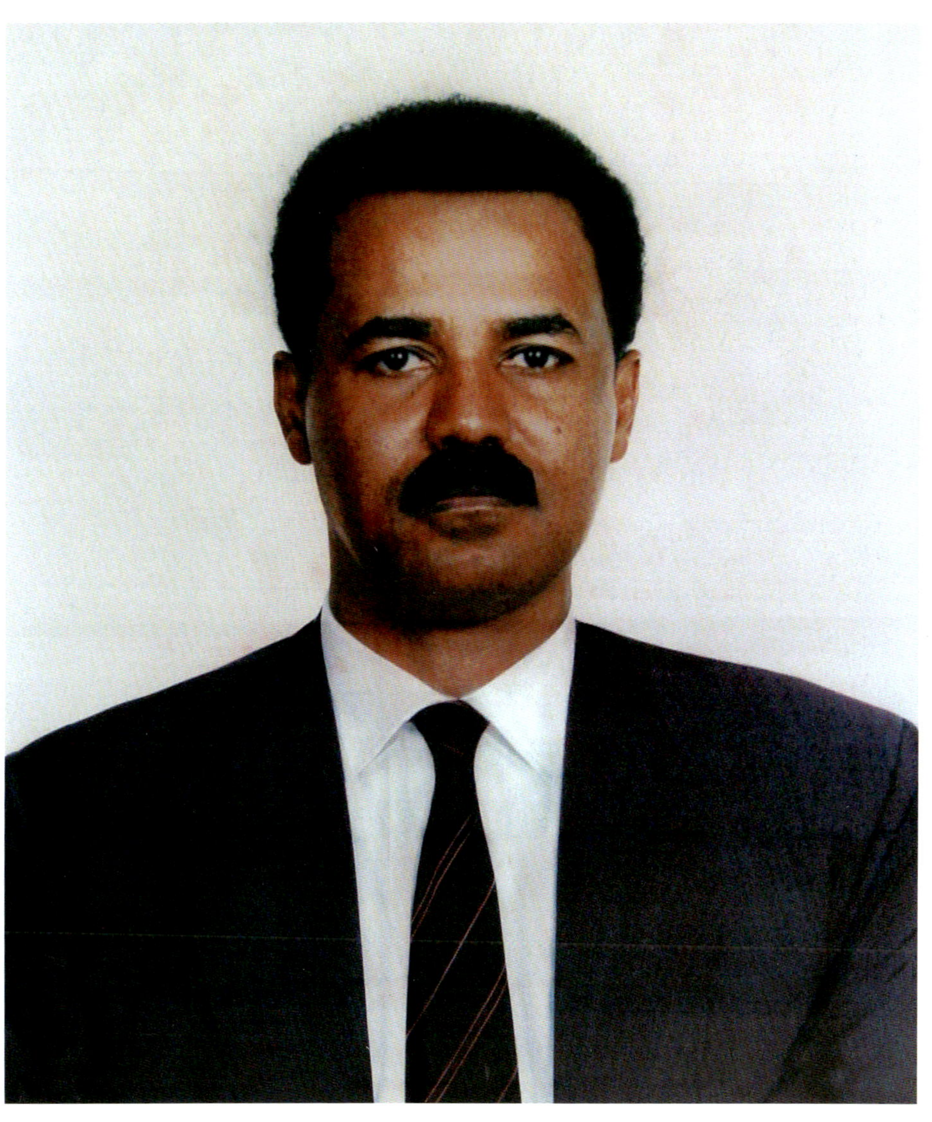

State of Eritrea – President Isaias Afwerki

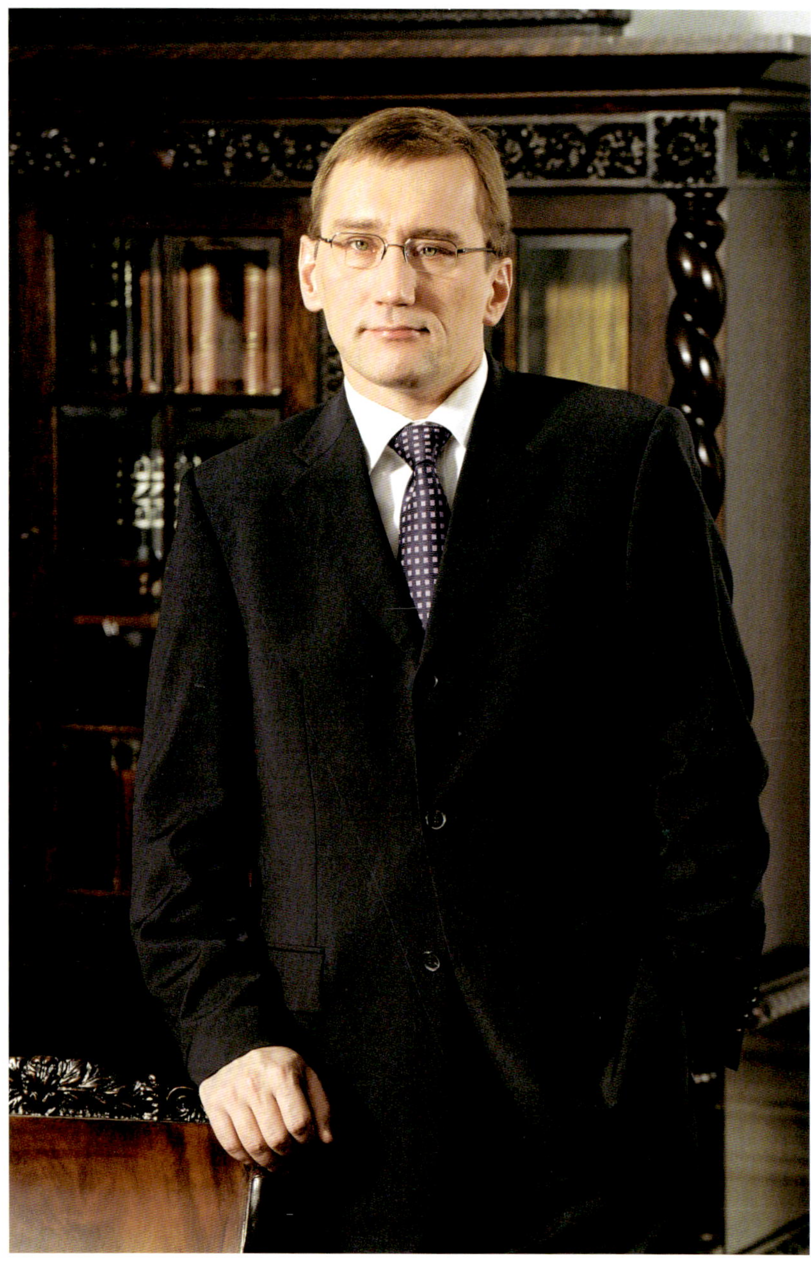

Republic of Estonia – Prime Minister Juhan Parts

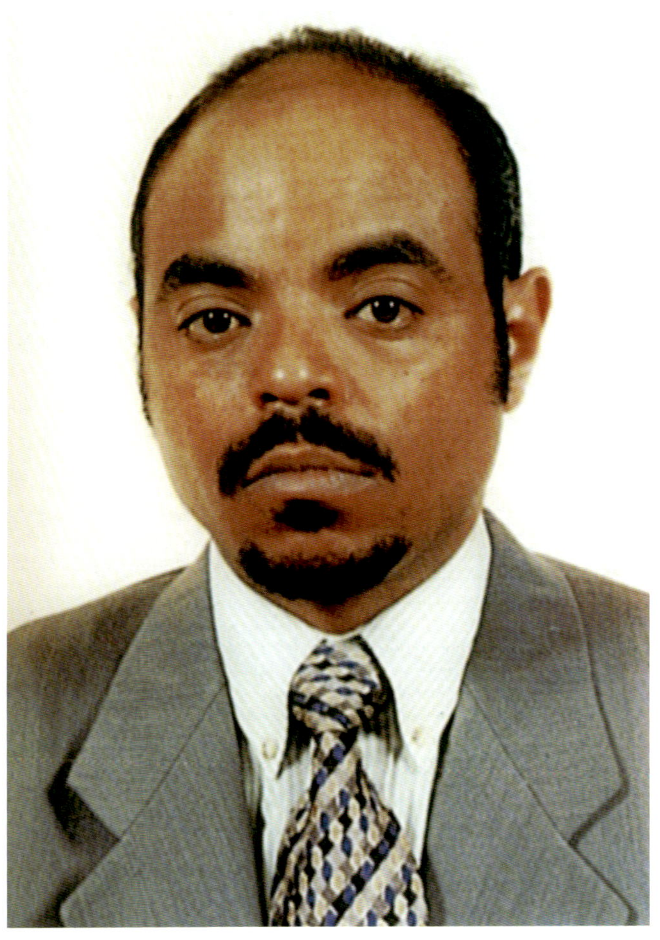

Federal Democratic Republic of Ethiopia – Prime Minister Meles Zenawi

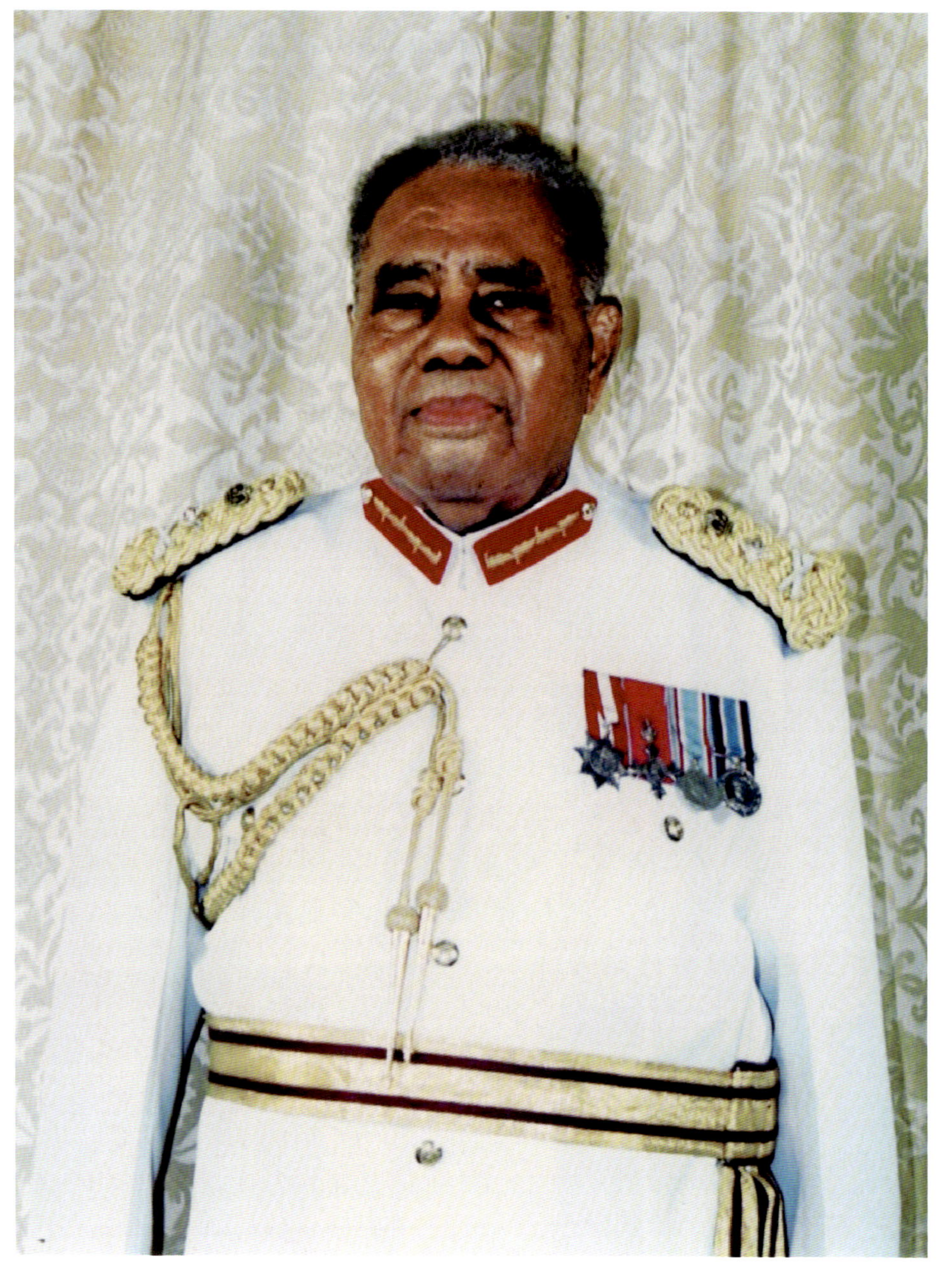

Republic of the Fiji Islands – President Ratu Josefa Iloilovatu

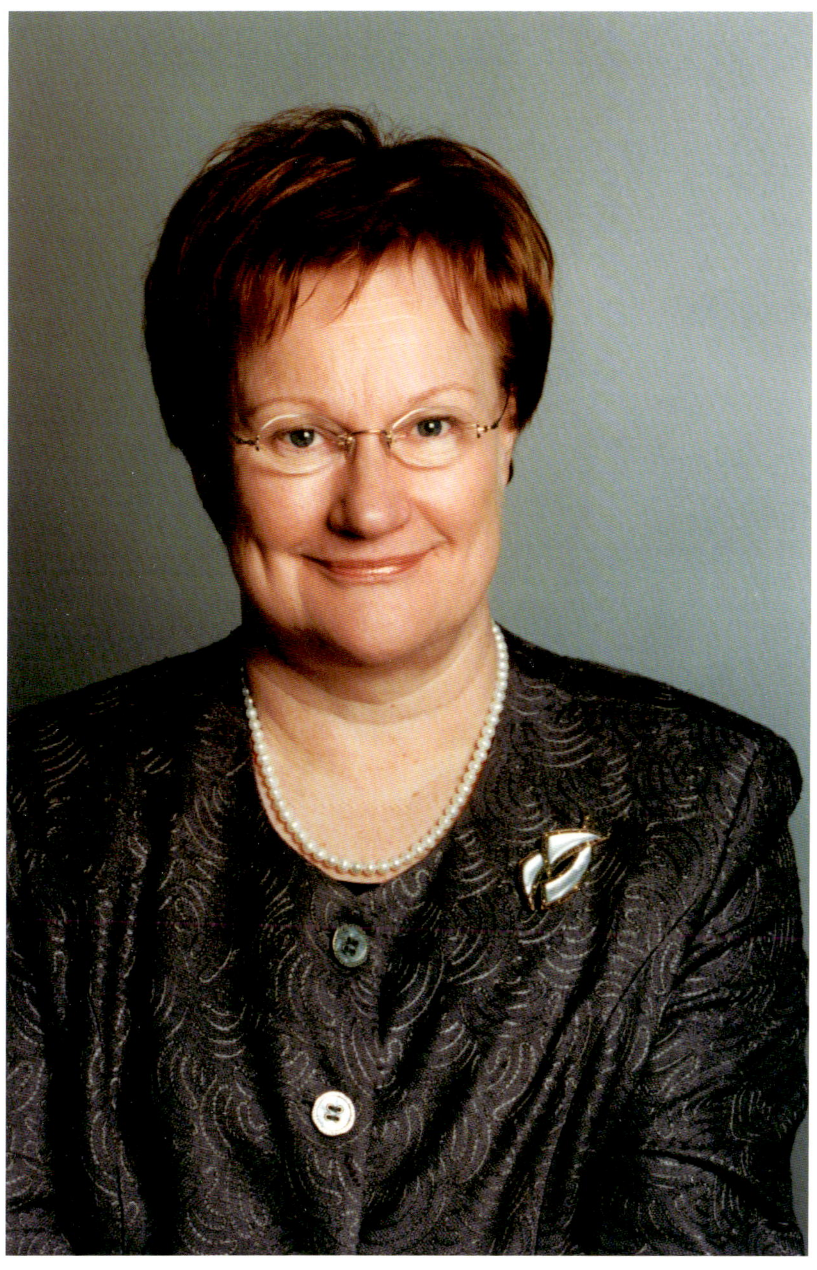

Republic of Finland – President Tarja Halonen

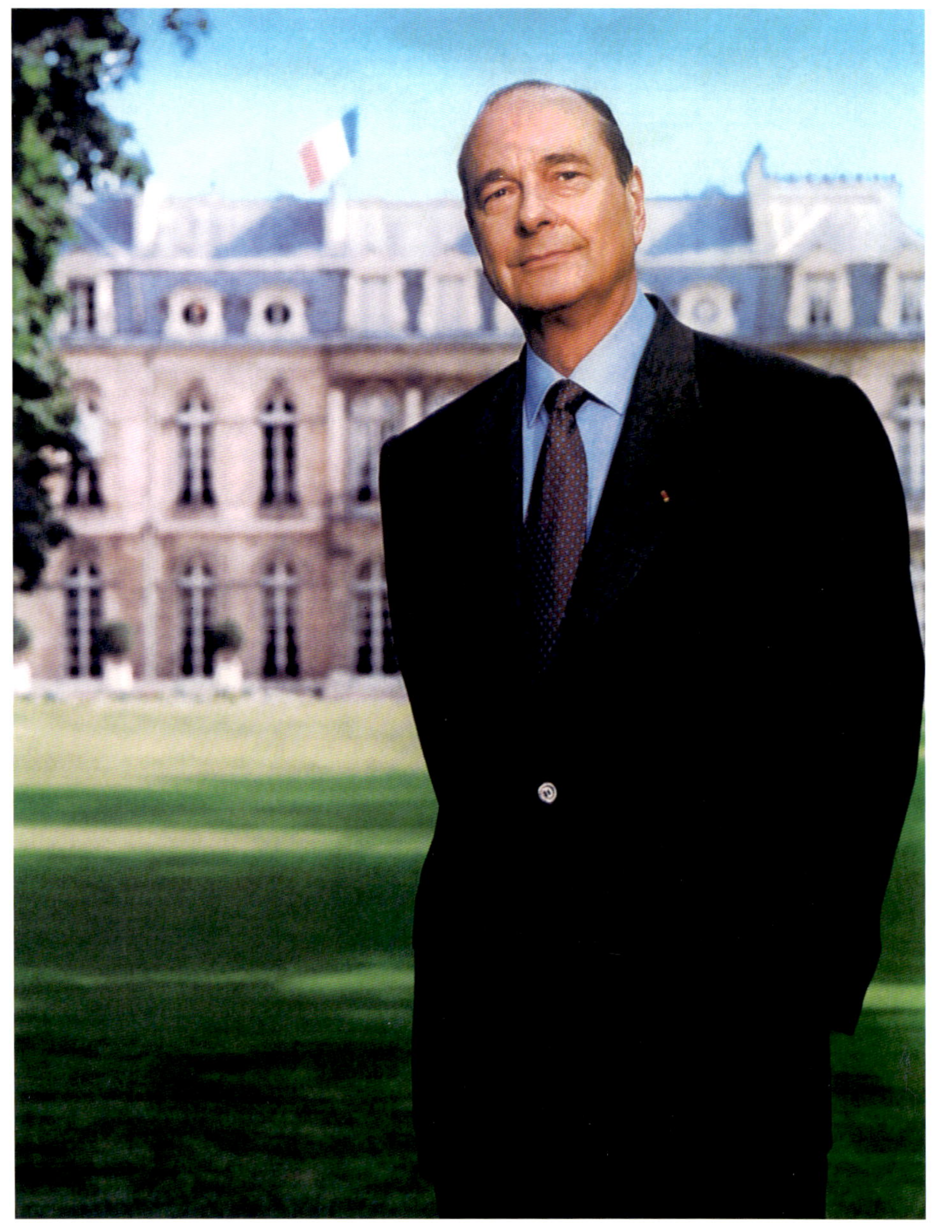

Republic of France – President Jacques Chirac

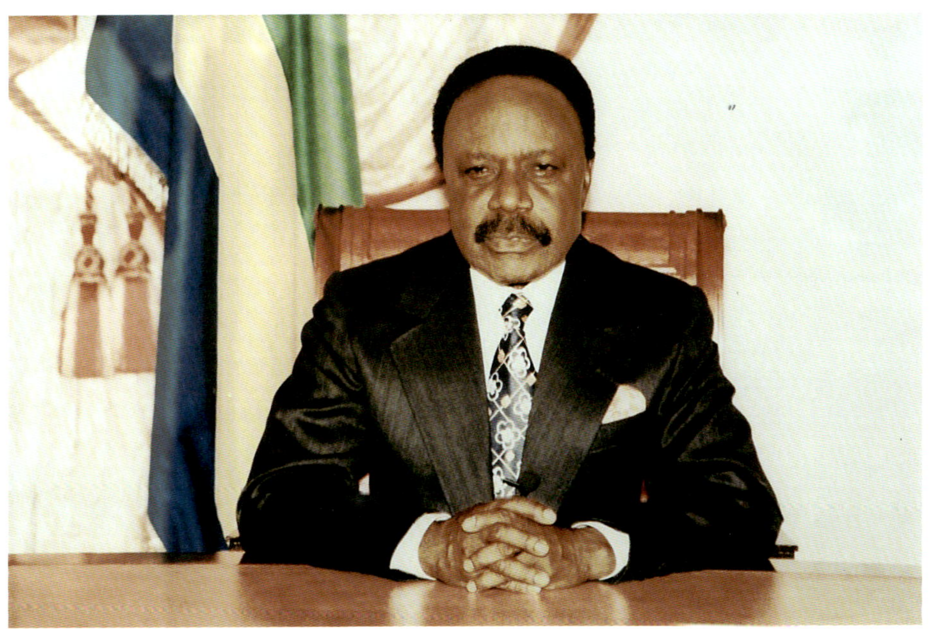

Republic of Gabon – President El Hadj Omar Bongo Ondimba

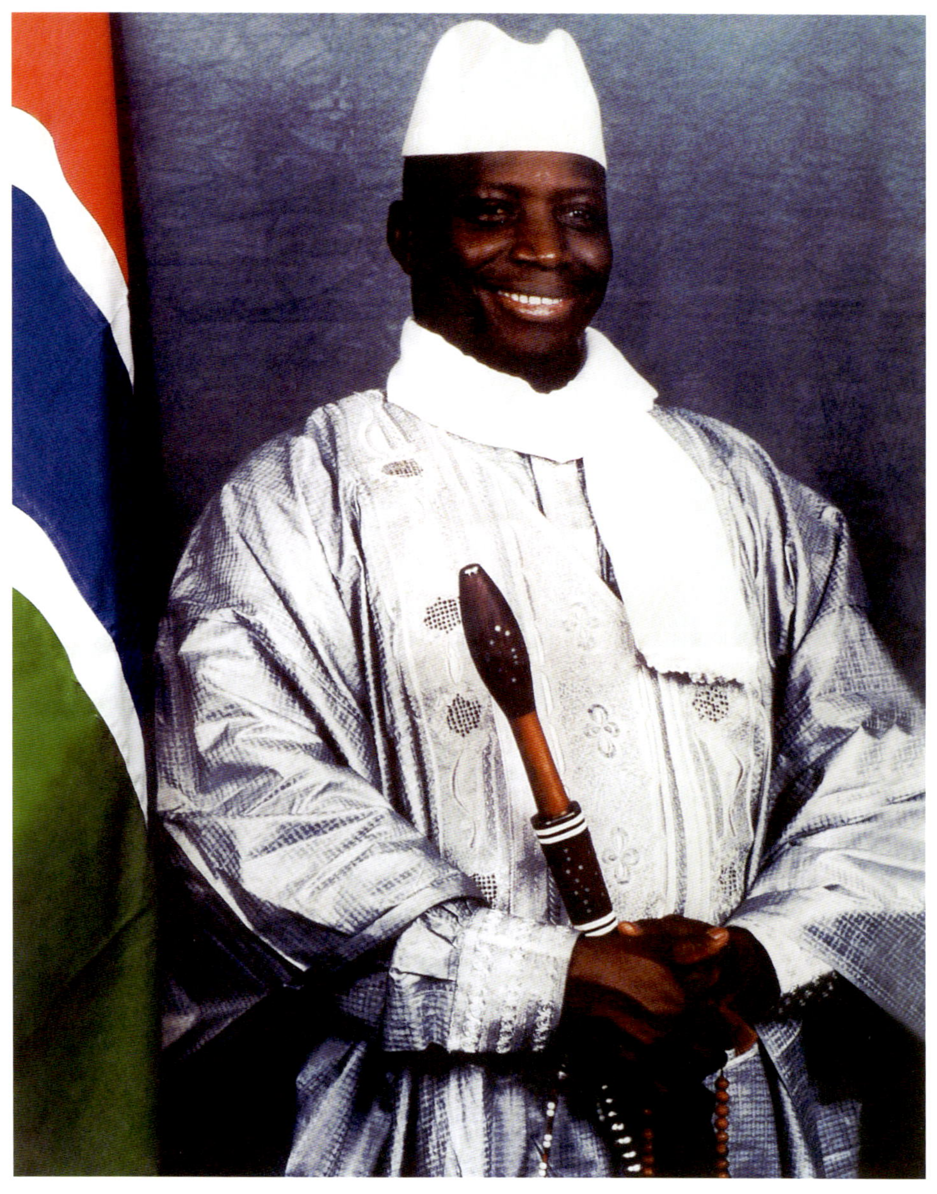

Republic of The Gambia – President Alhaji Yahya A. J.J. Jammeh

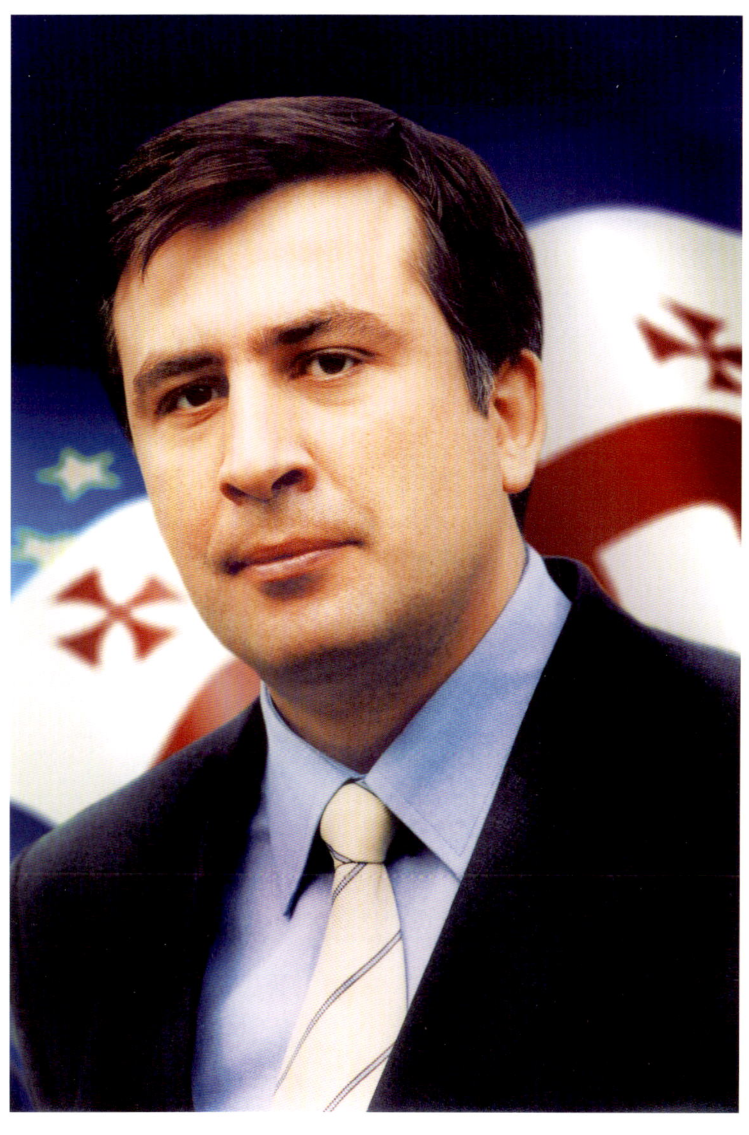

Georgia – President Mikhail Saakashvili

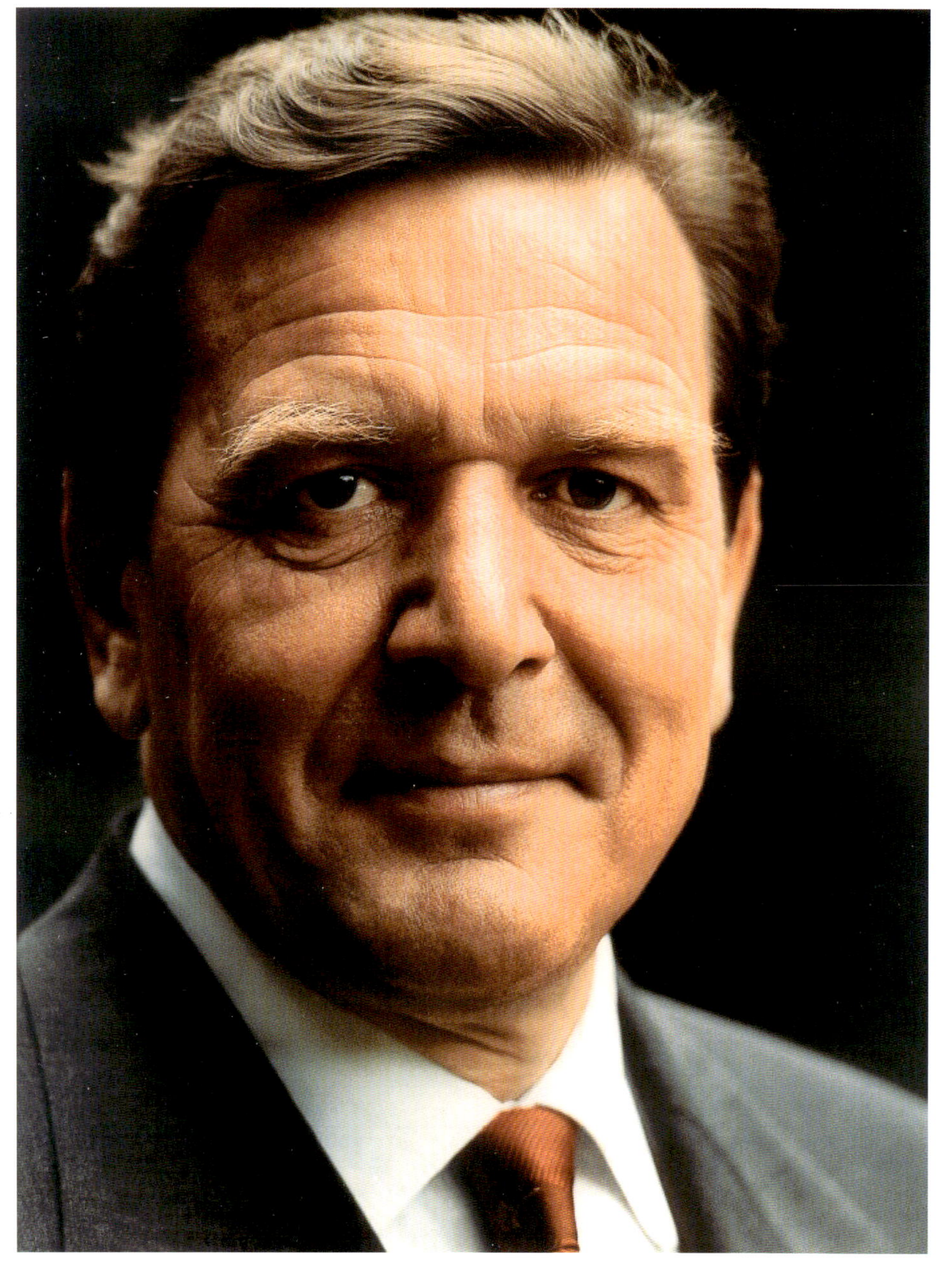

Federal Republic of Germany – Chancellor Gerhard Schröder

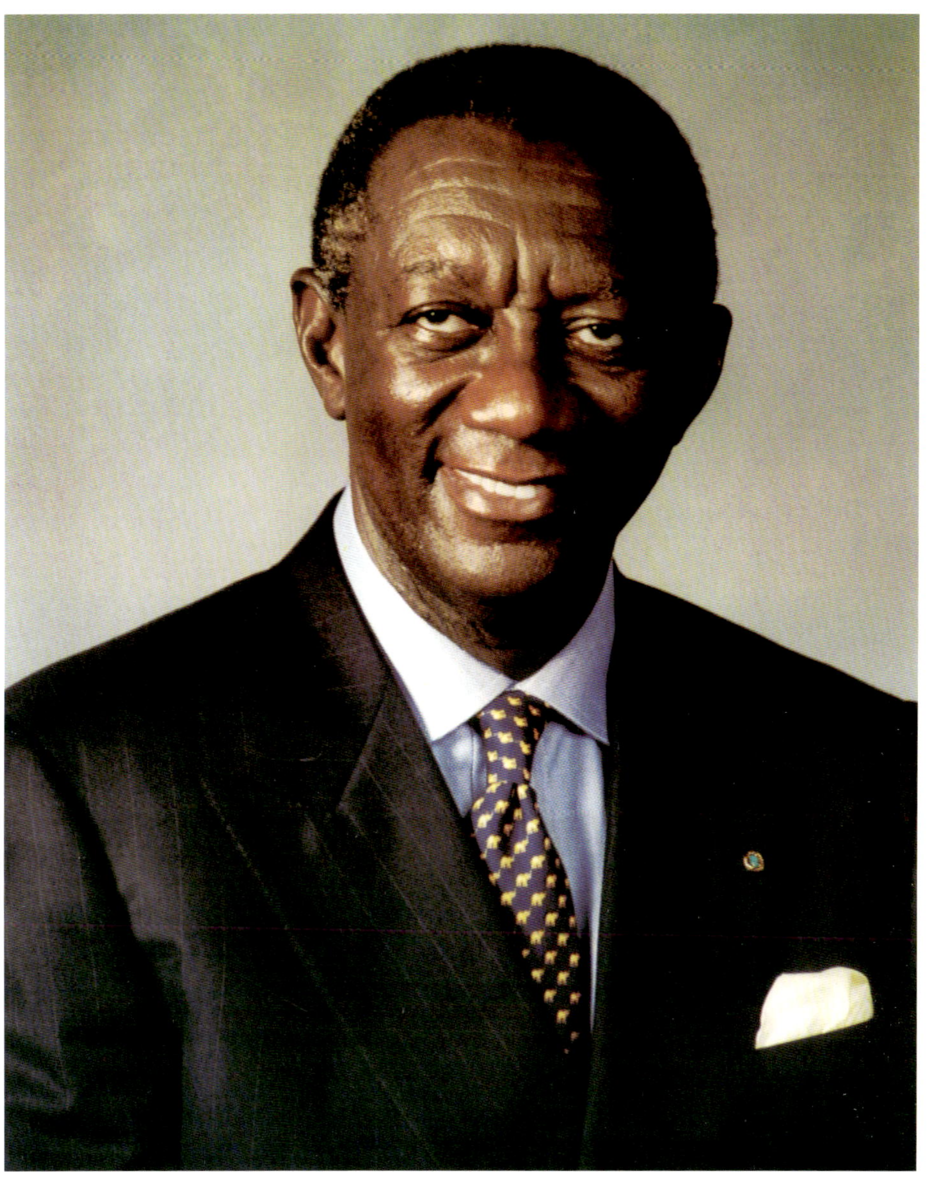

Republic of Ghana – President John Agyekum Kufuor

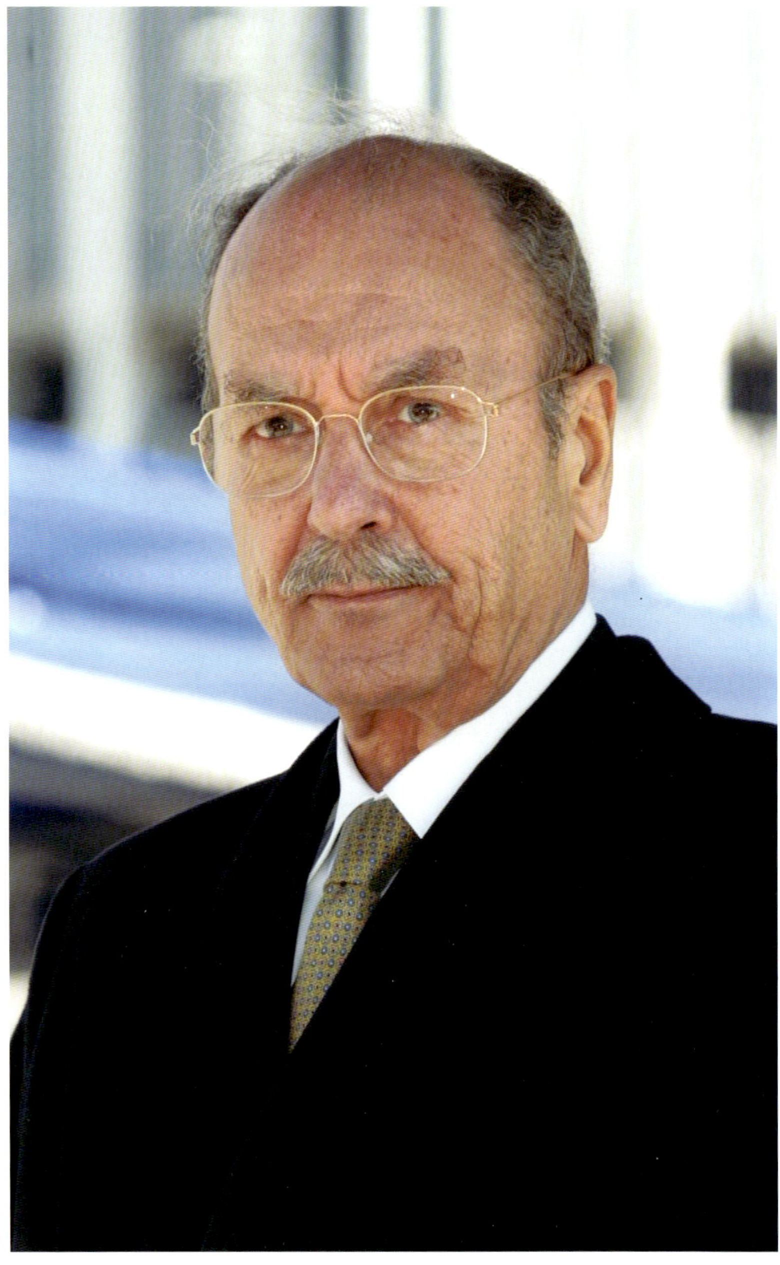

64

Republic of Greece – President Konstandinos Stephanopoulos

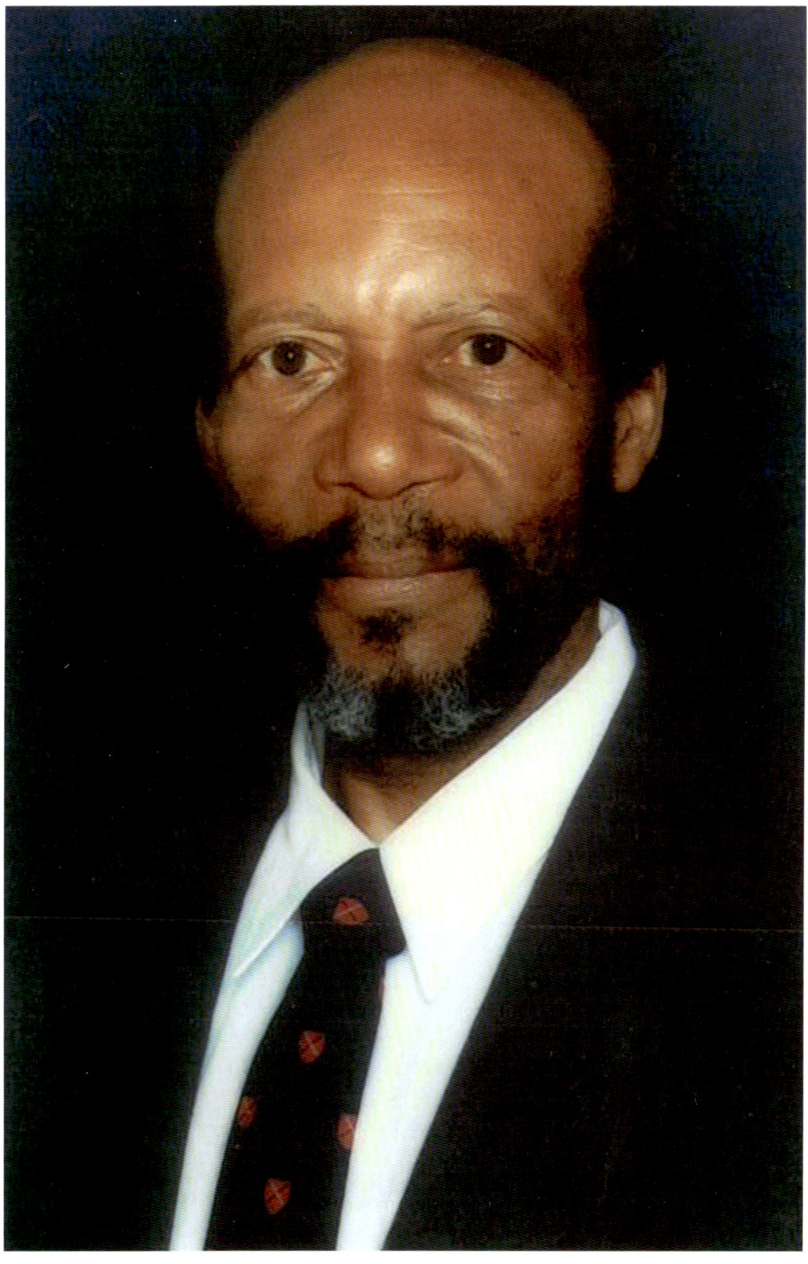

Grenada – Governor General Sir Daniel Charles Williams

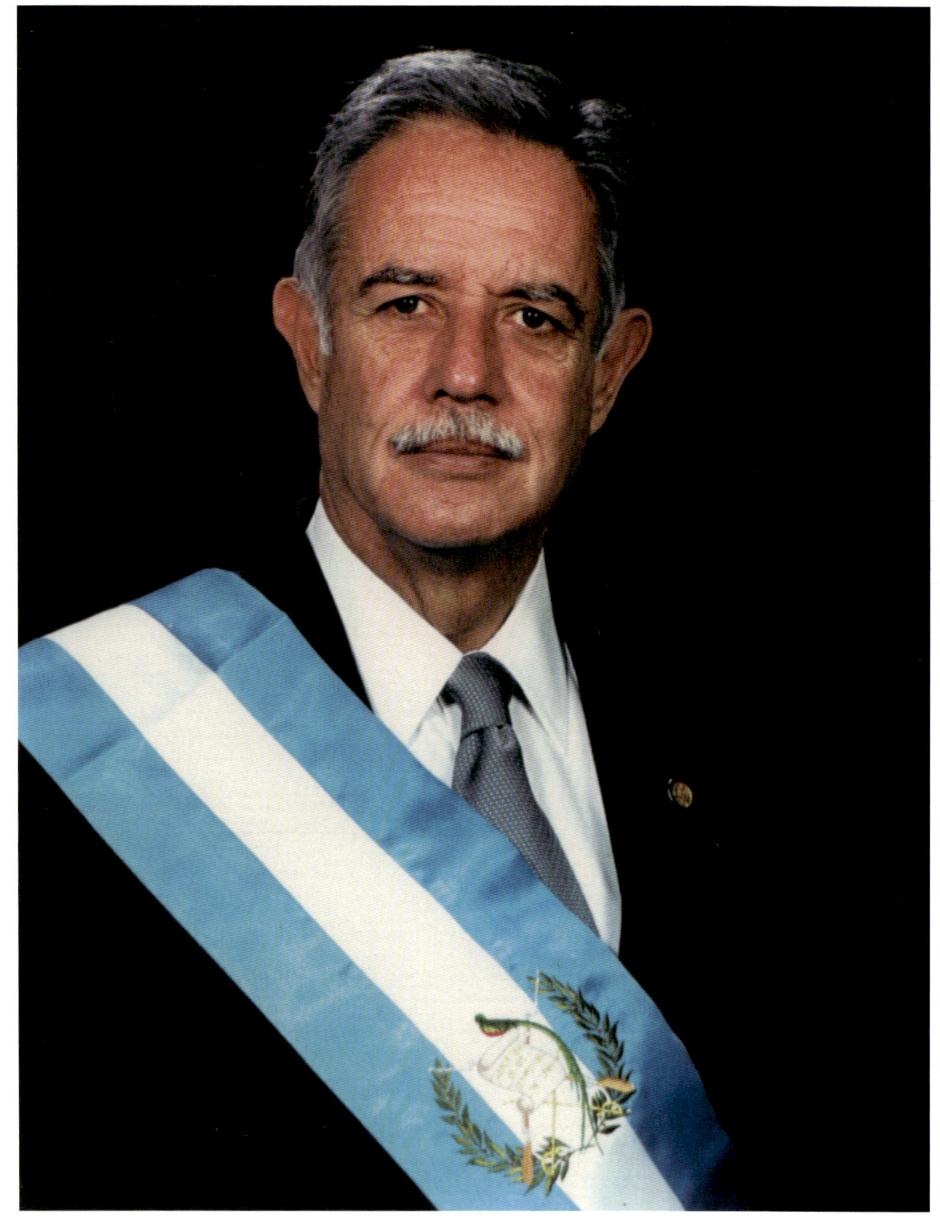

Republic of Guatemala – President Oscar Berger

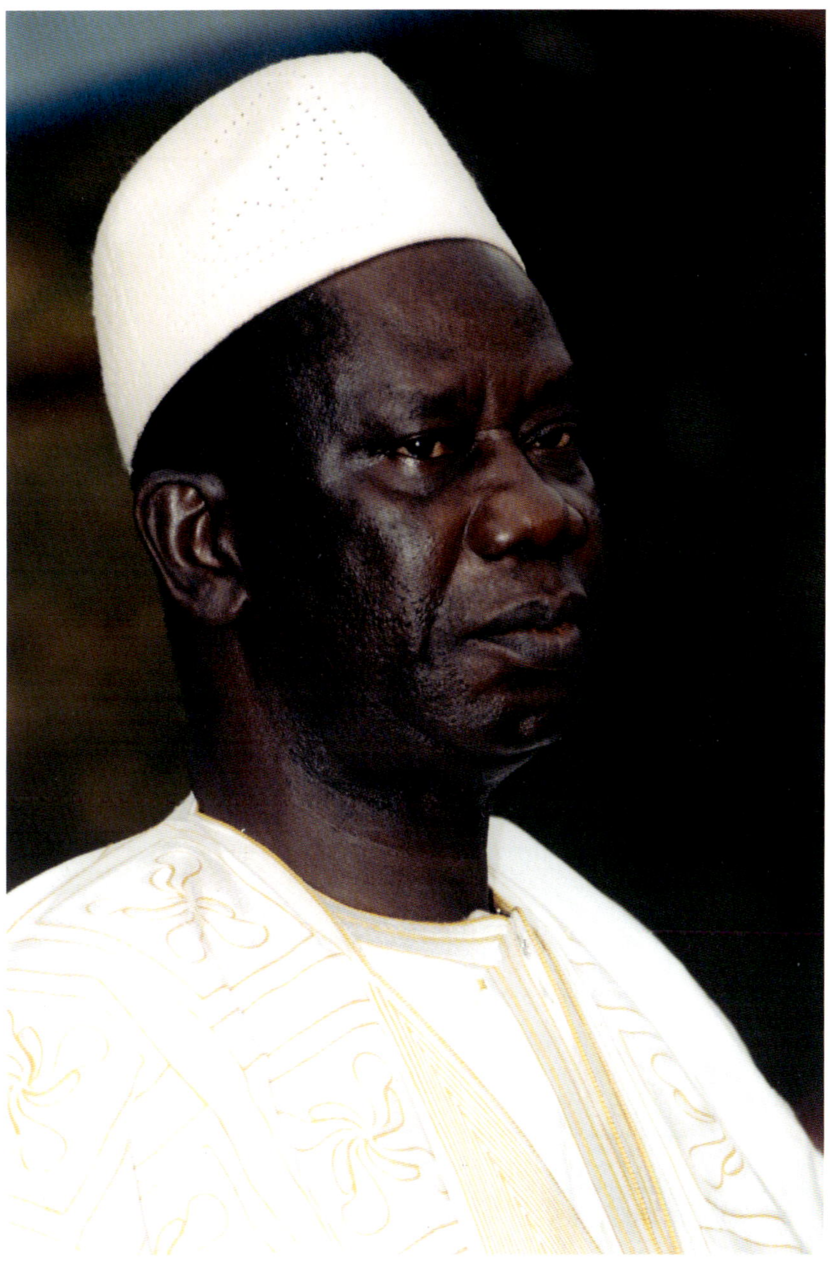

Republic of Guinea – President Lansana Conté

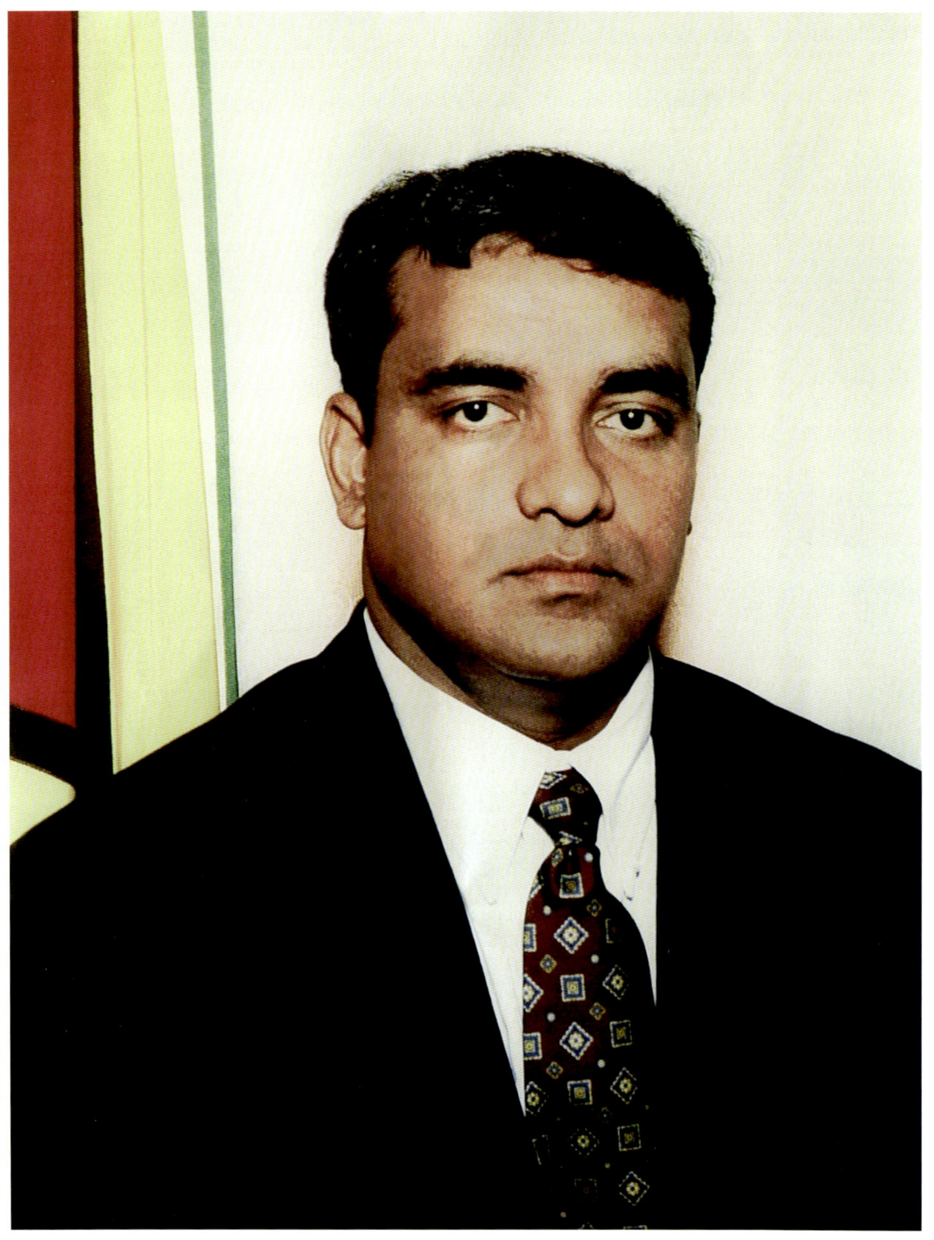

Republic of Guyana – President Bharrat Jagdeo

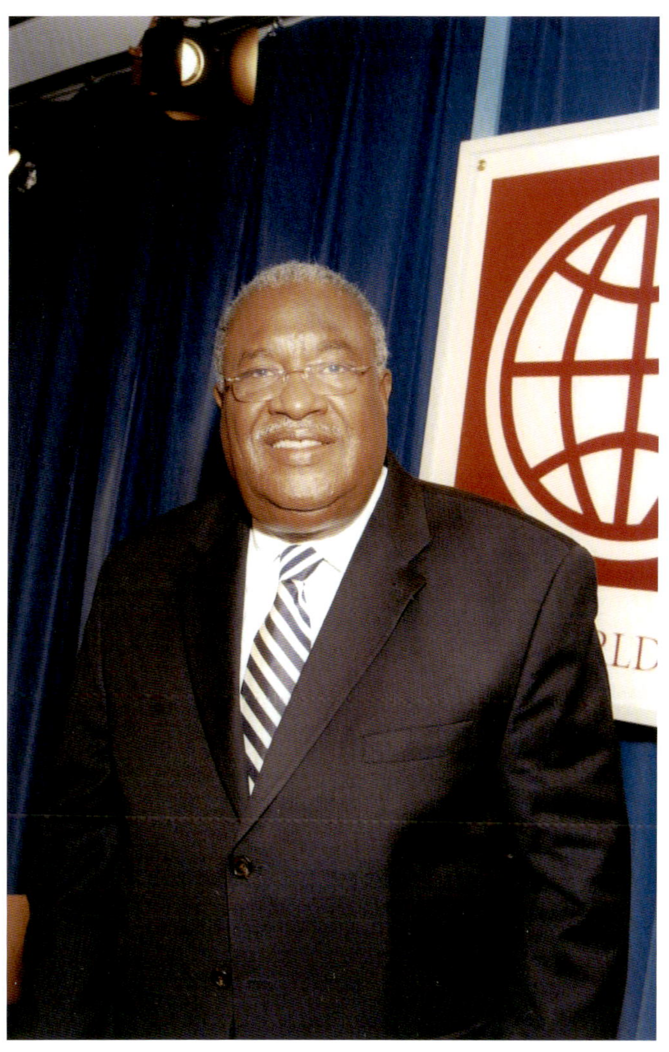

Republic of Haiti – Interim Prime Minister Gérard Latortue

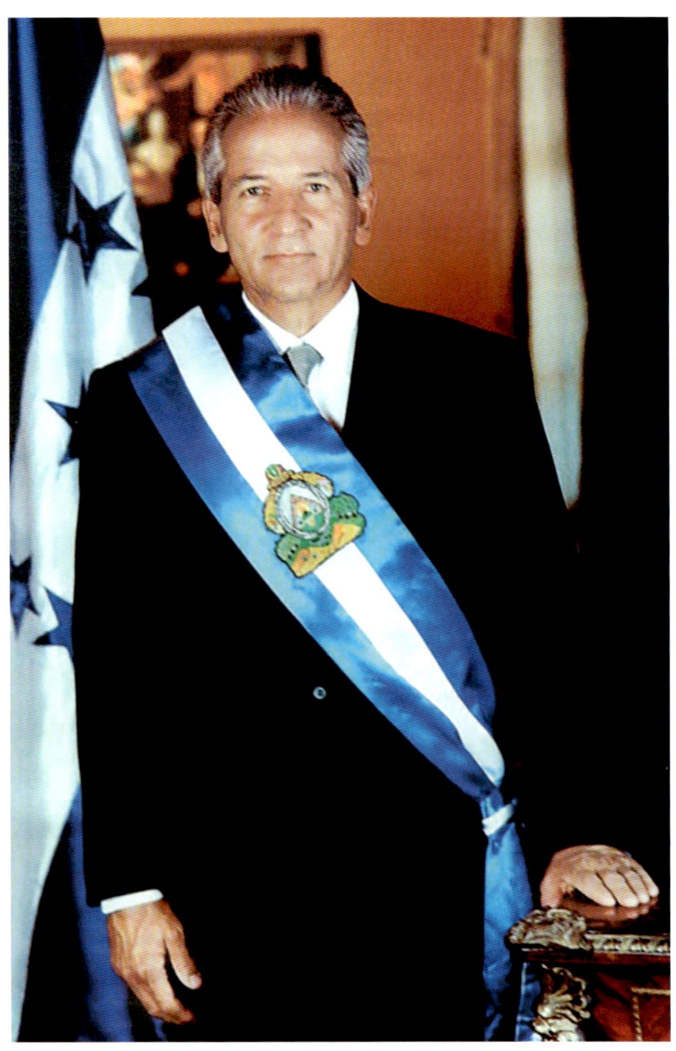

Republic of Honduras – President Ricardo Maduro

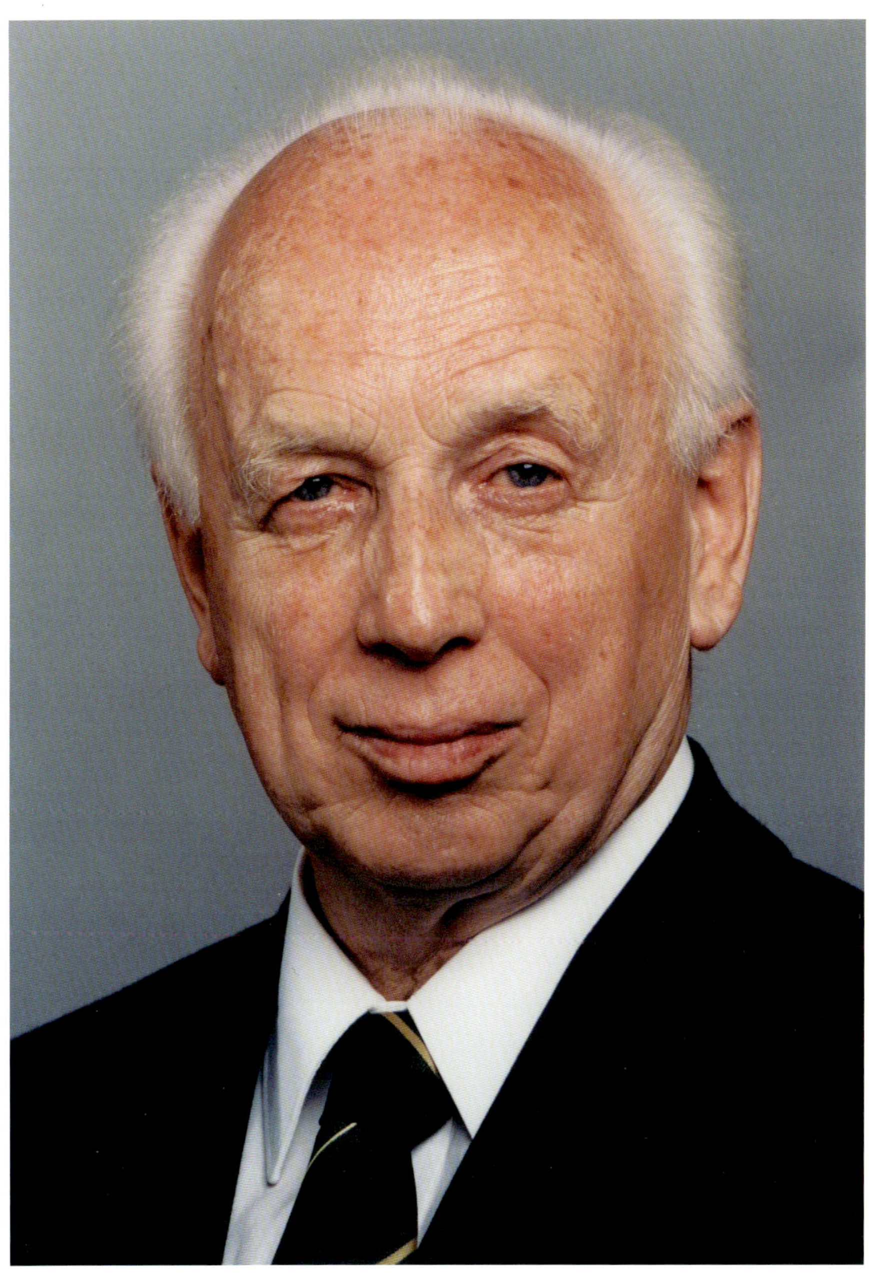

Hungary – President Ferenc Mádl

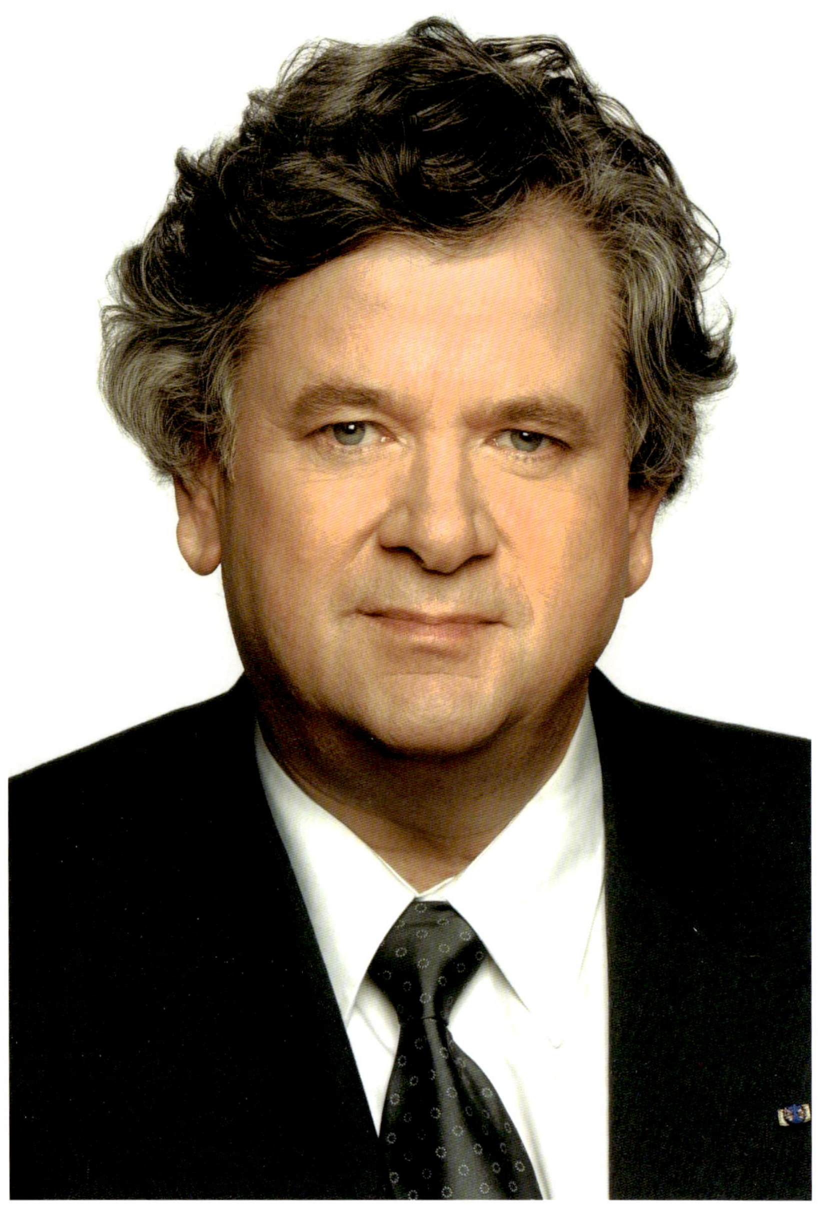

Republic of Iceland – Prime Minister David Oddsson

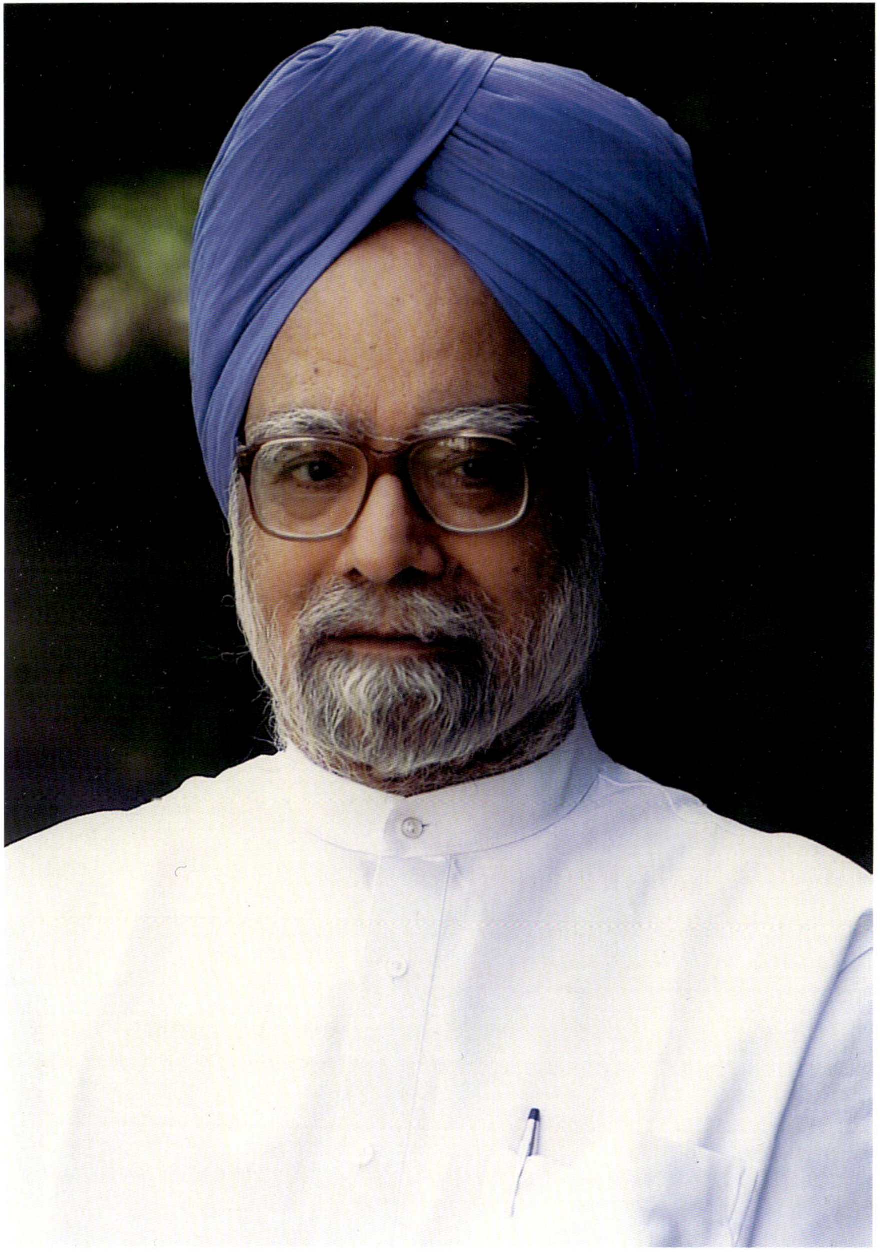

Republic of India – Prime Minister Manmohan Singh

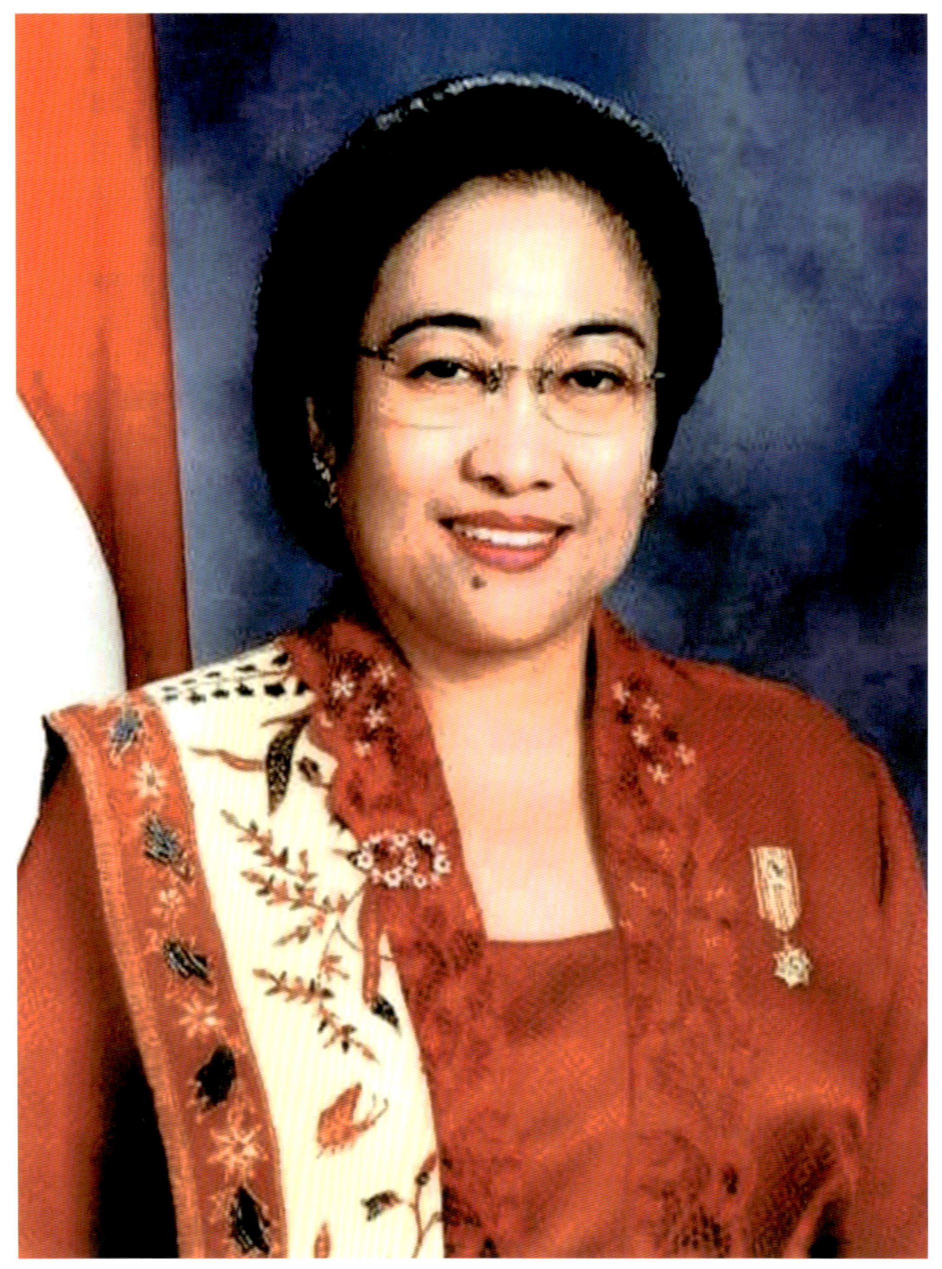

Republic of Indonesia – President Megawati Sukarnoputri

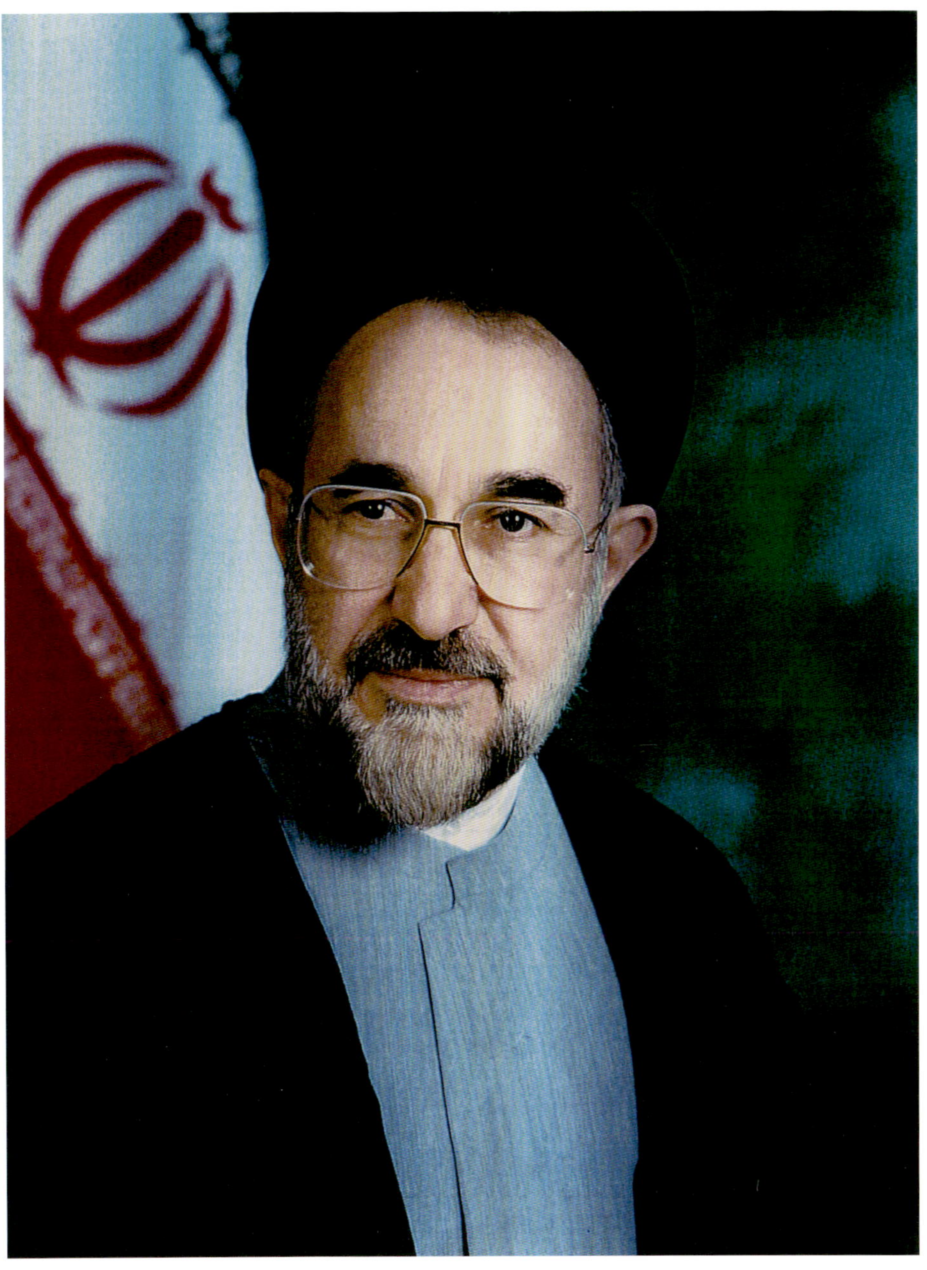

Islamic Republic of Iran – President Seyyed Mohammad Khatami

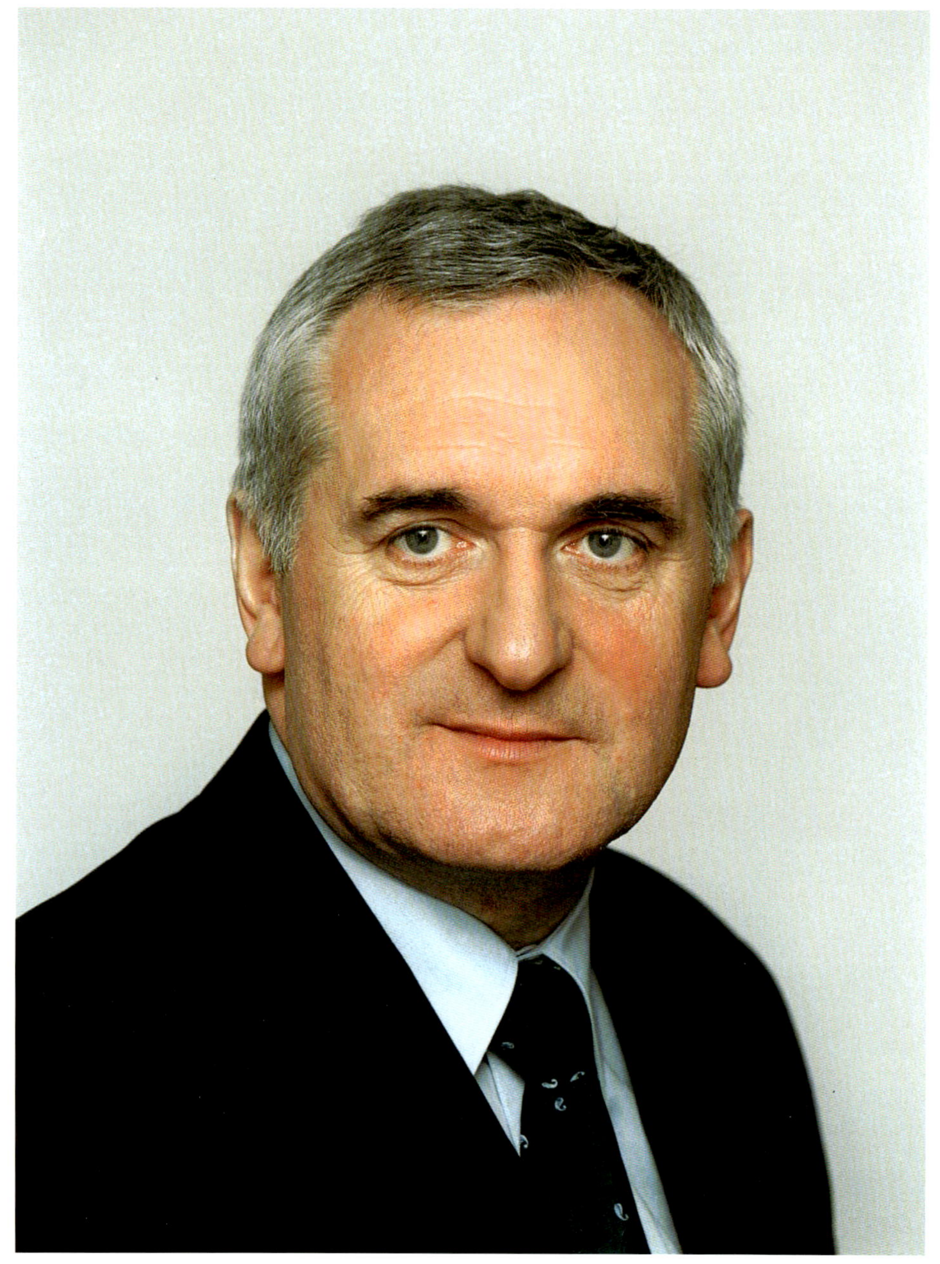

Ireland – Prime Minister Bertie Ahern

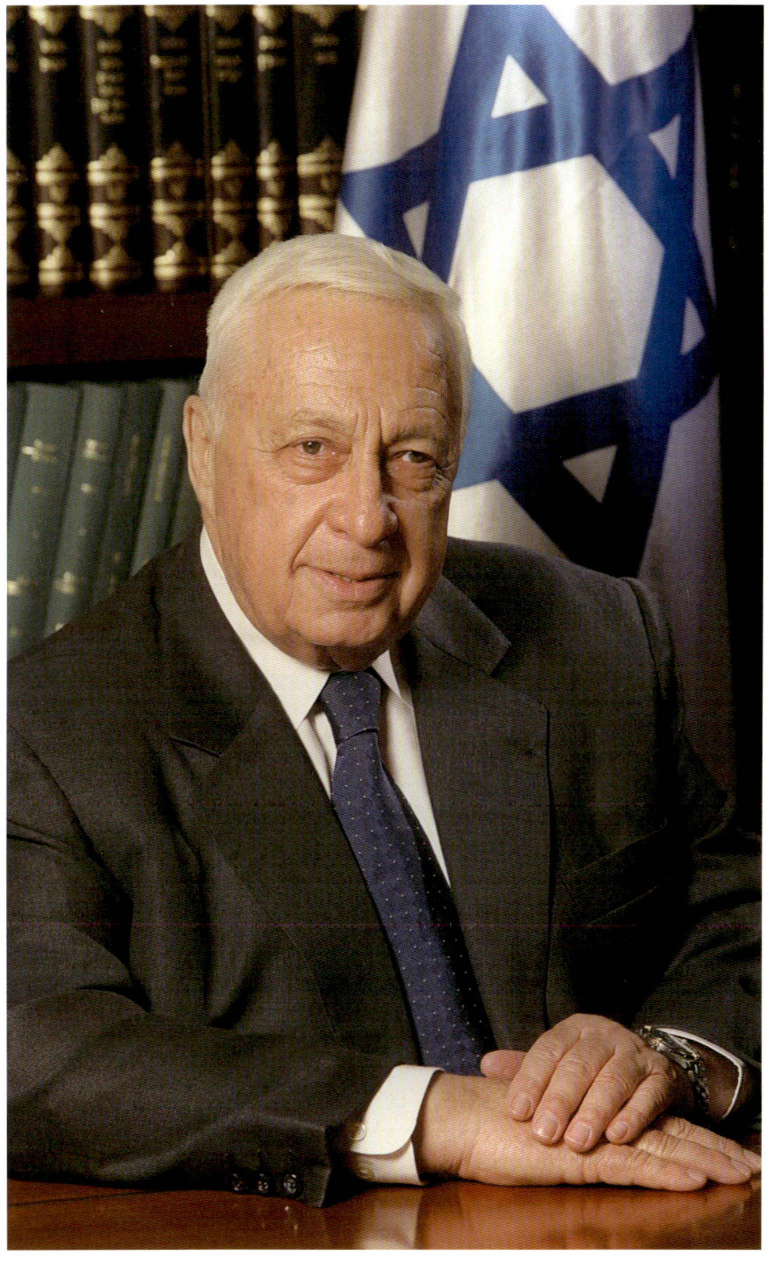

State of Israel – Prime Minister Ariel Sharon

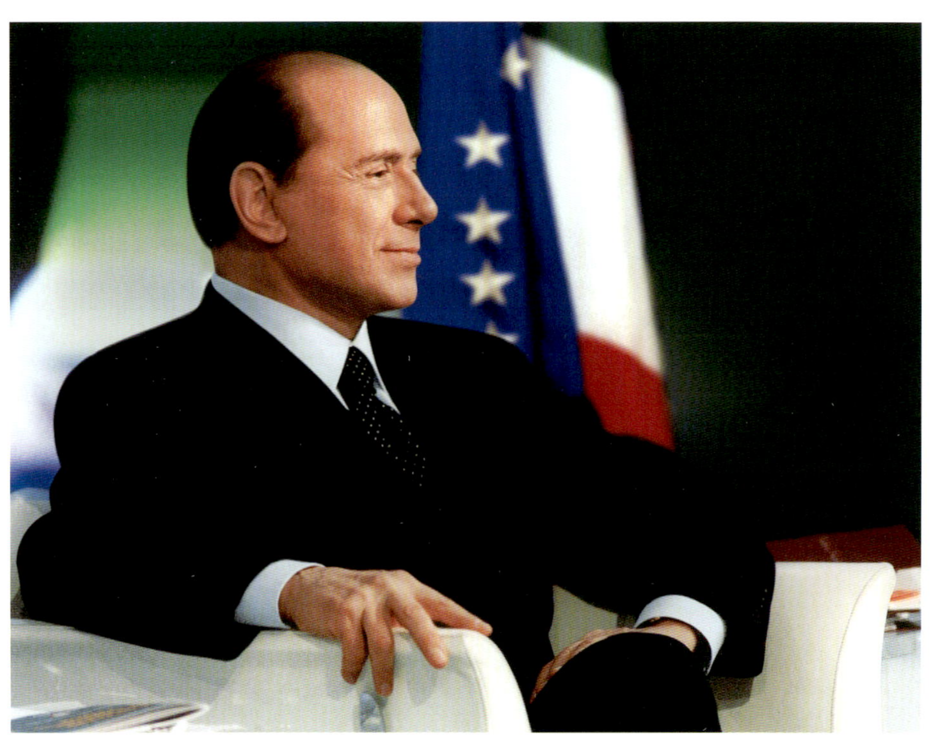

Republic of Italy – Prime Minister Silvio Berlusconi

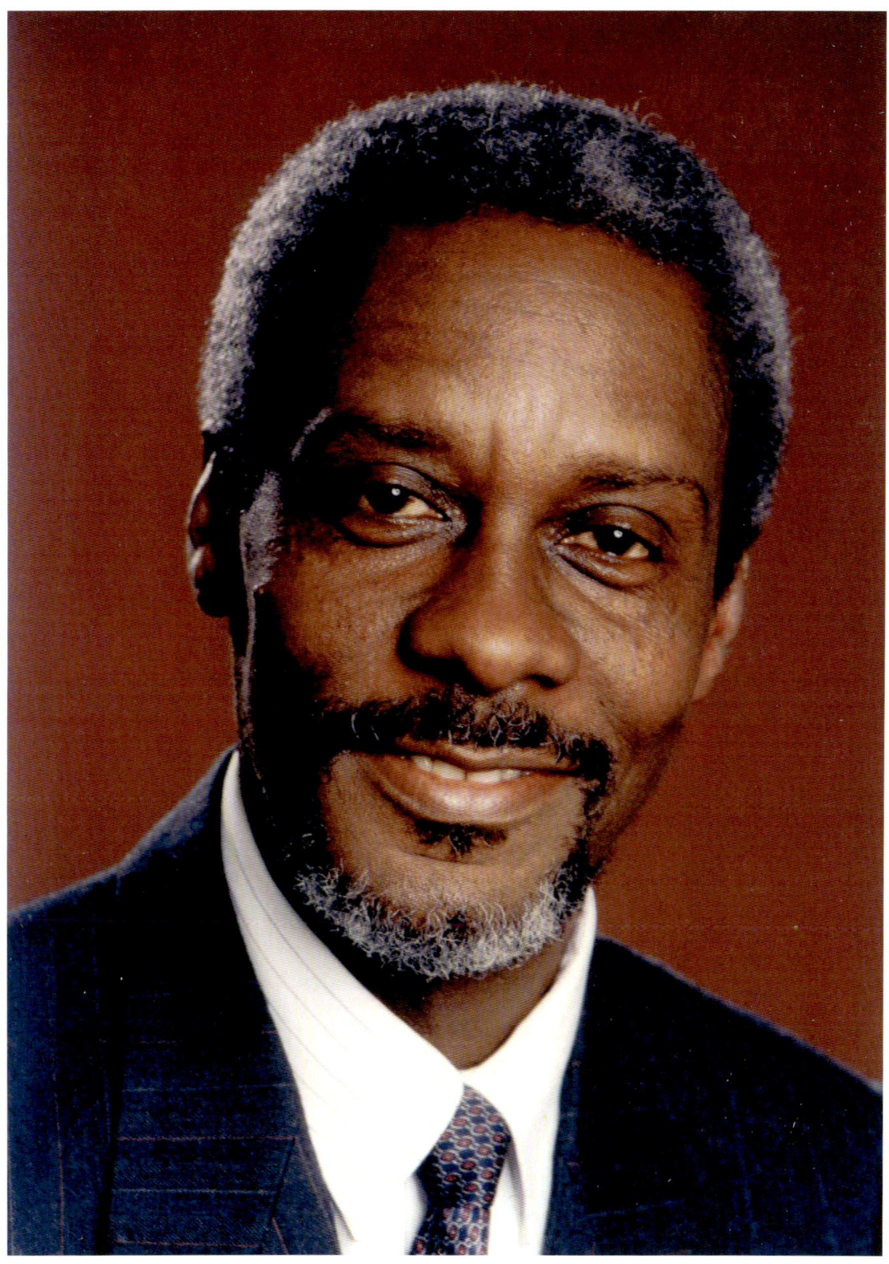

Jamaica – Prime Minister P.J. Patterson

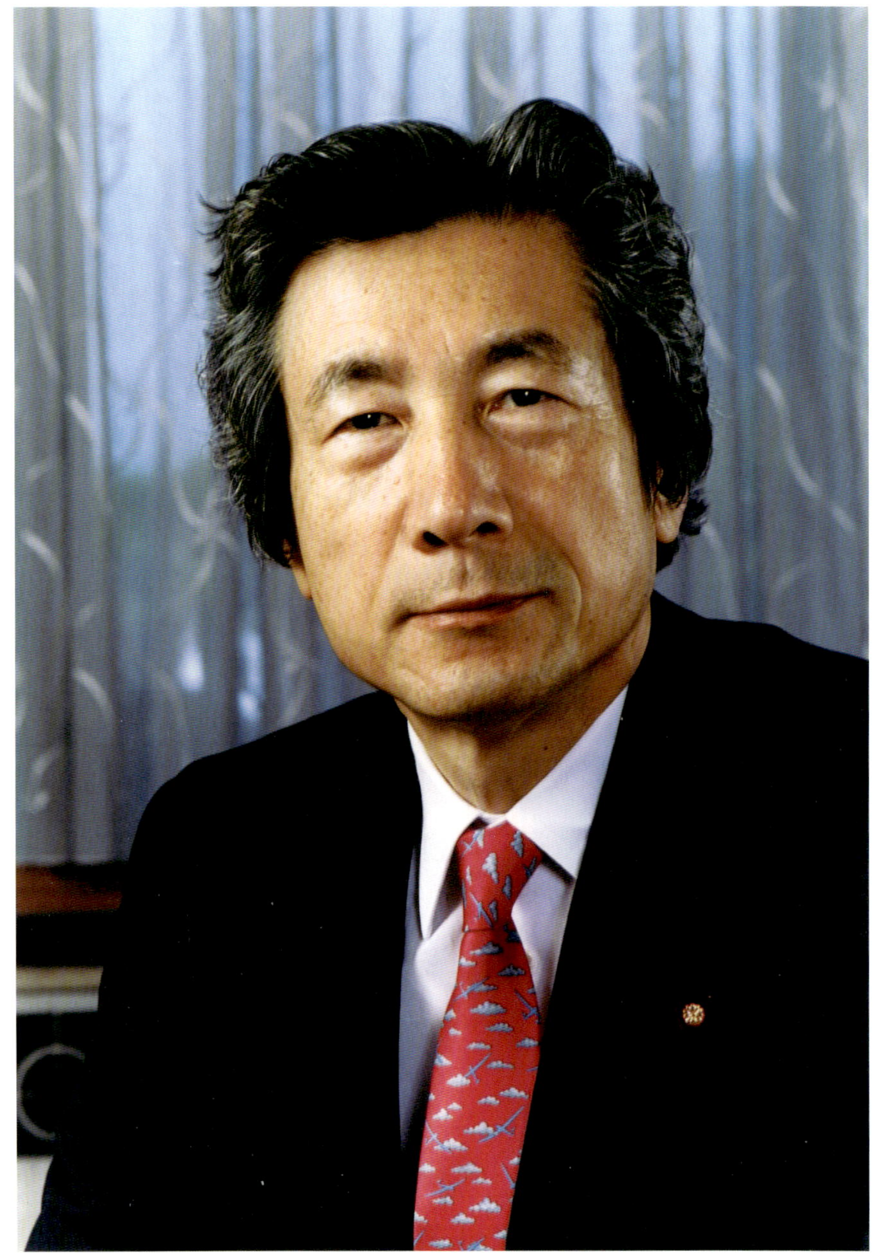

Japan – Prime Minister Junichiro Koizumi

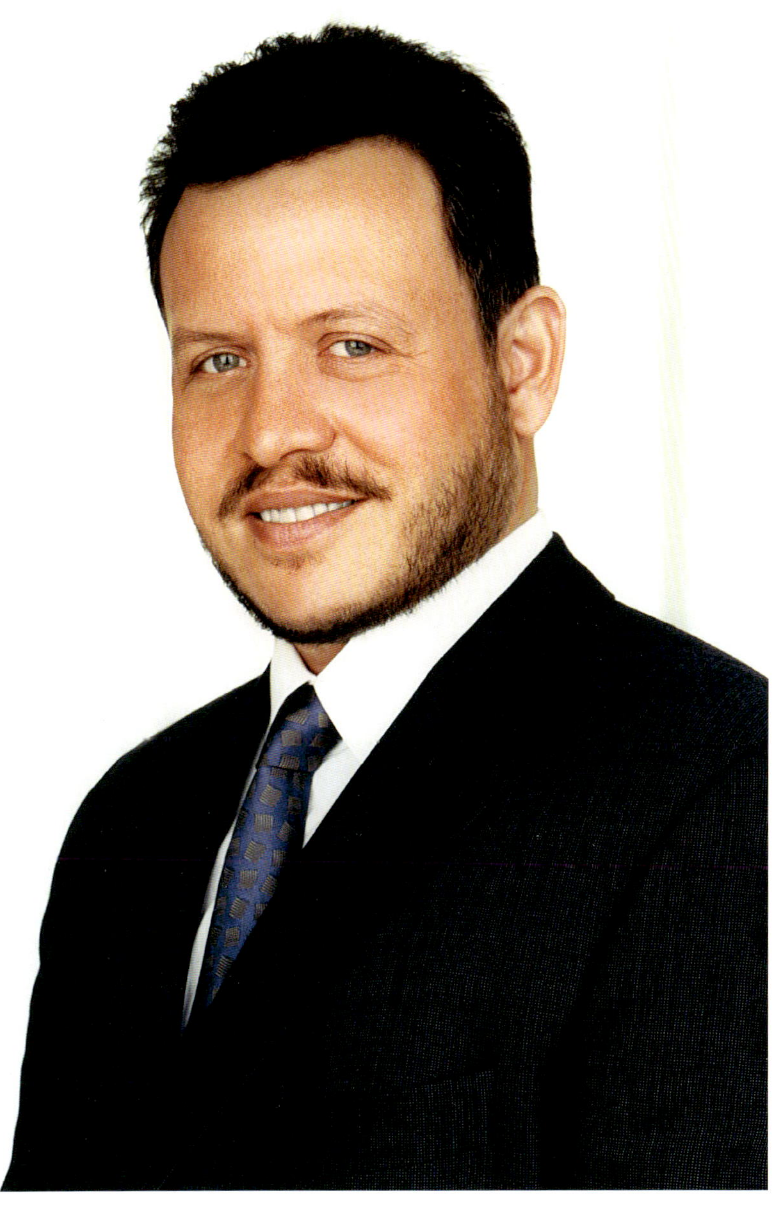

Hashemite Kingdom of Jordan – King Abdullah II

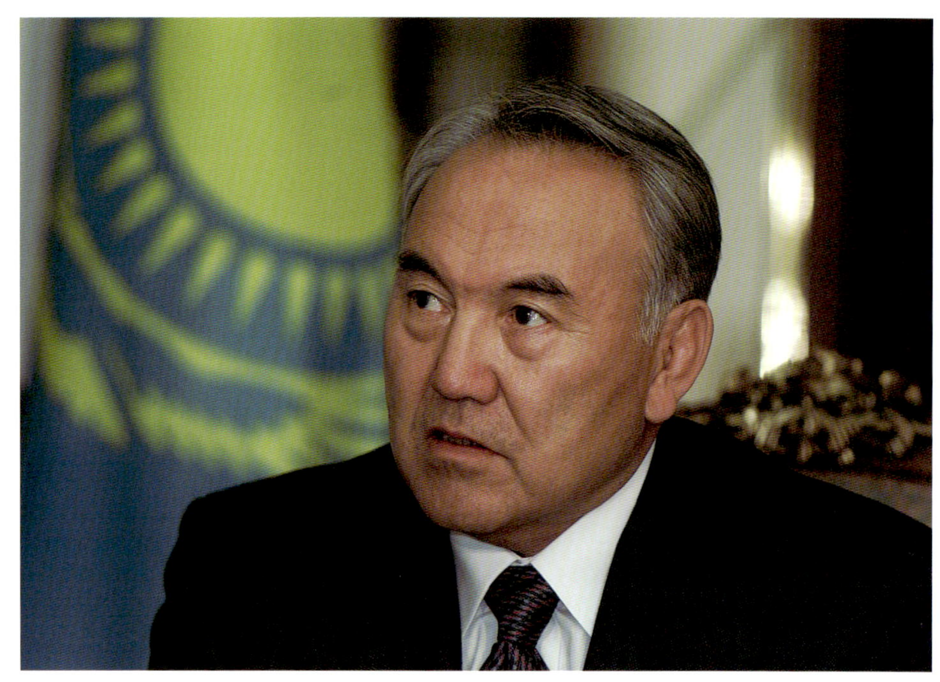

Republic of Kazakhstan – President Nursultan Nazarbayev

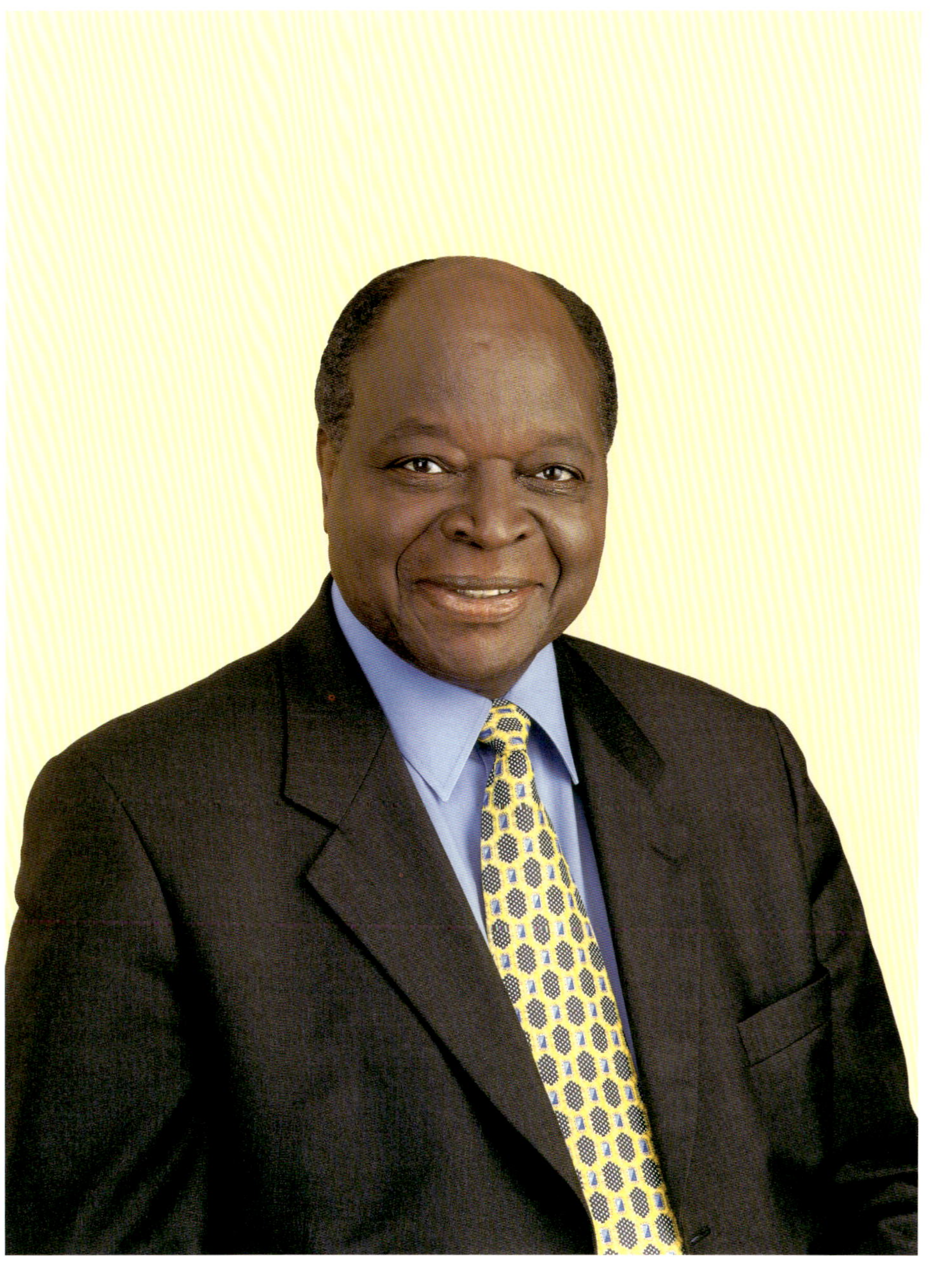

Republic of Kenya – President Mwai Kibaki

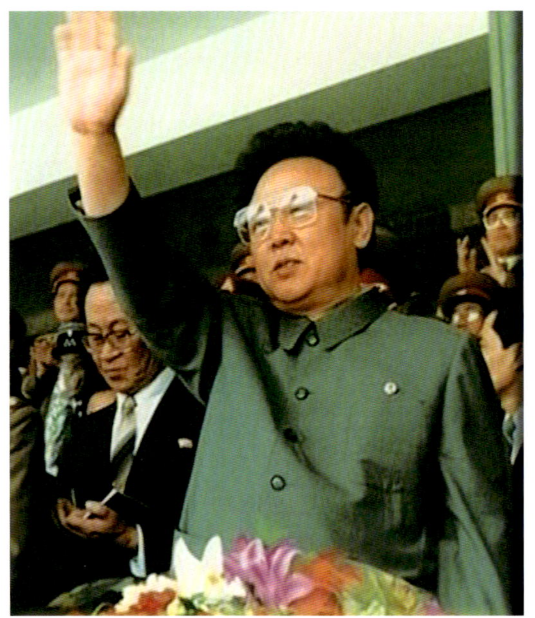

Democratic People's Republic of Korea – Chairman of the National Defence Commission
Kim Chong-il

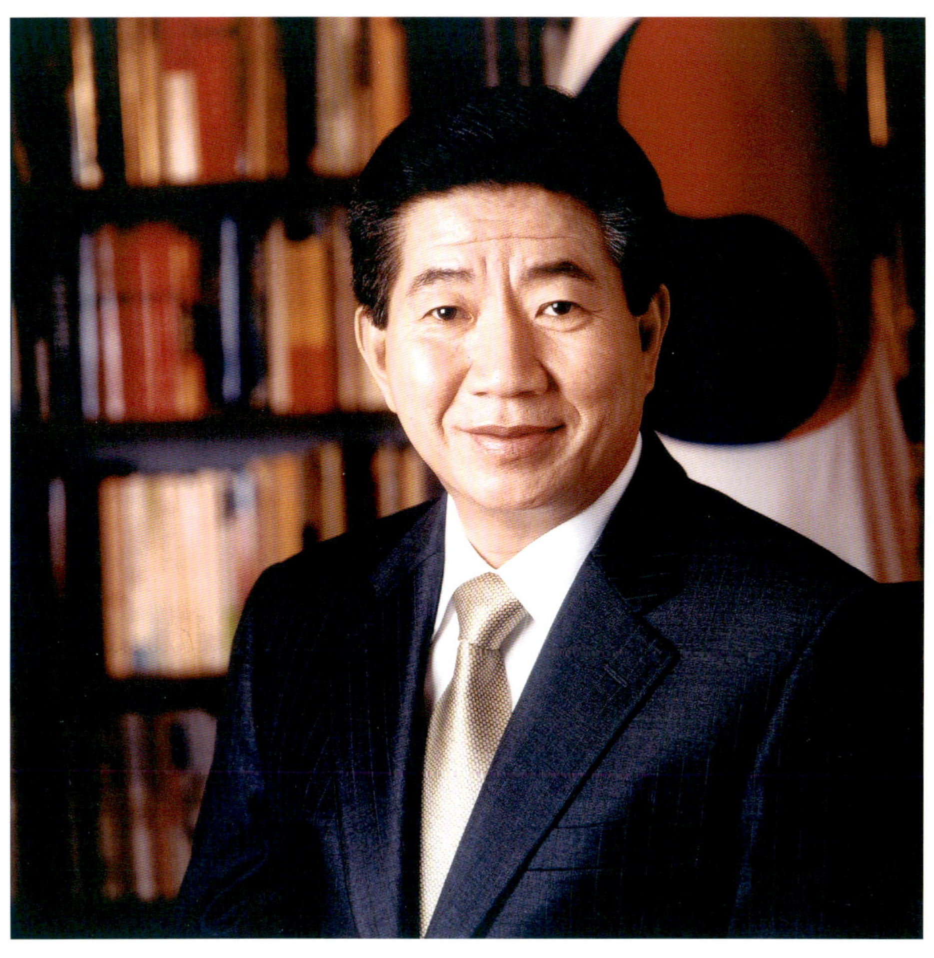

85

Republic of Korea – President Roh Moo-hyun

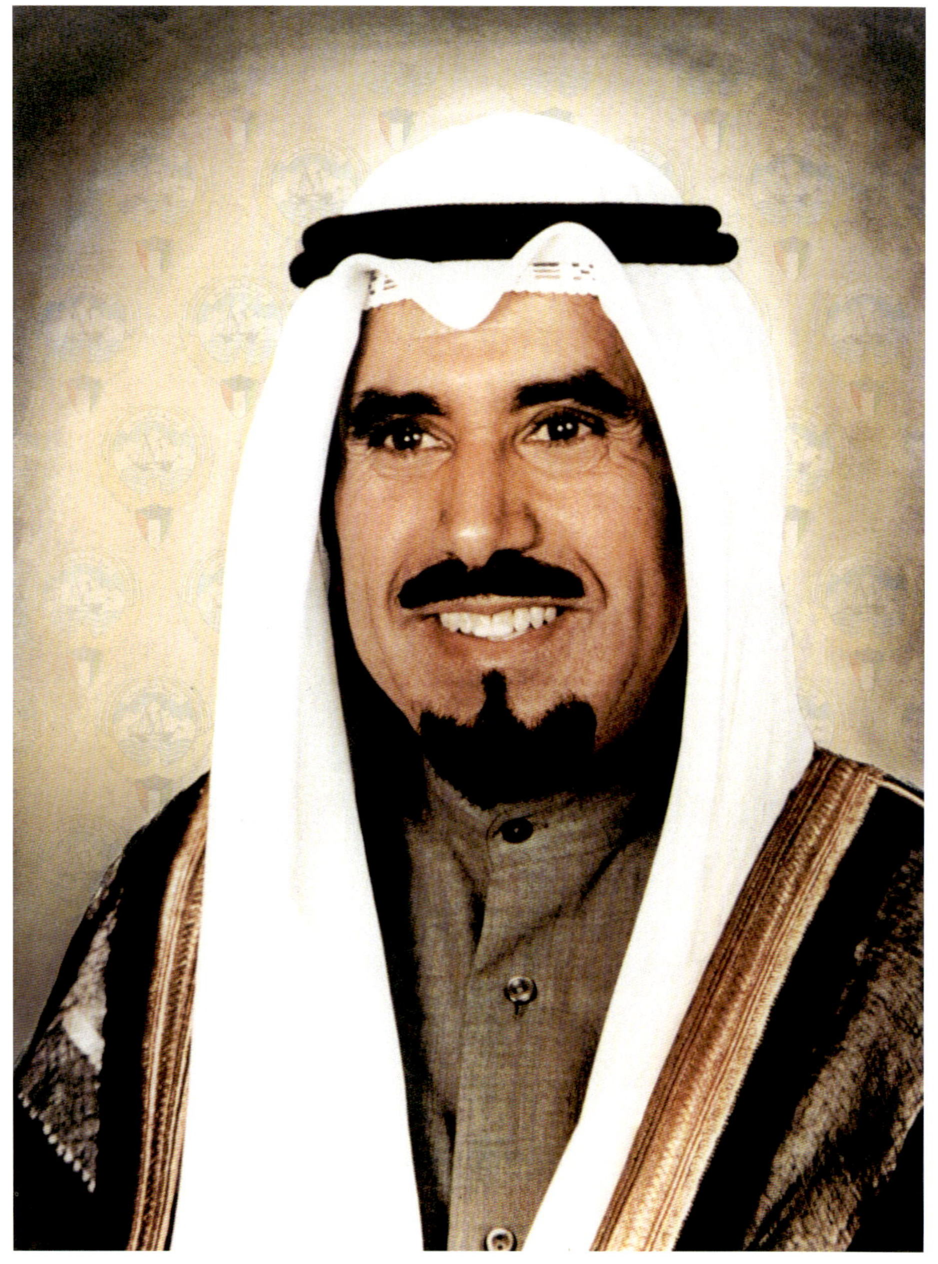

State of Kuwait – Emir Jaber Al-Ahmad Al-Jaber Al Sabah

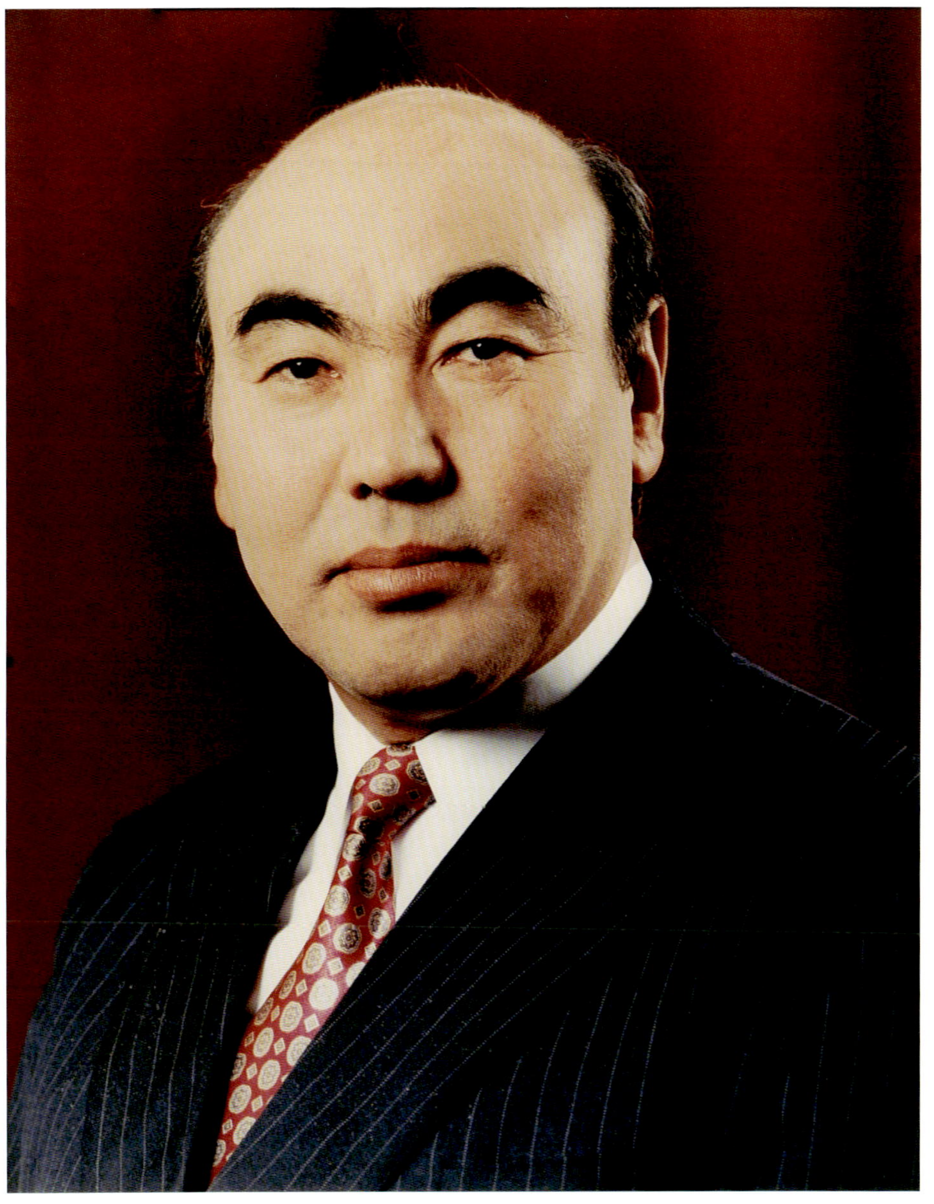

87

Republic of Kyrgyzstan – President Askar Akayev

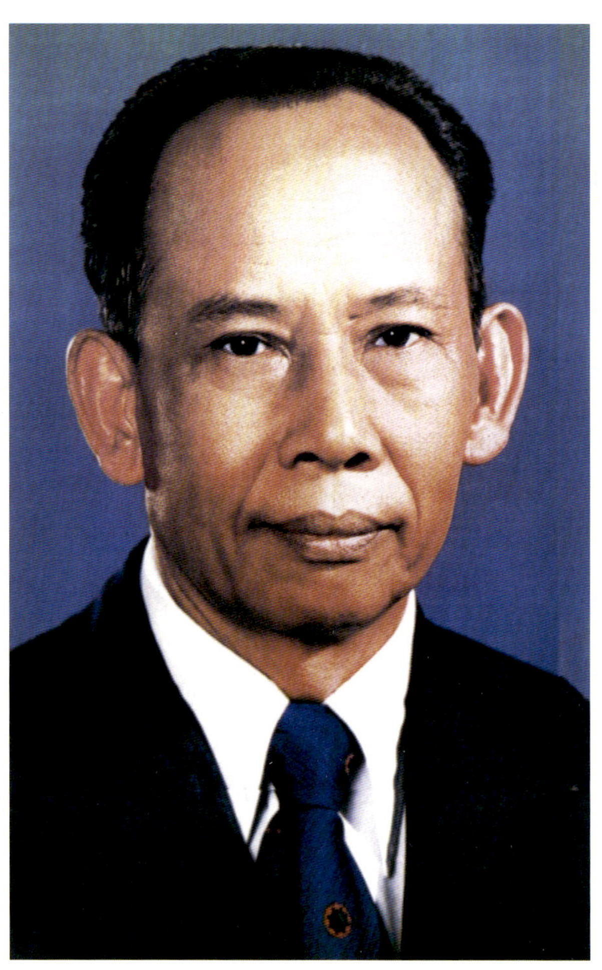

Lao People's Democratic Republic – President Khamtai Siphandone

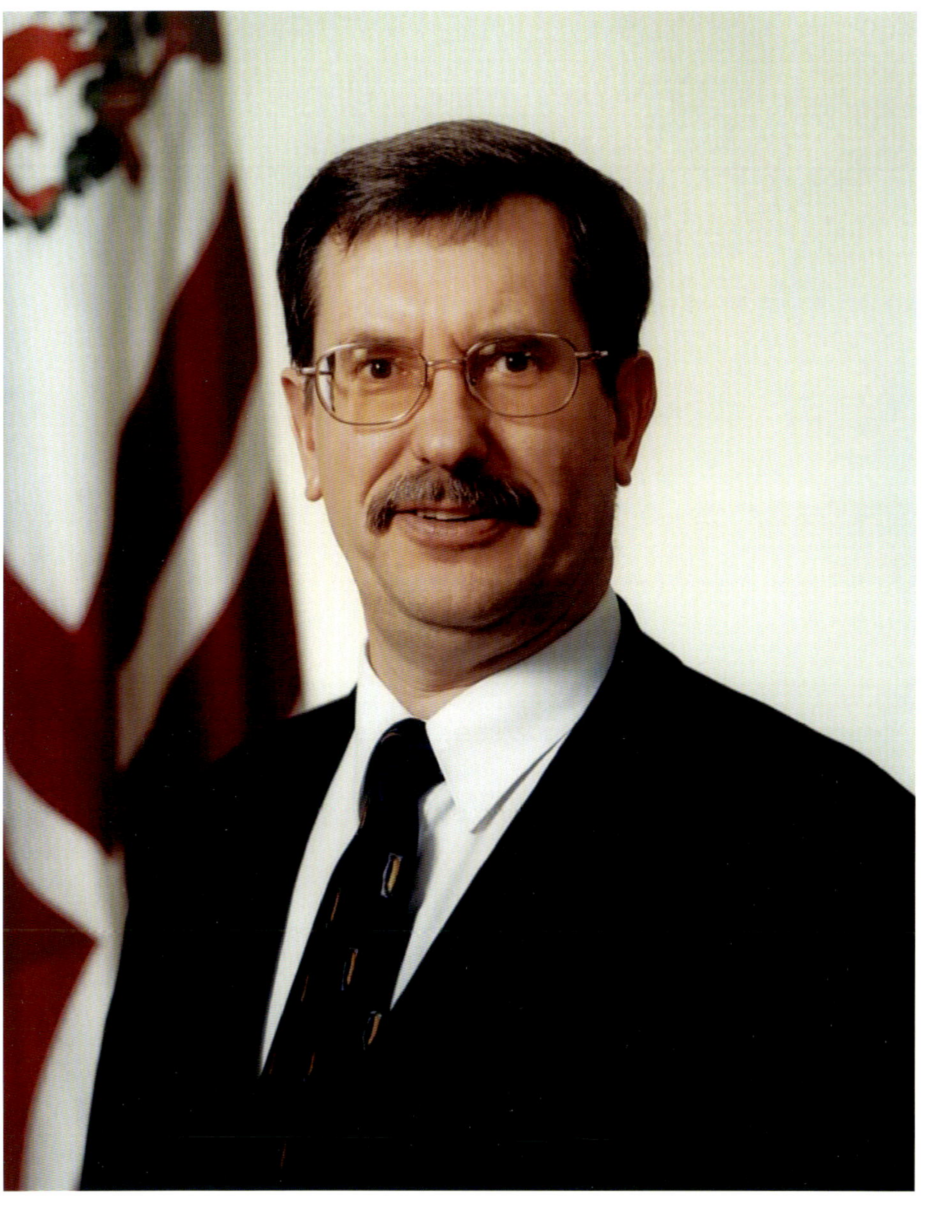

Republic of Latvia – Prime Minister Indulis Emsis

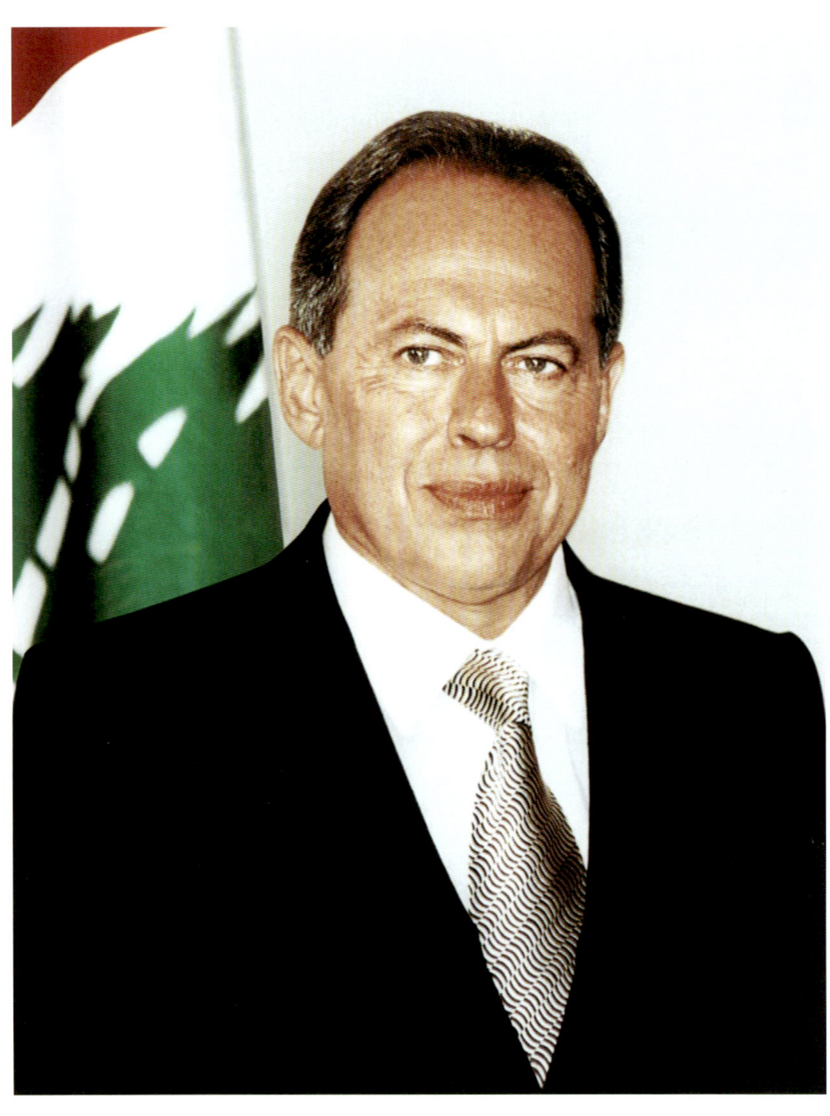

Republic of Lebanon – President Emile Lahoud

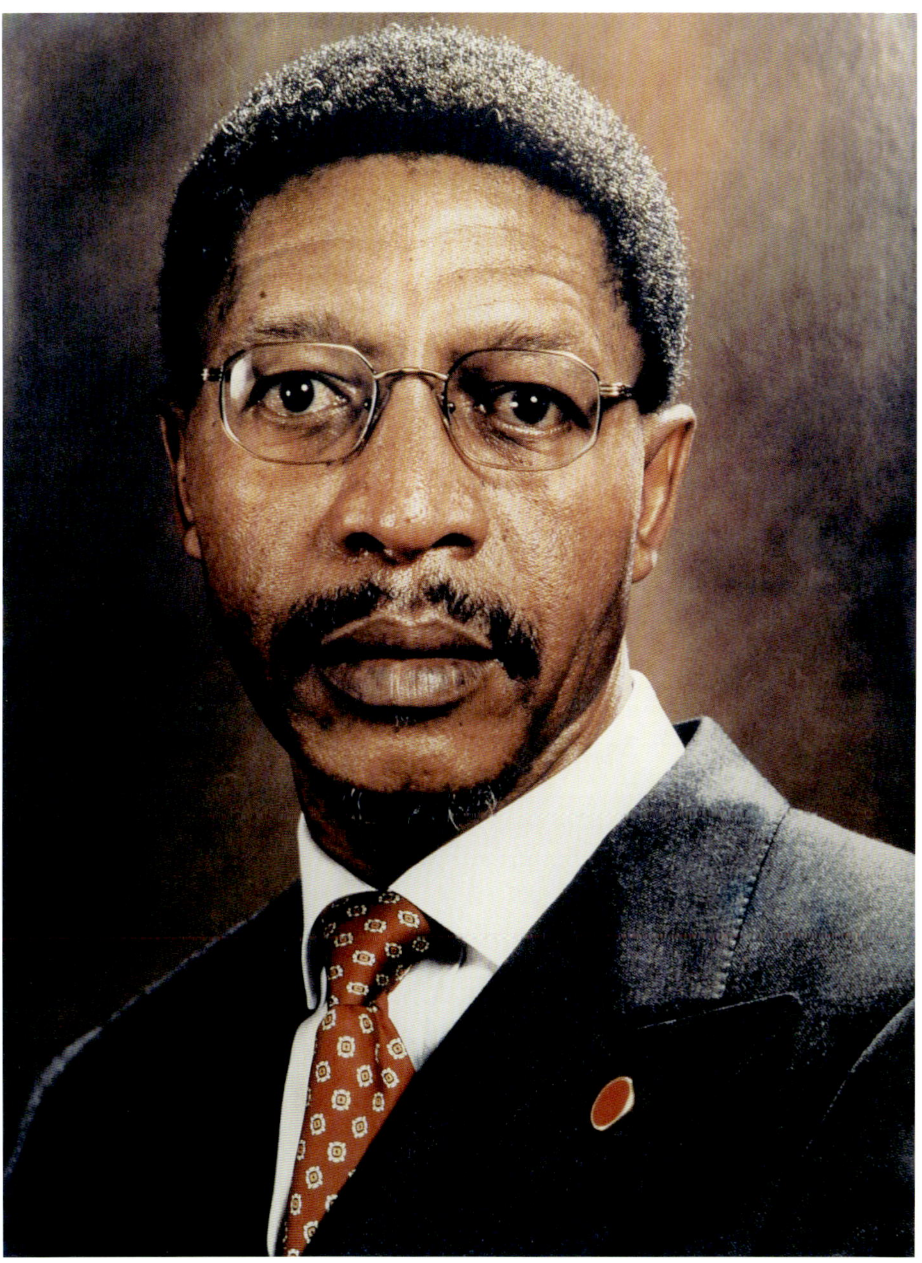

Kingdom of Lesotho – Prime Minister Bethuel Pakalitha Mosisili

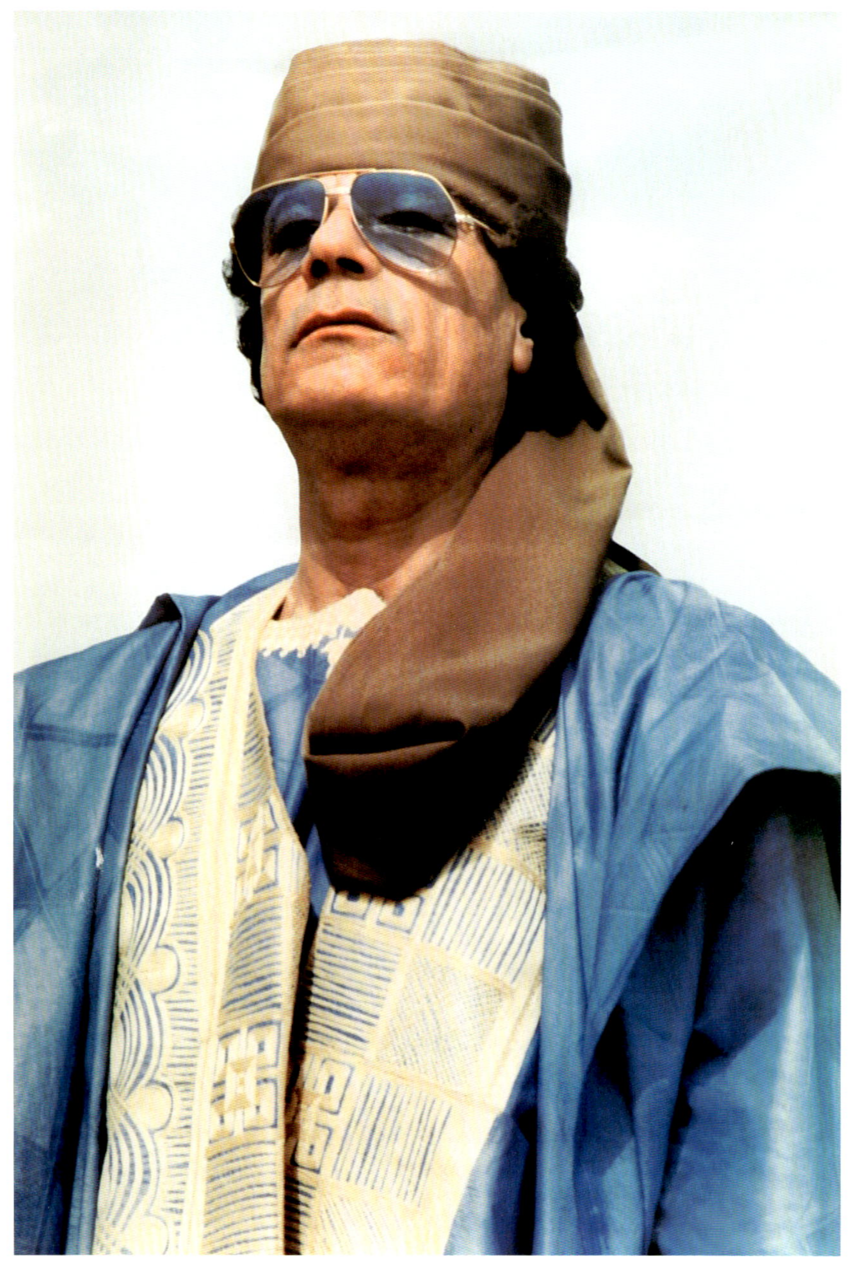

The Great Socialist People's Libyan Arab Jamahiriya – Colonel Muamar Al Qadhafi
Leader of the Great Al Fatah Revolution

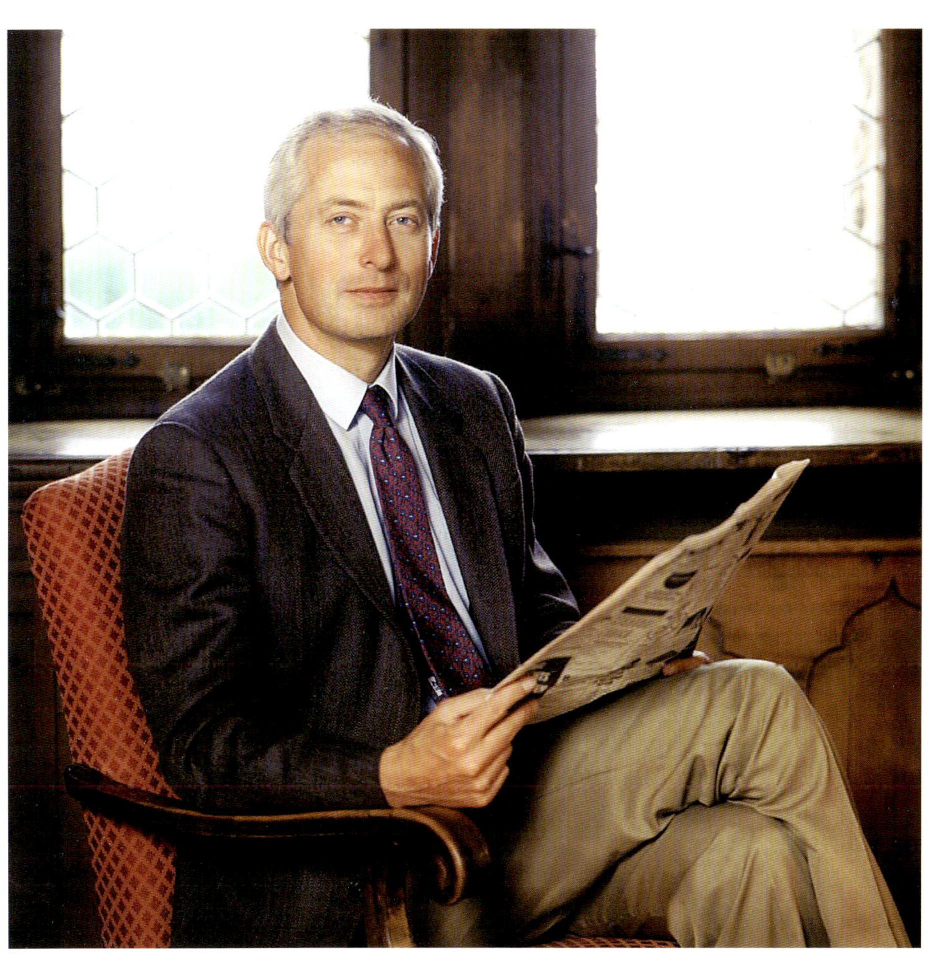

Principality of Liechtenstein – Prince Hans Adam II

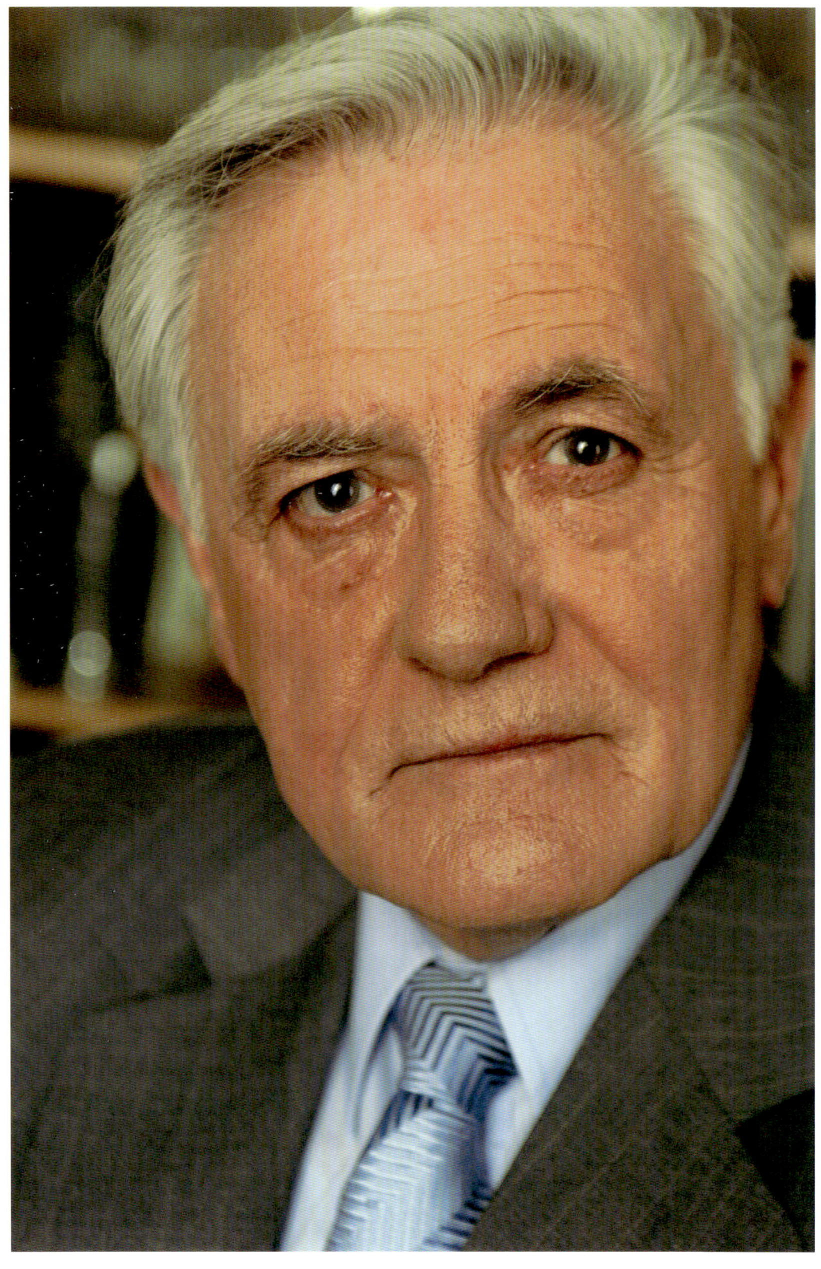

Republic of Lithuania – President Vladas Adamkus

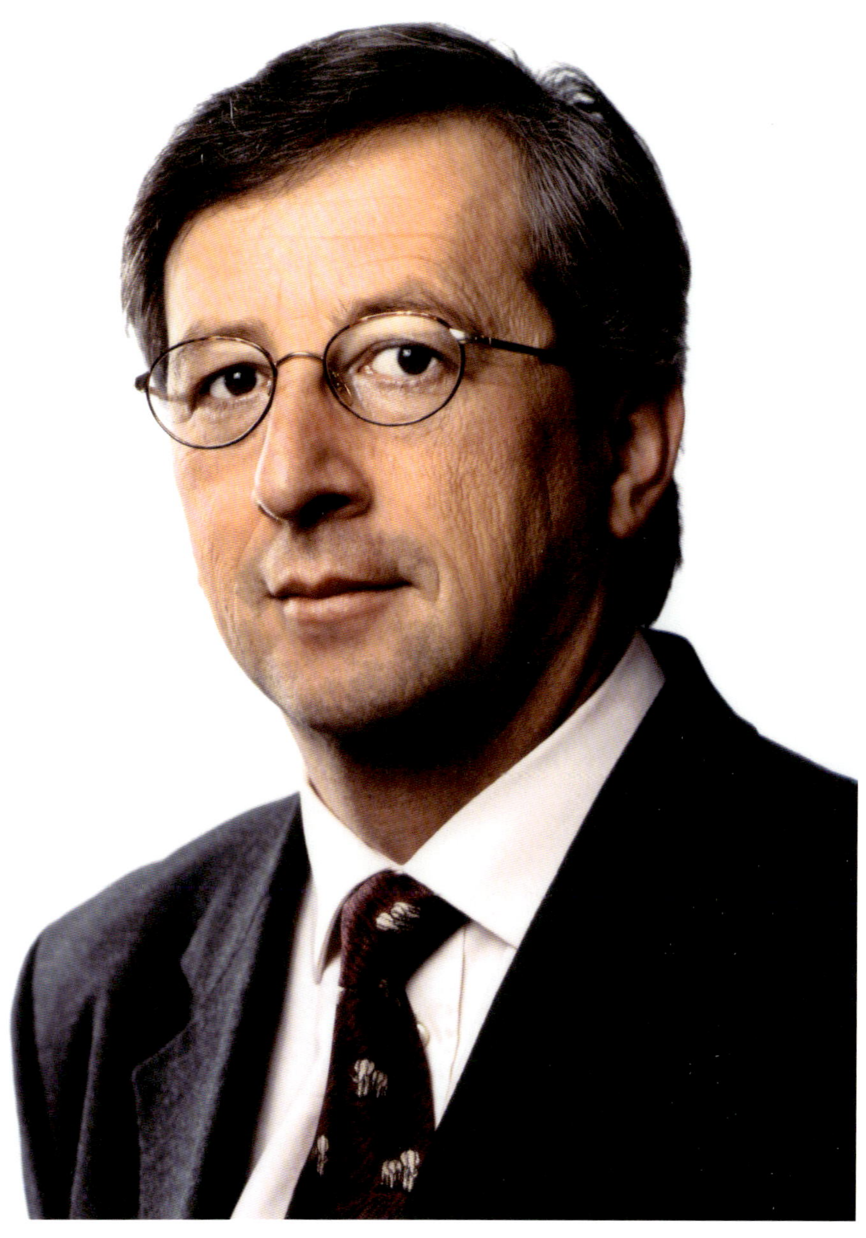

Grand Duchy of Luxembourg – Prime Minister Jean-Claude Juncker

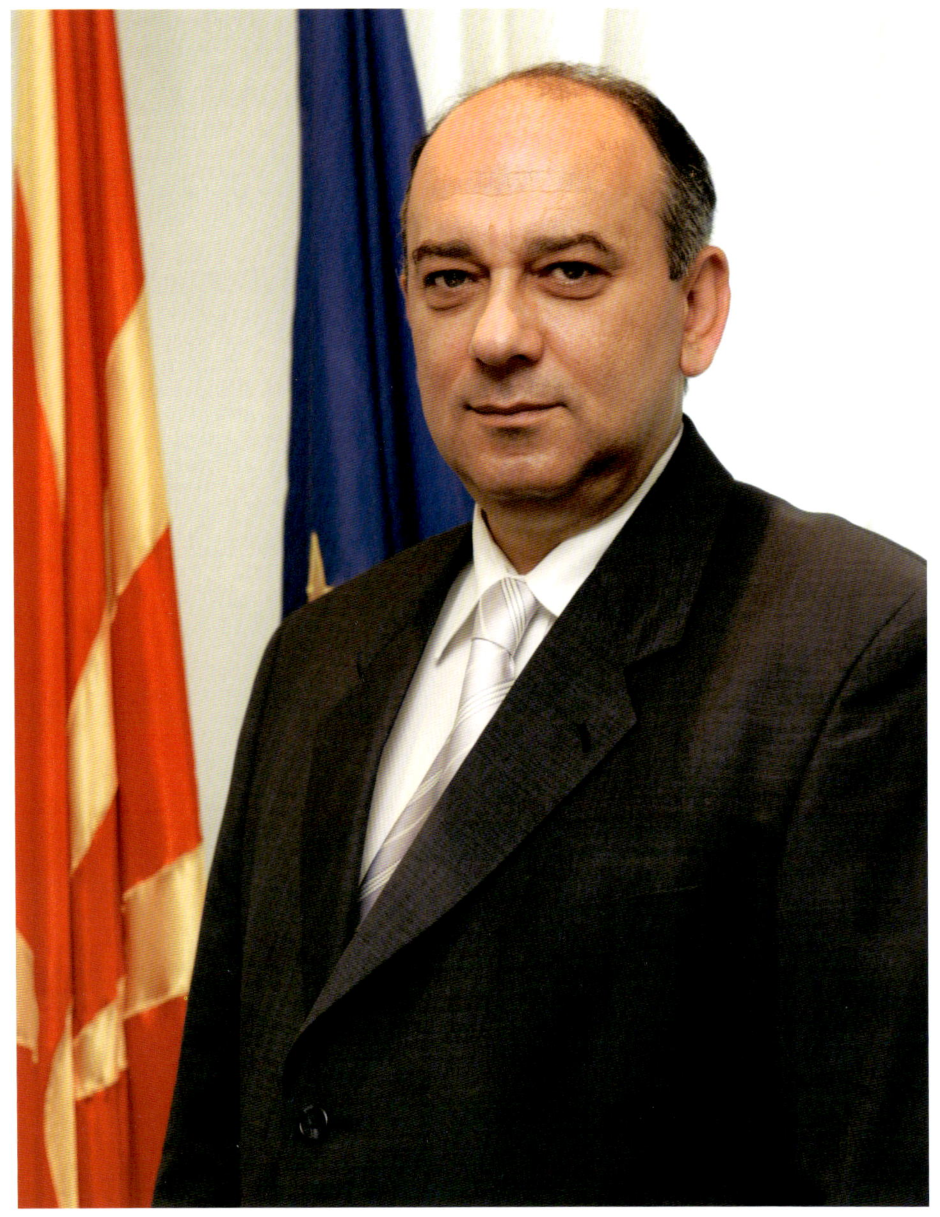

The Former Yugolslav Republic of Macedonia – Prime Minister Hari Kostov

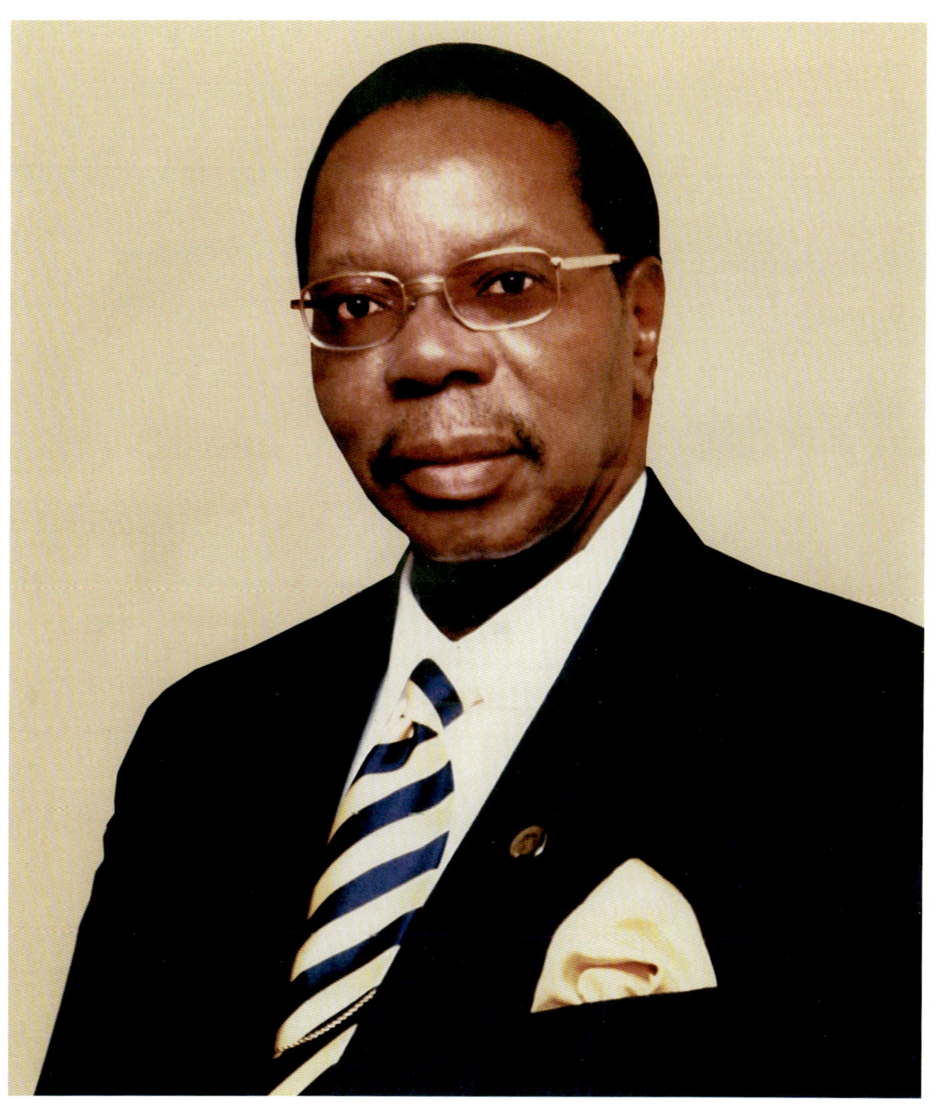

Republic of Malawi – President Bingu wa Mutharika

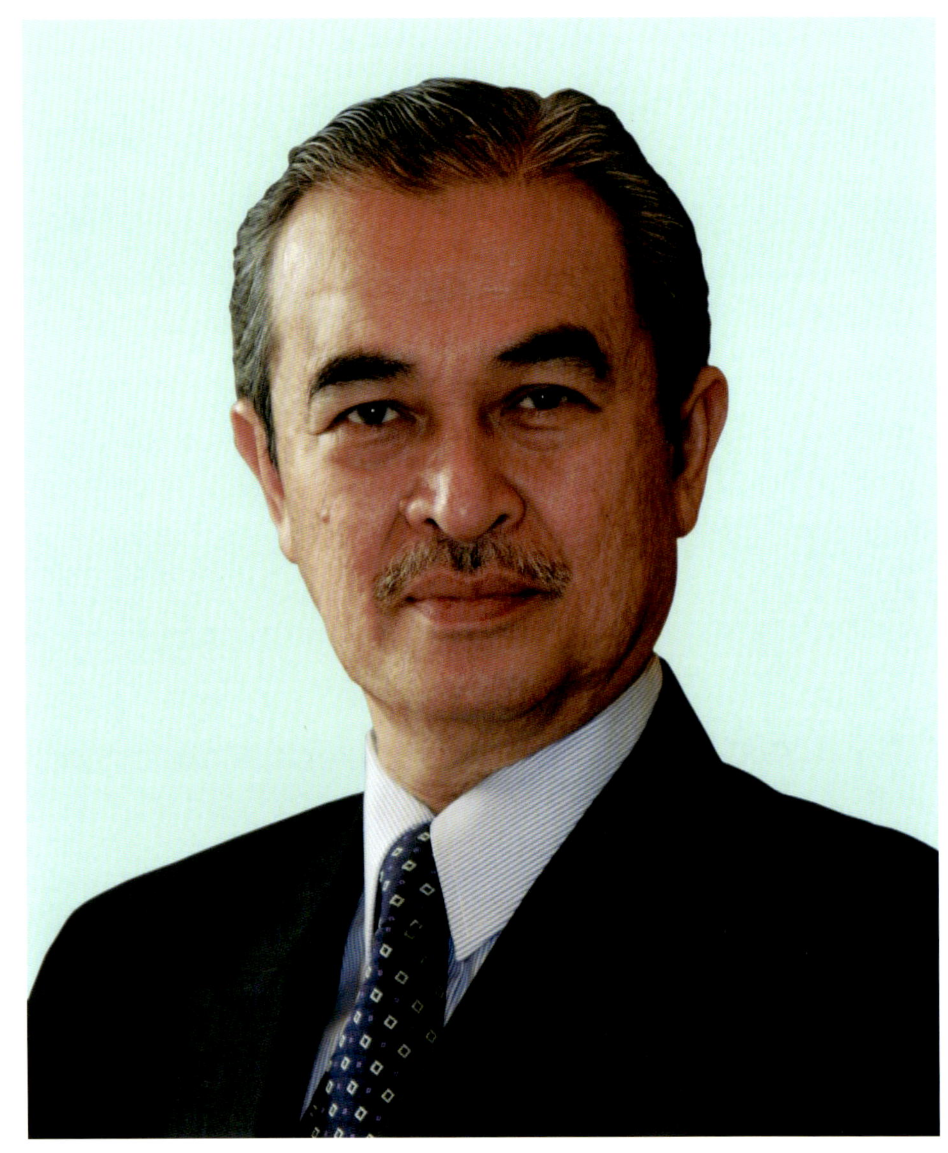

Malaysia – Prime Minister Dato' Seri Abdullah Ahmad Badawi

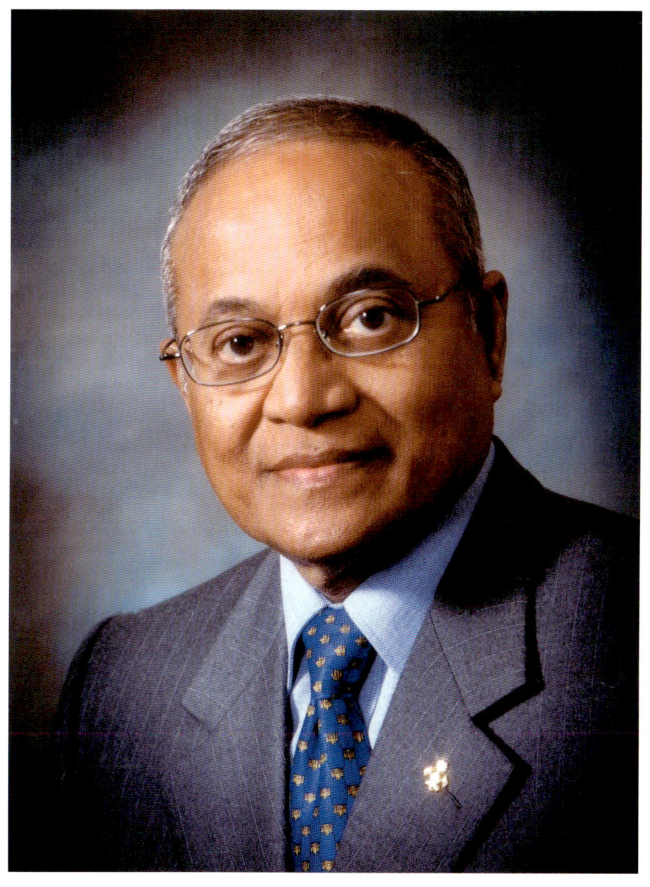

Republic of Maldives – President Maumoon Abdul Gayoom

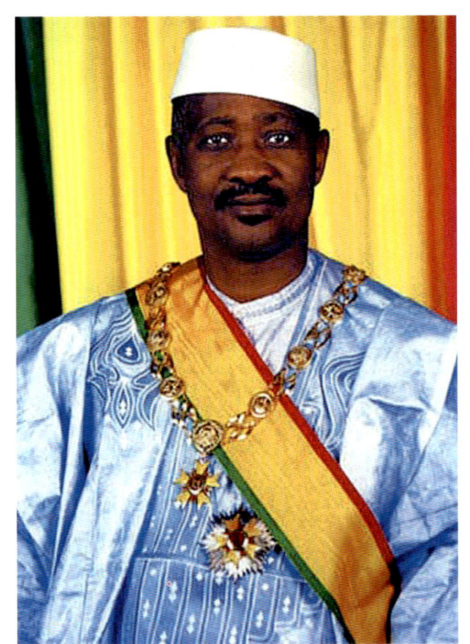

Republic of Mali – President Amadou Toumani Touré

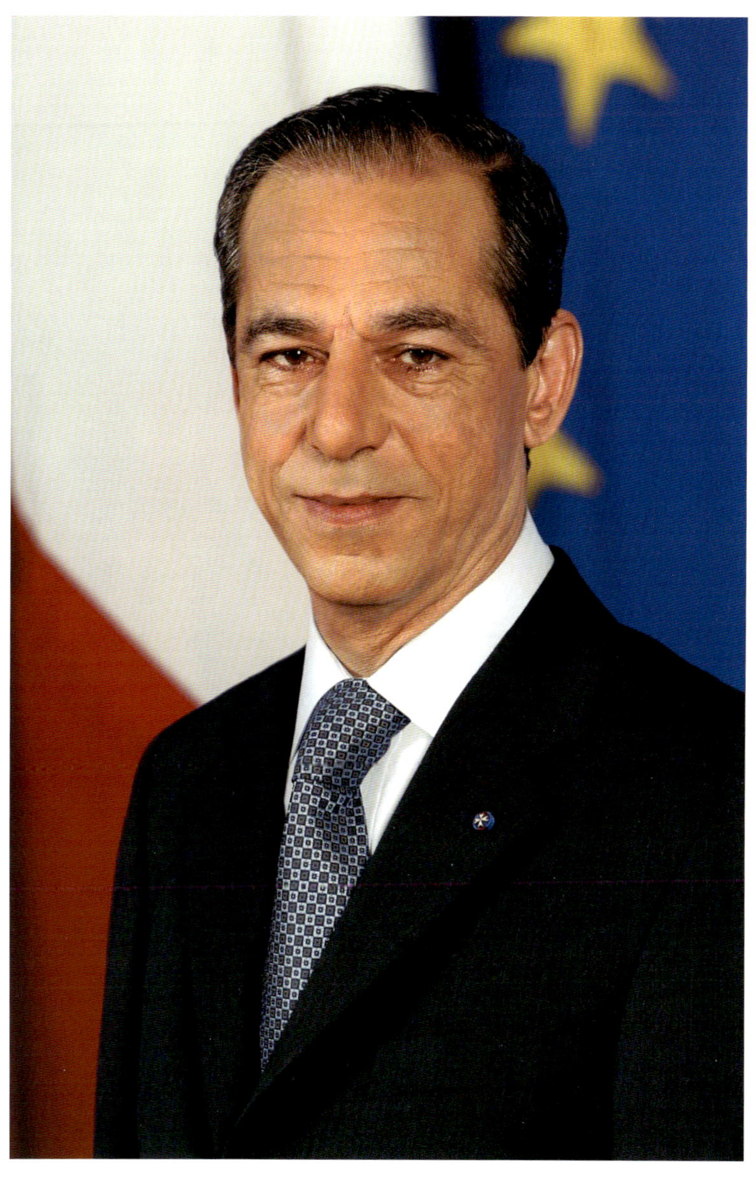

Republic of Malta – Prime Minister Lawrence Gonzi

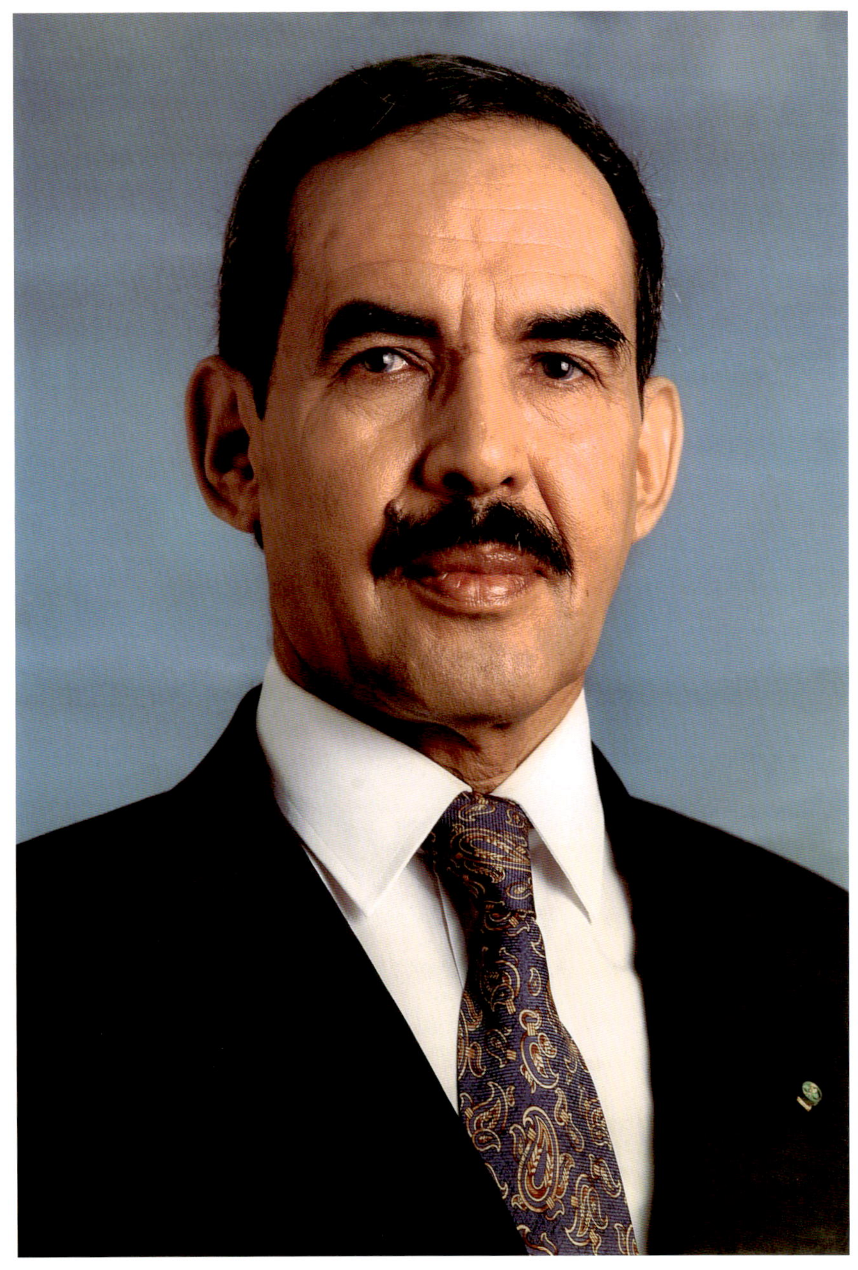

Islamic Republic of Mauritania – President Maaouya Ould Sidi Ahmed Taya

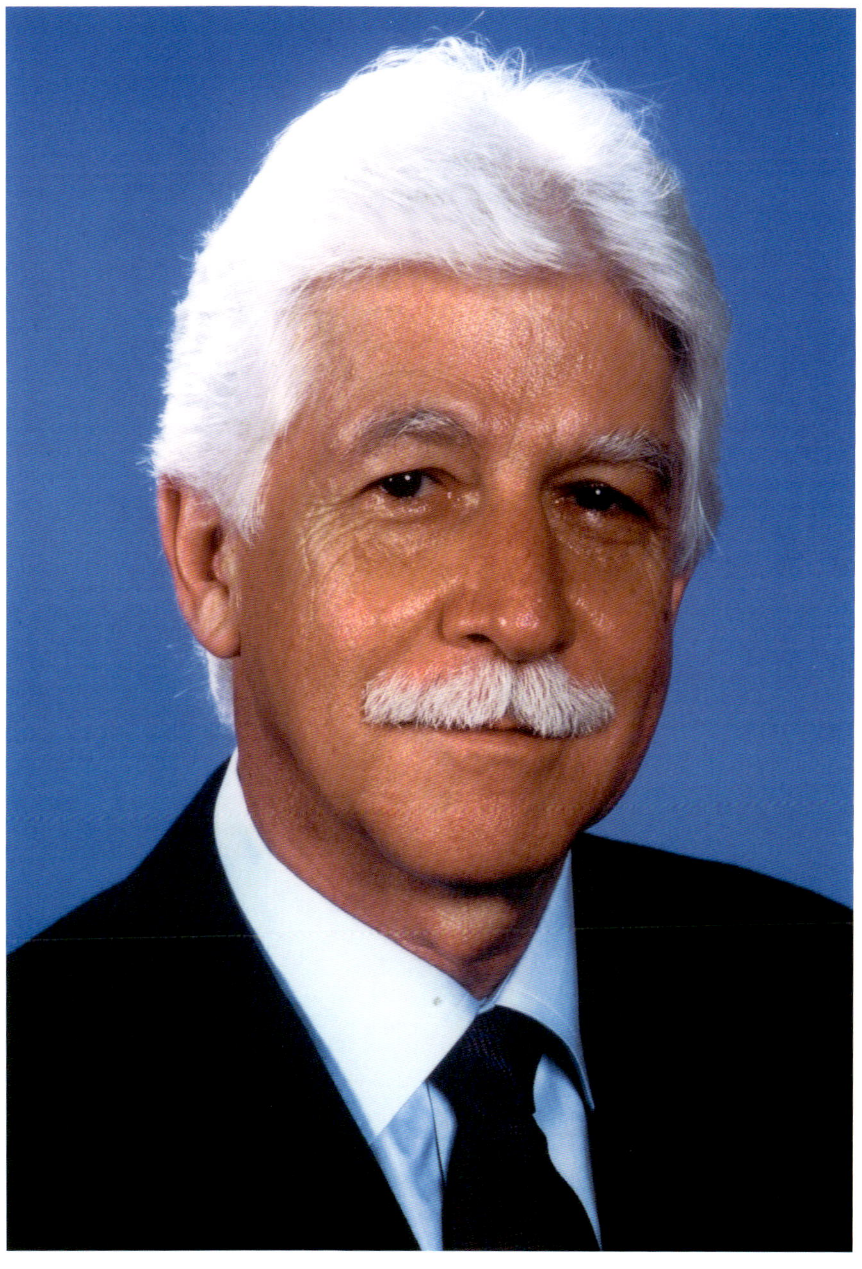

Republic of Mauritius – Prime Minister Paul Raymond Bérenger

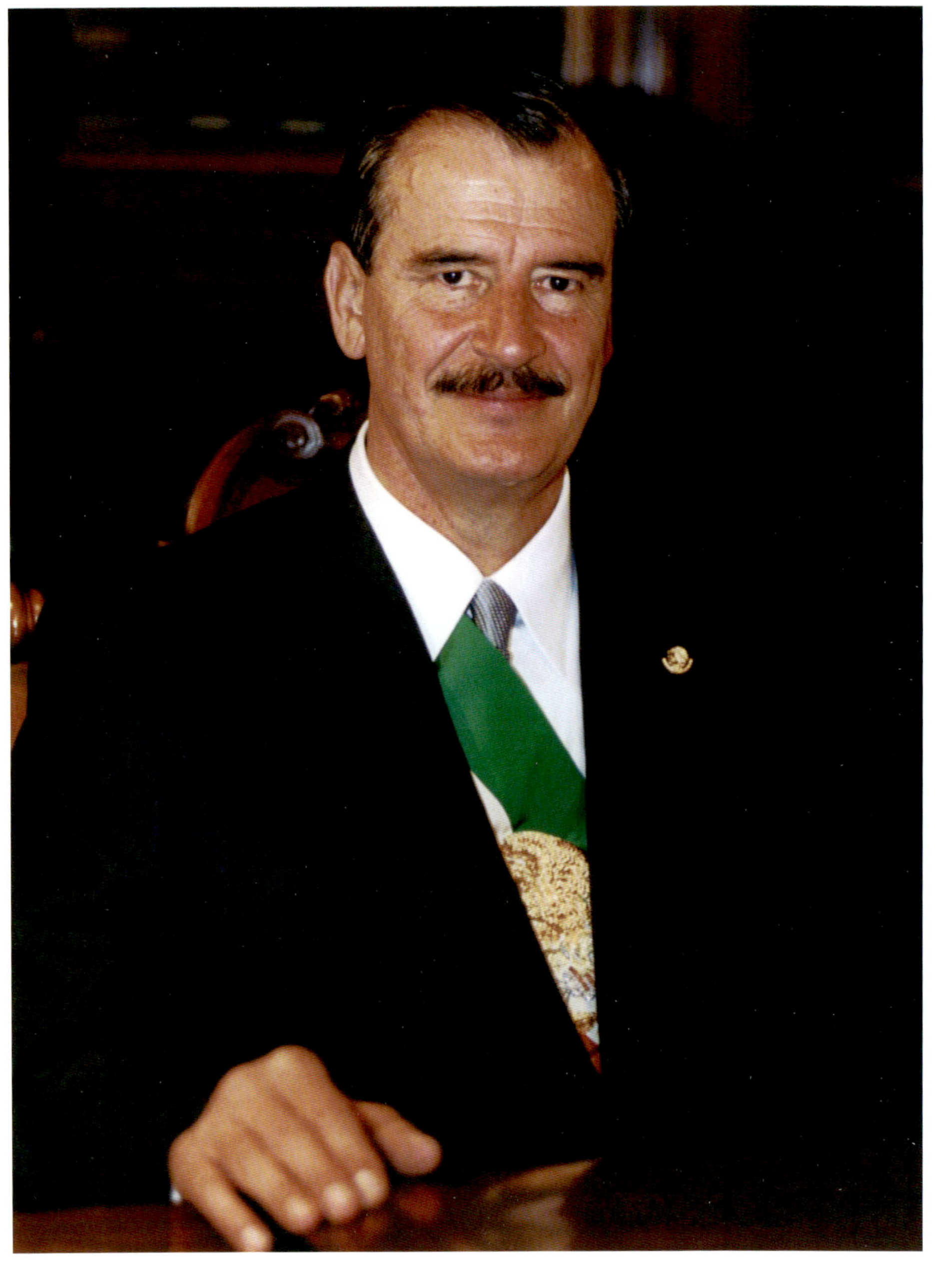

Mexico – President Vincente Fox Quesada

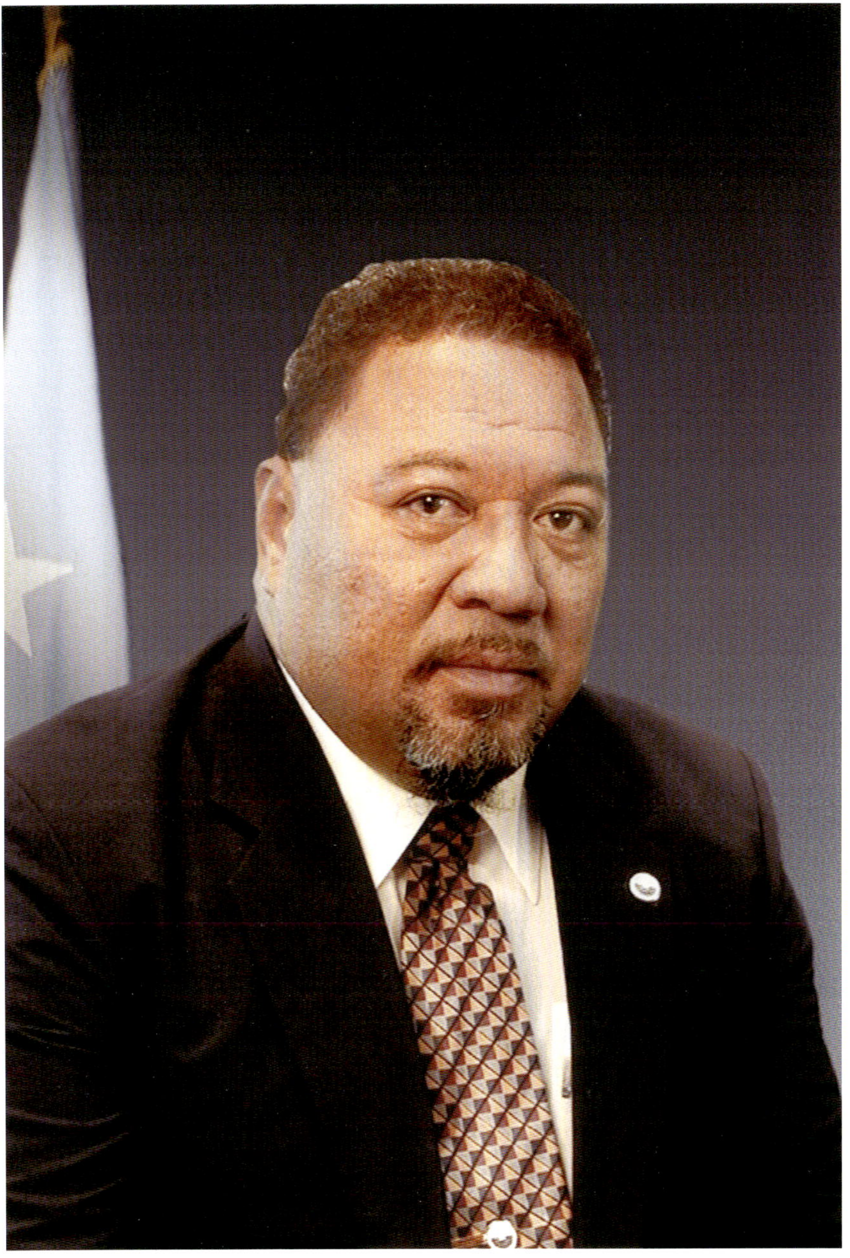

Federated States of Micronesia – President Joseph J. Urusemal

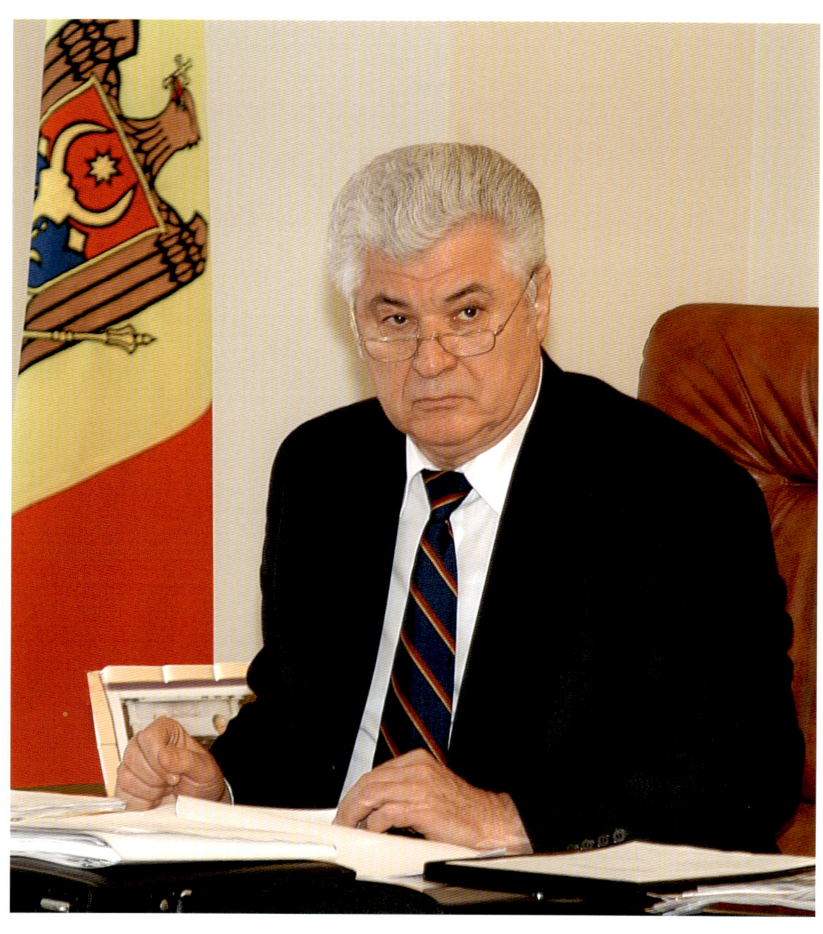

Republic of Moldova – President Vladimir Voronin

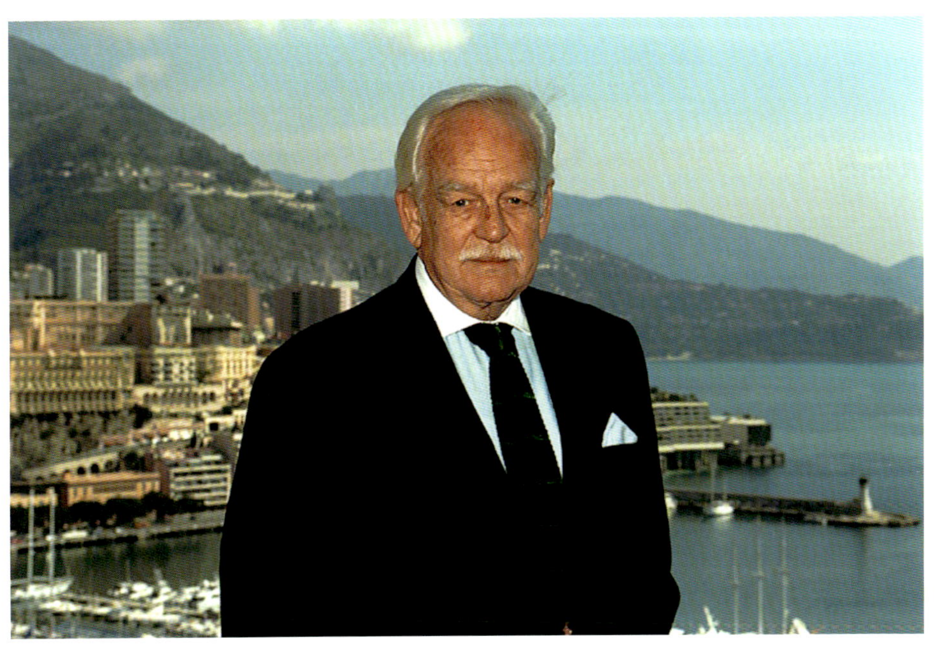

Principality of Monaco – Prince Rainier III

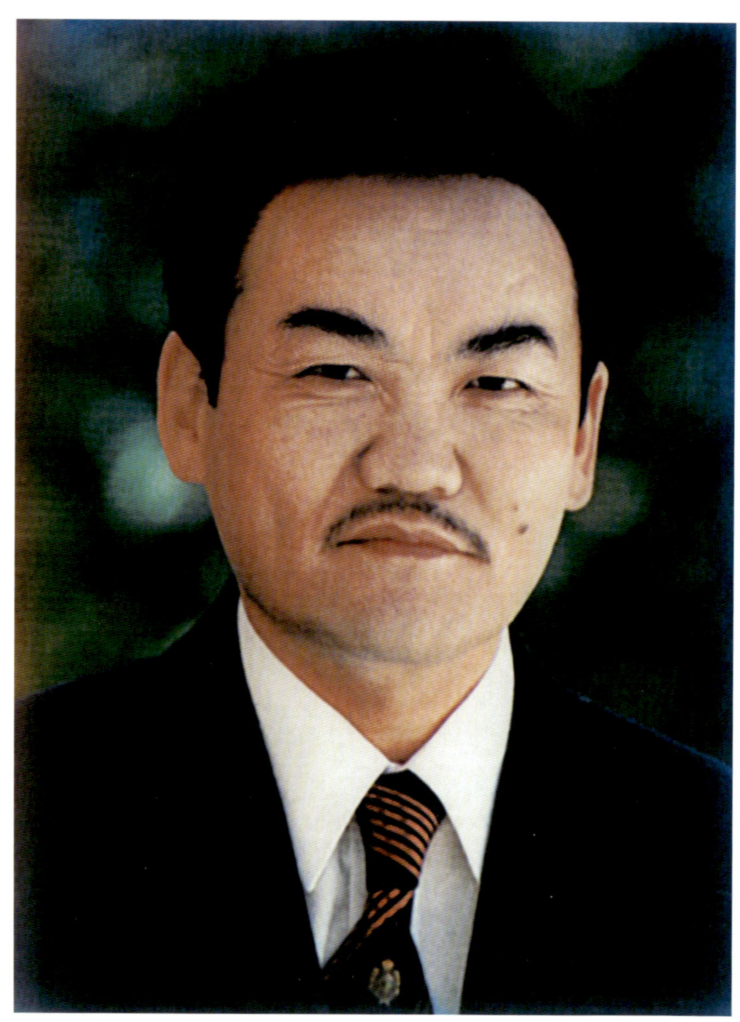

Mongolia – President Natsagiin Bagabandi

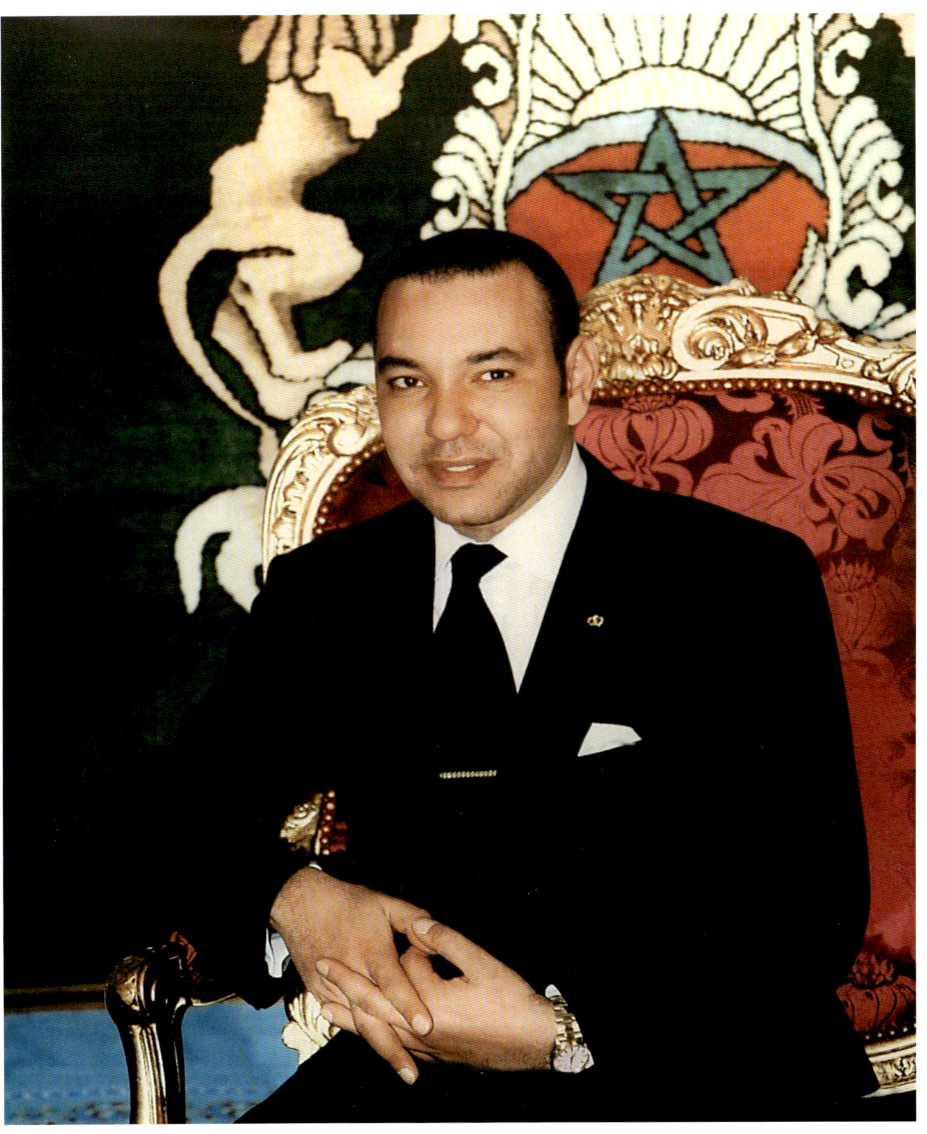

Kingdom of Morocco – King Mohammed VI

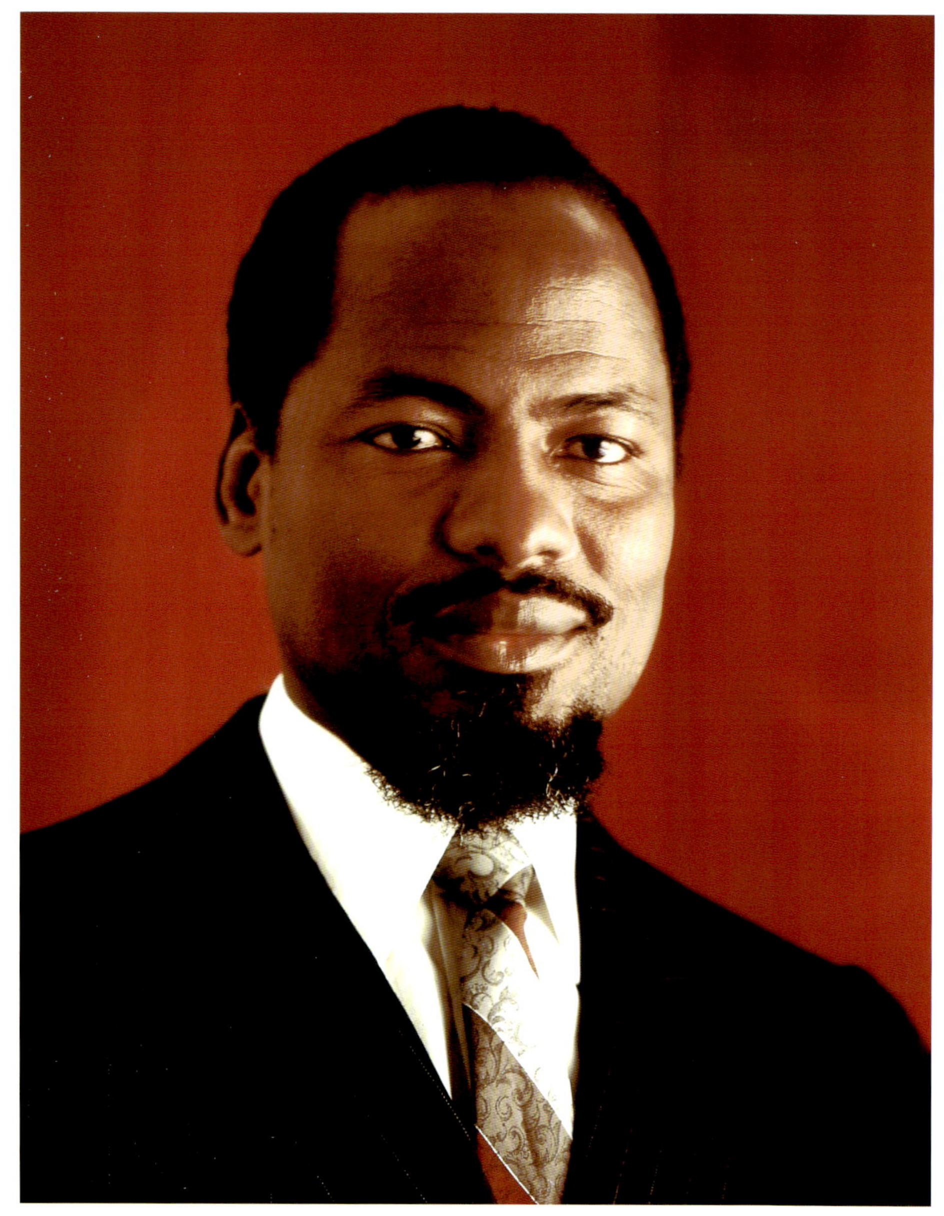

Republic of Mozambique – President Joaquim Alberto Chissano

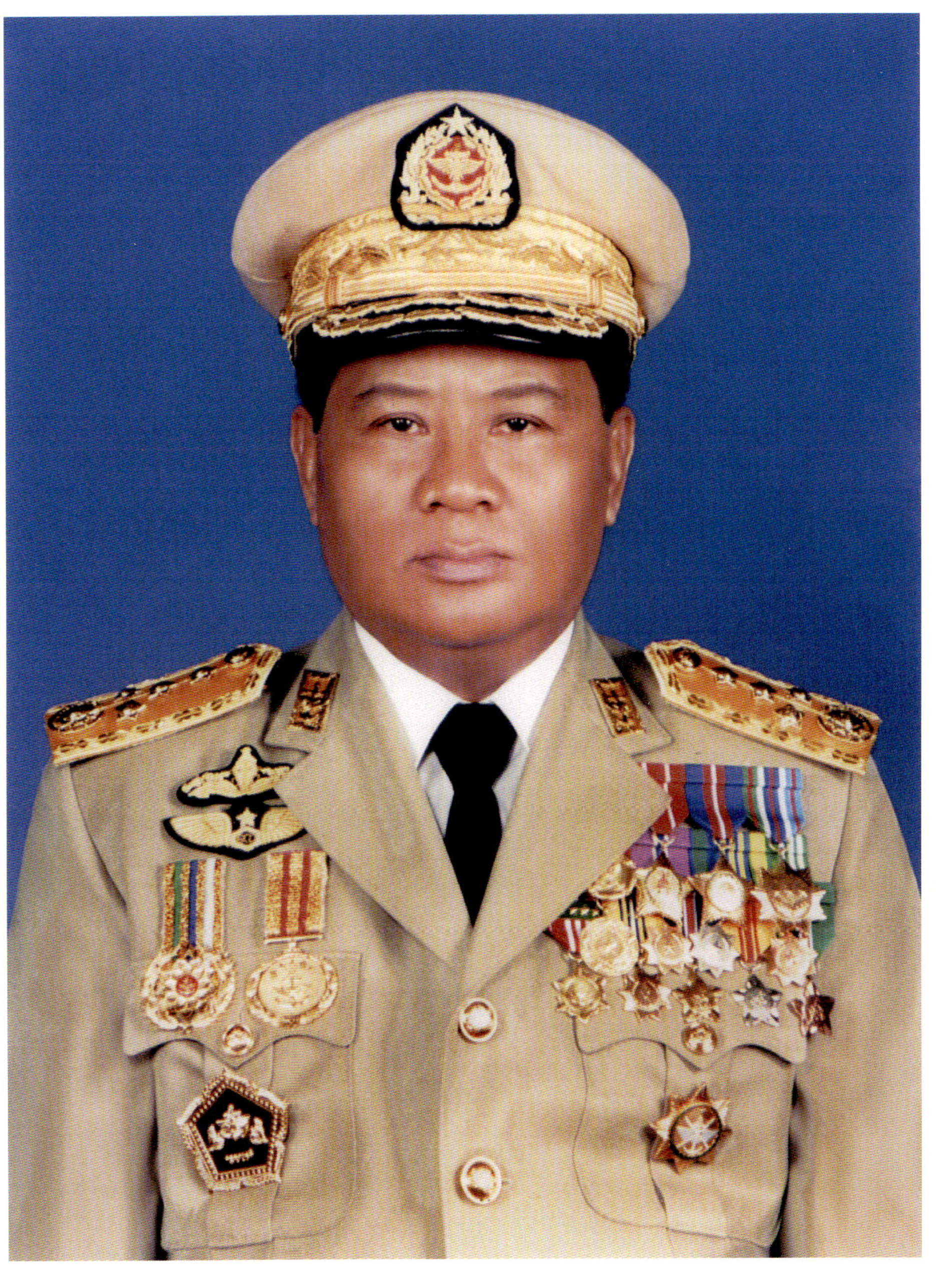

Myanmar – Chairman of the State Peace and Development Council General Than Shwe, Sr.

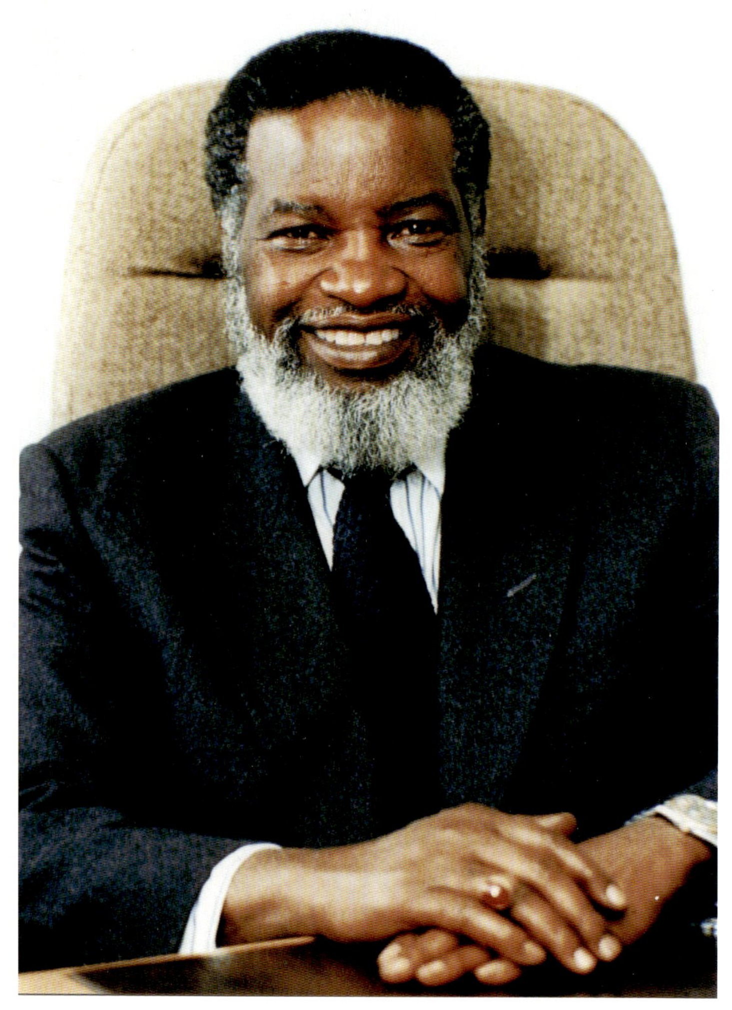

Republic of Namibia – President Sam Nujoma

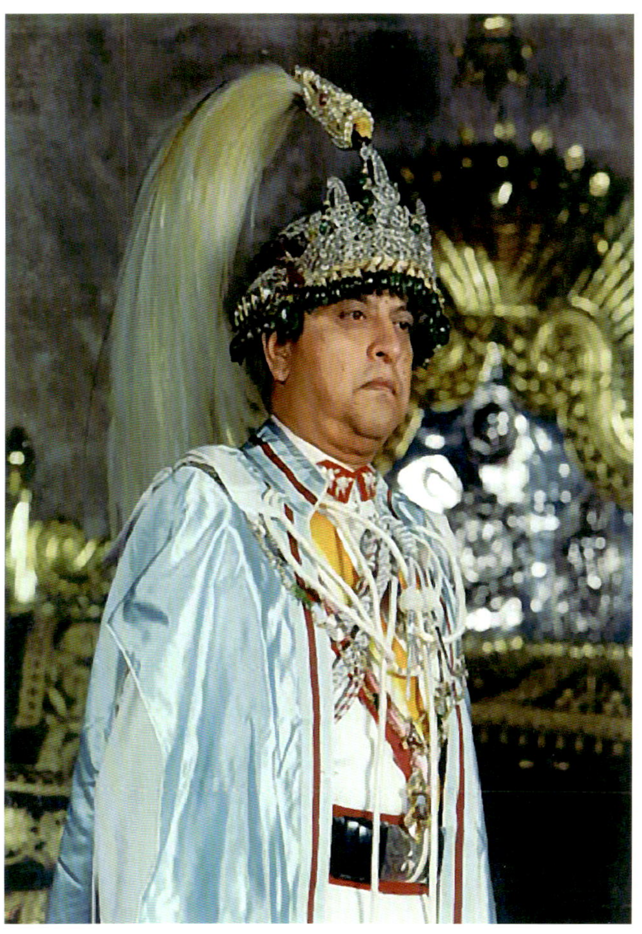

Kingdom of Nepal – King Gyanendra Bir Bikram Shah

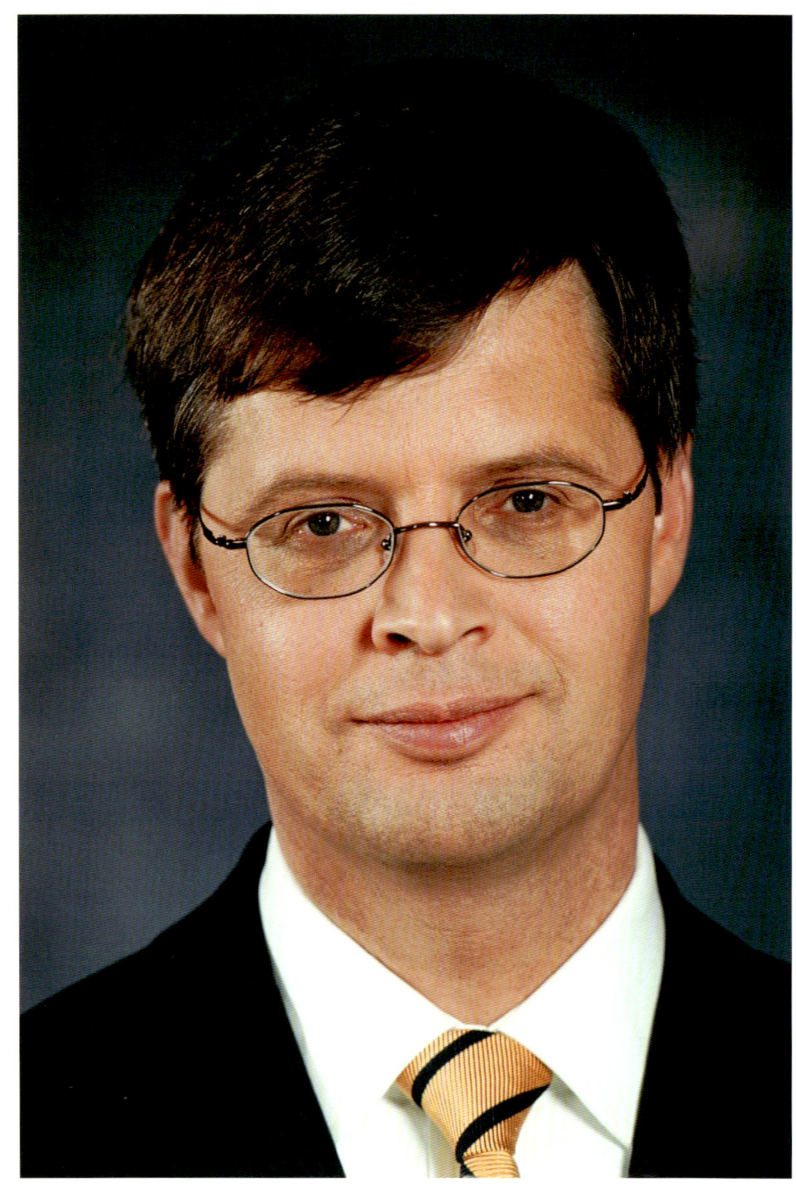

Kingdom of the Netherlands – Prime Minister Jan Peter Balkenende

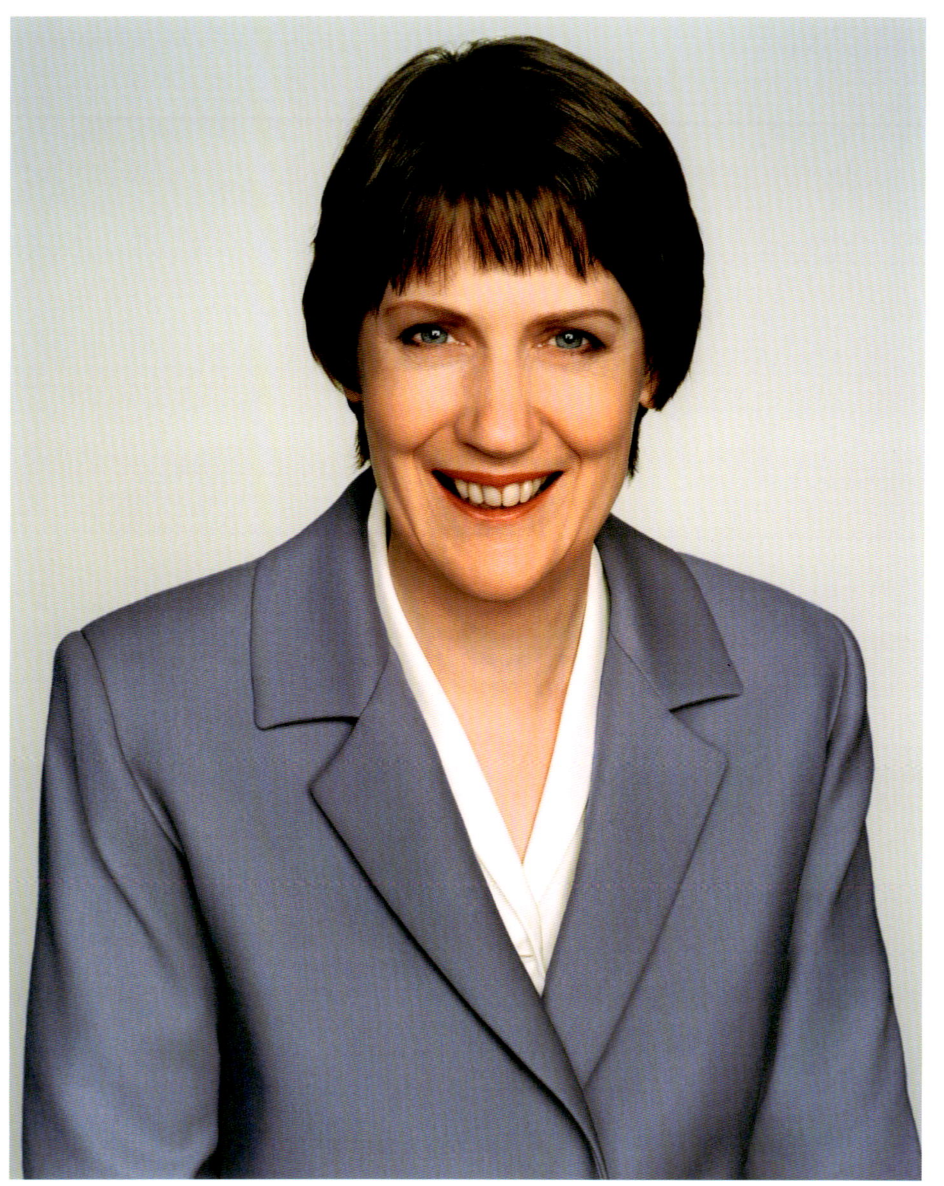

New Zealand – Prime Minister Helen Clark

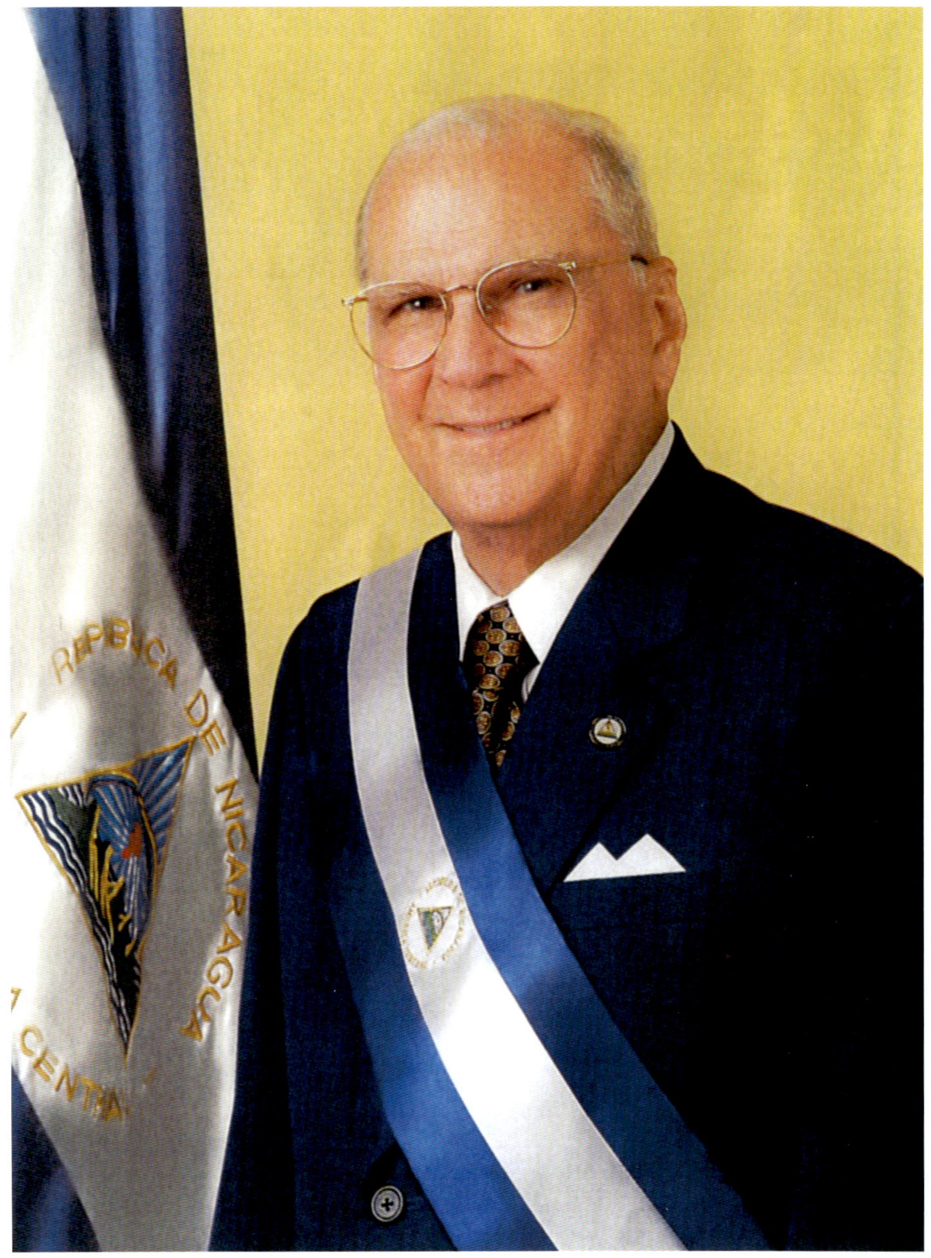

Republic of Nicaragua – President Enrique Bolaños Geyer

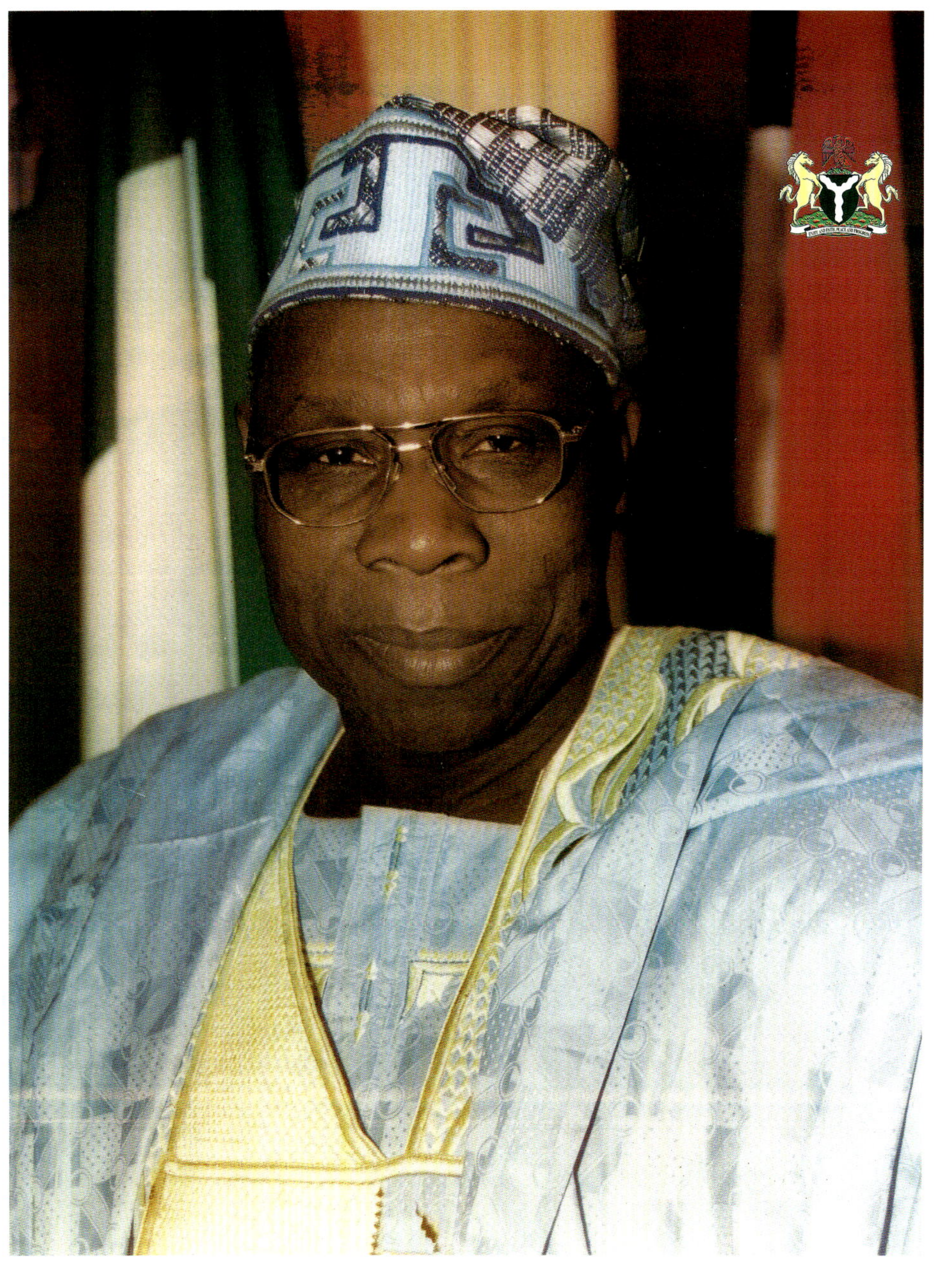

Federal Republic of Nigeria – President Olusegun Obasanjo

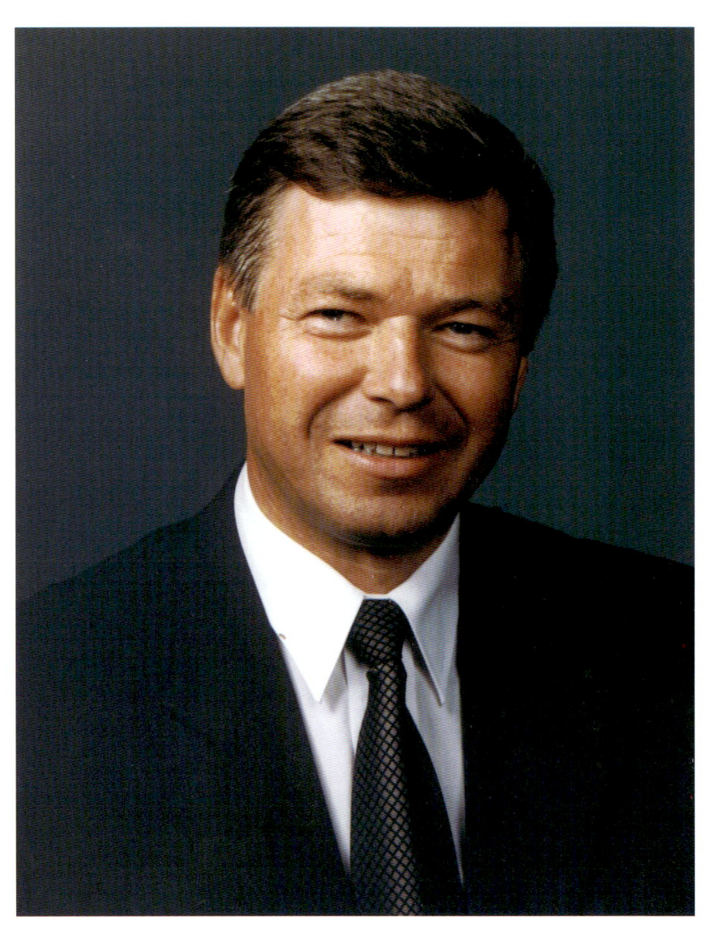

Kingdom of Norway – Prime Minister Kjell Magne Bondevik

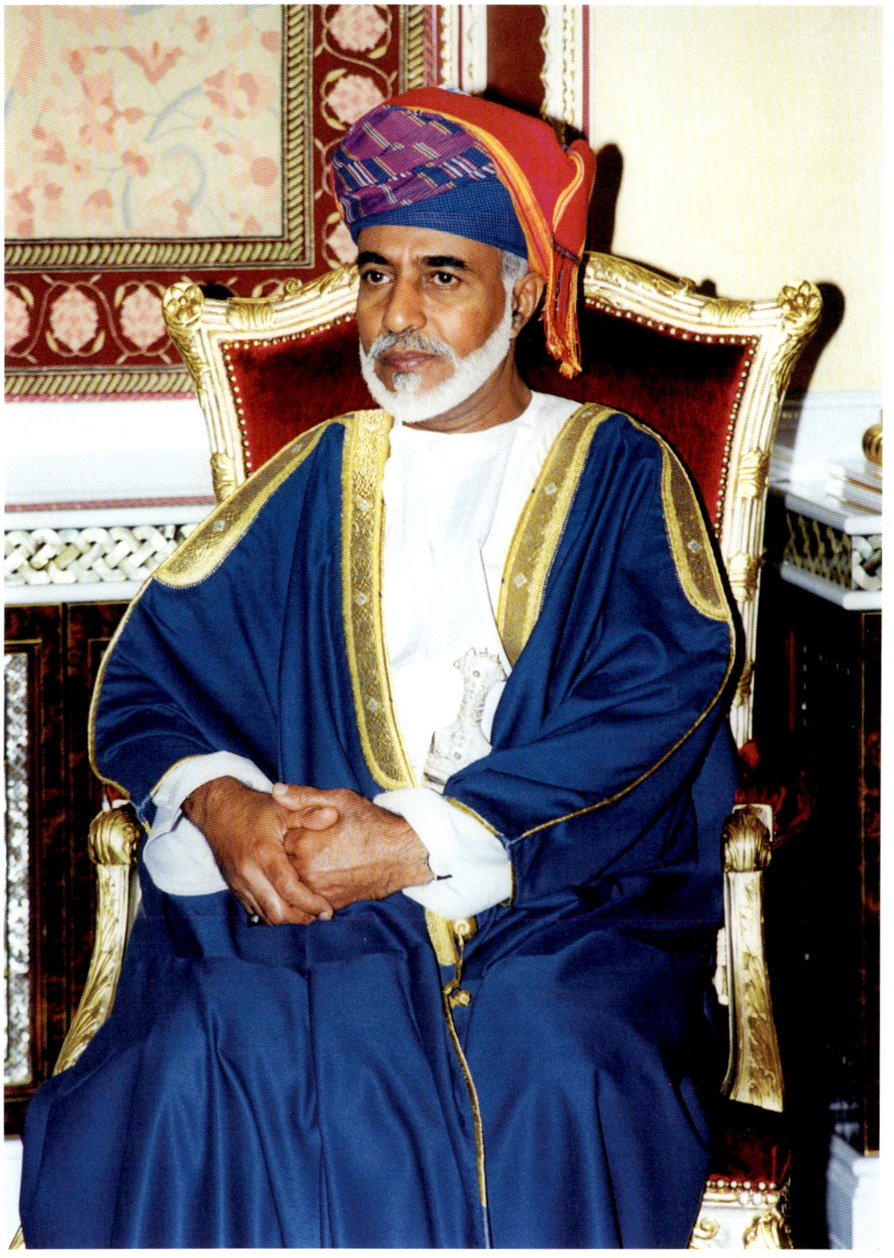

Sultanate of Oman – Sultan and Prime Minister Qaboos Bin Said Al Said

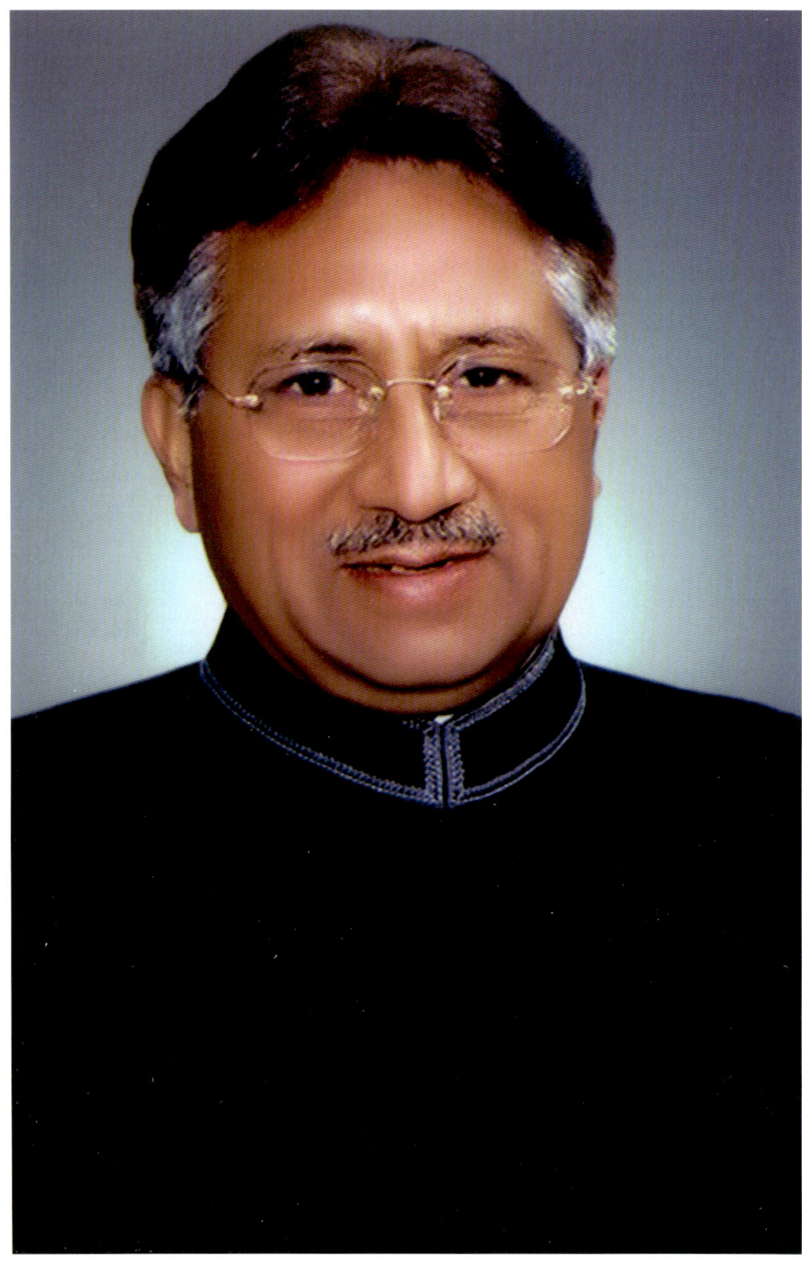

Islamic Republic of Pakistan – President Perves Musharraf

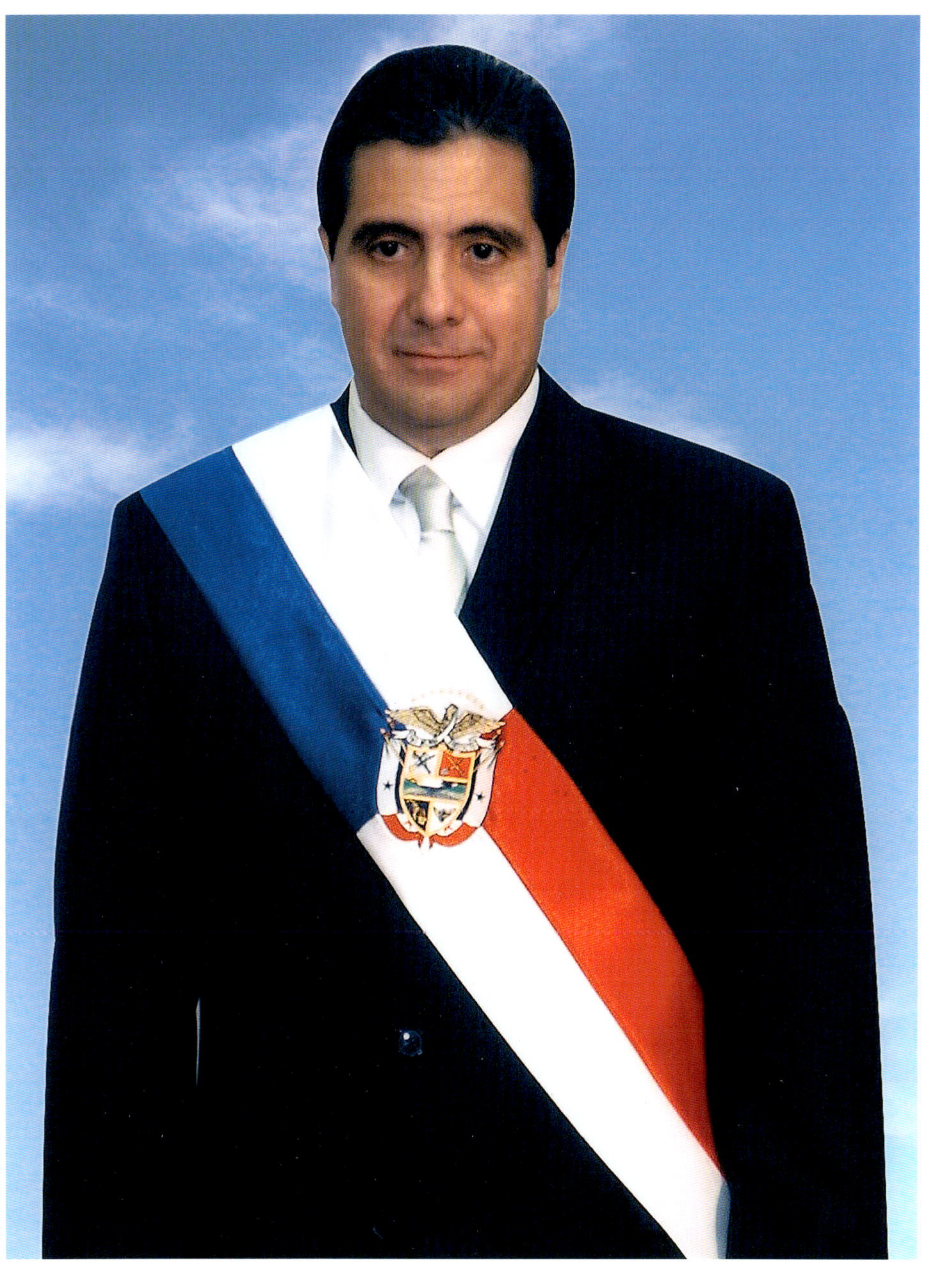

Republic of Panama – President Martin Torrijos Espino

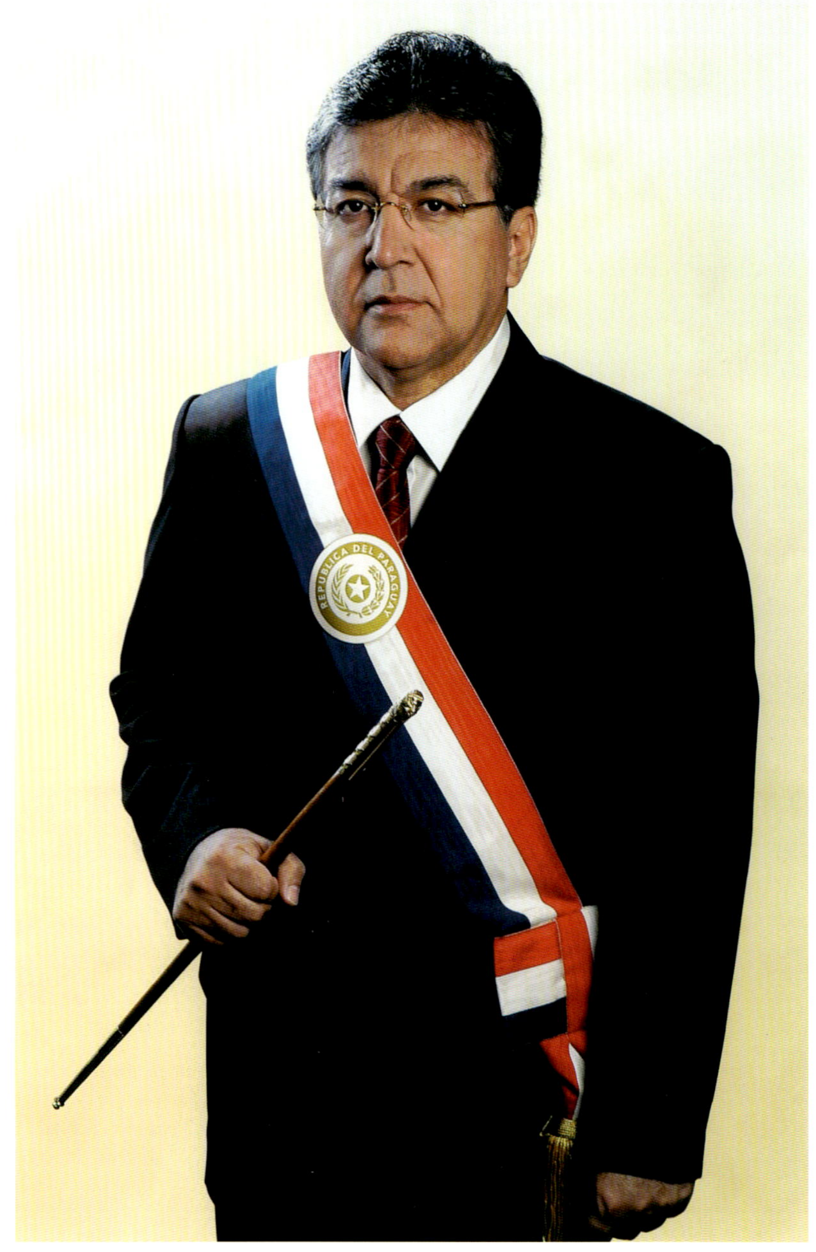

Republic of Paraguay – President Nicanor Duarte Frutos

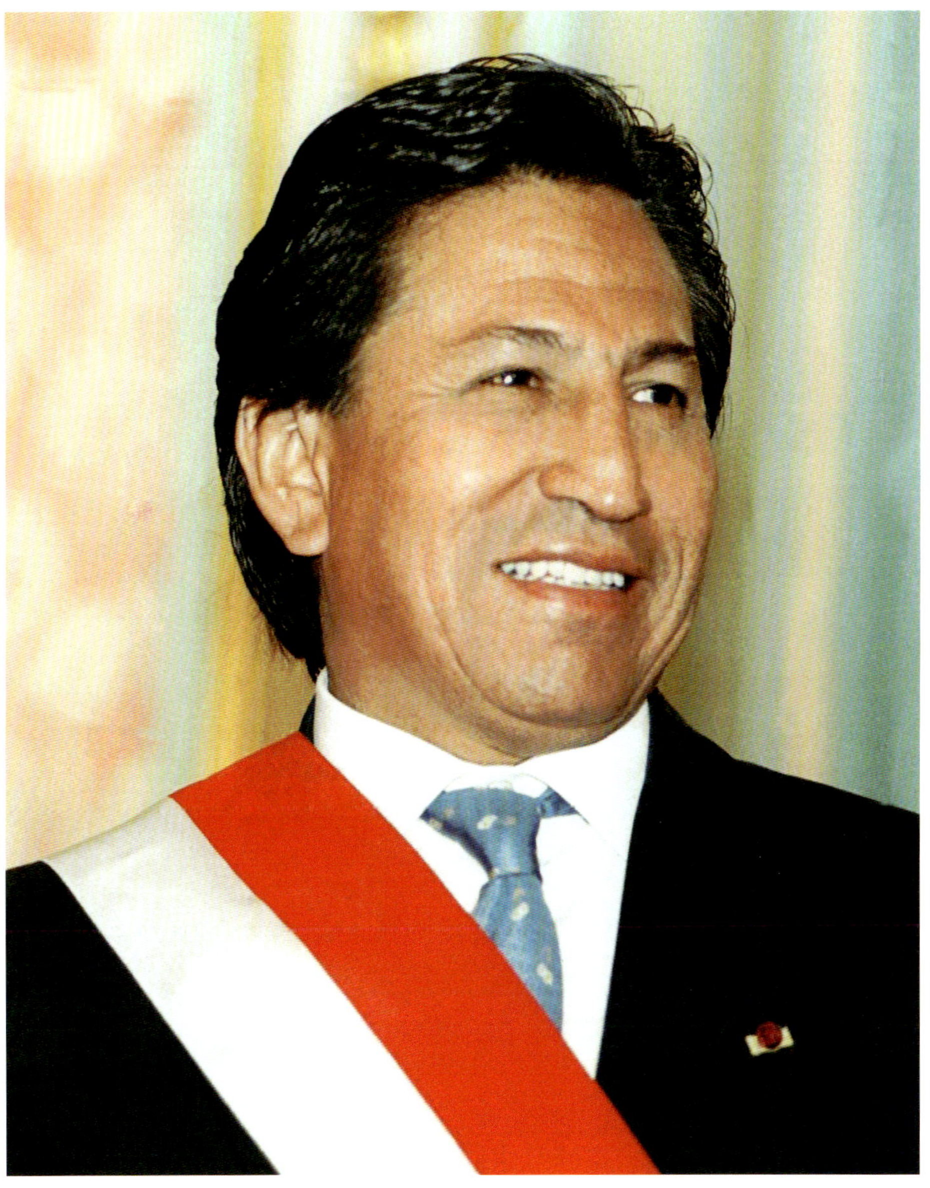

Republic of Peru – President Alejandro Toledo

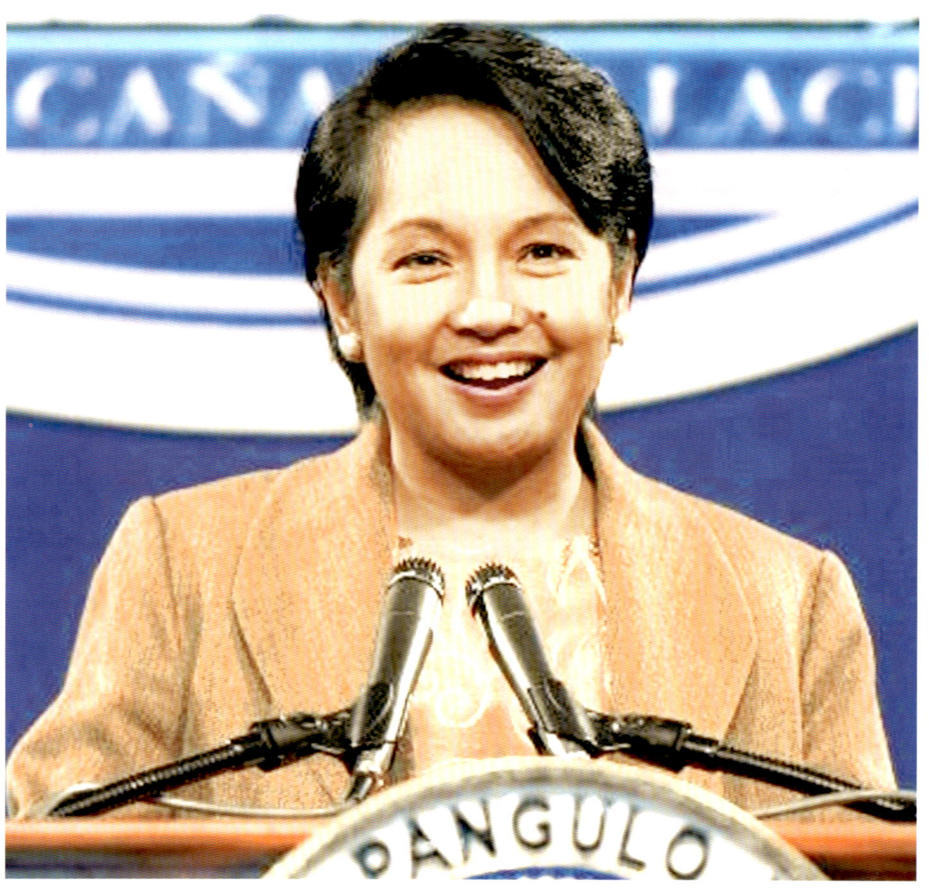

Republic of the Philippines – President Gloria Macapagal-Arroyo

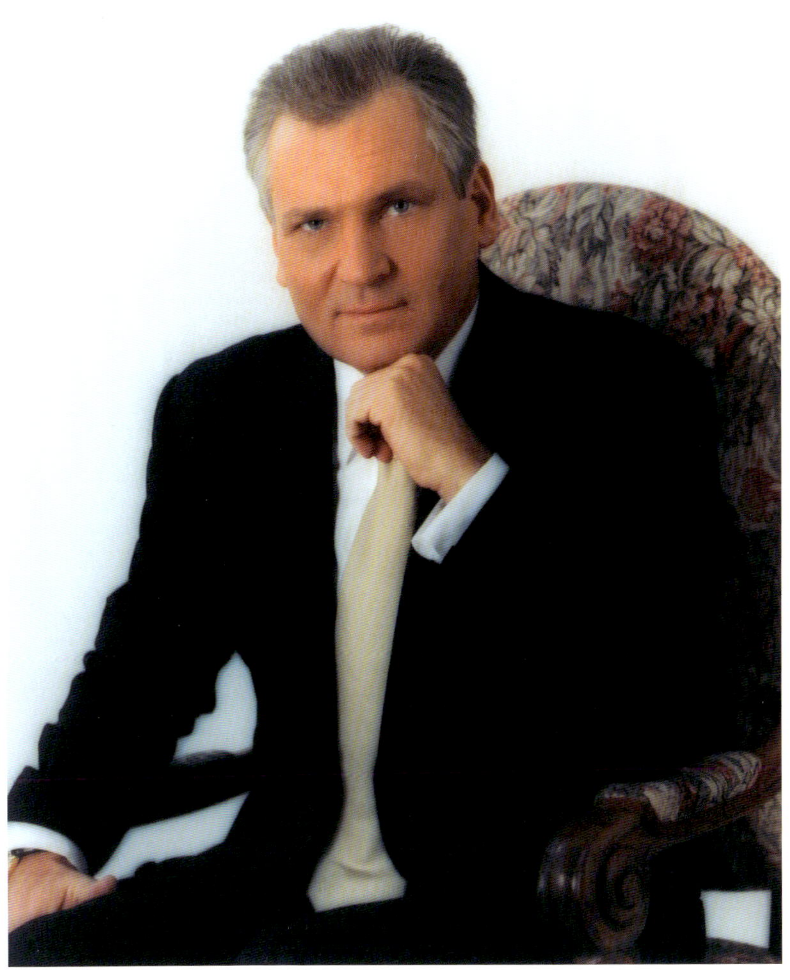

Republic of Poland – President Aleksander Kwasniewski

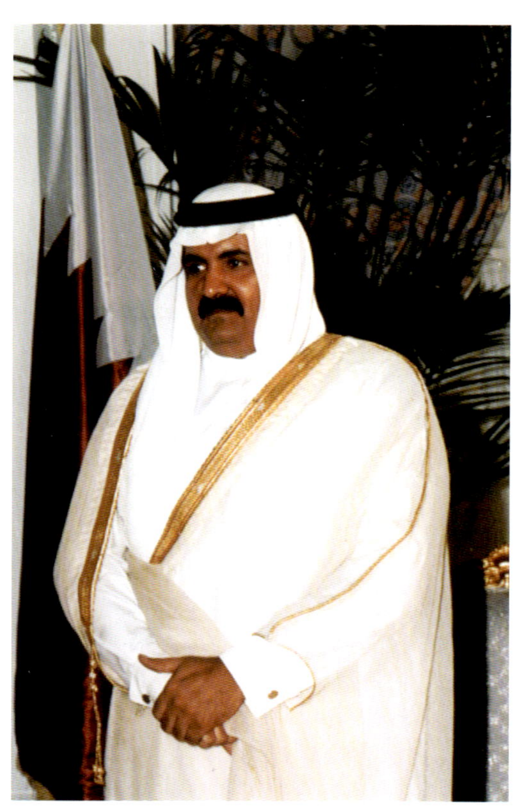

State of Qatar – Emir Hamad Bin Khalifa Al Thani

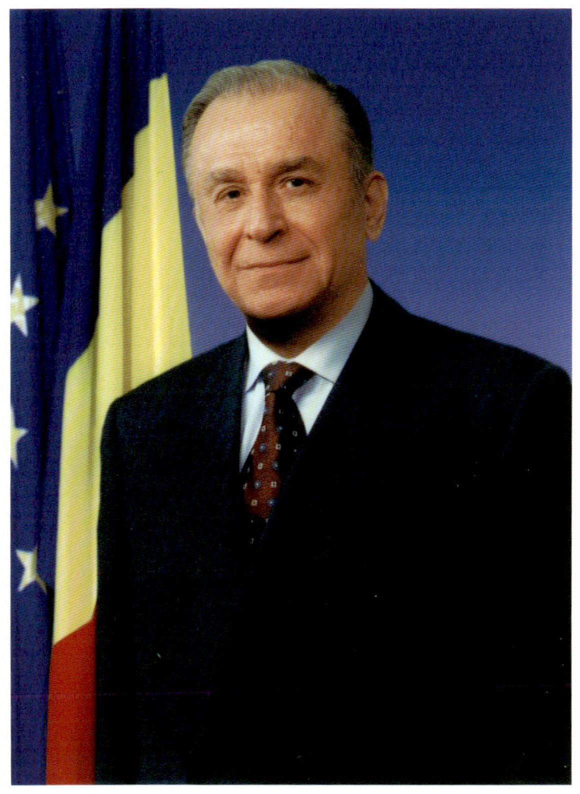

Romania – President Ion Iliescu

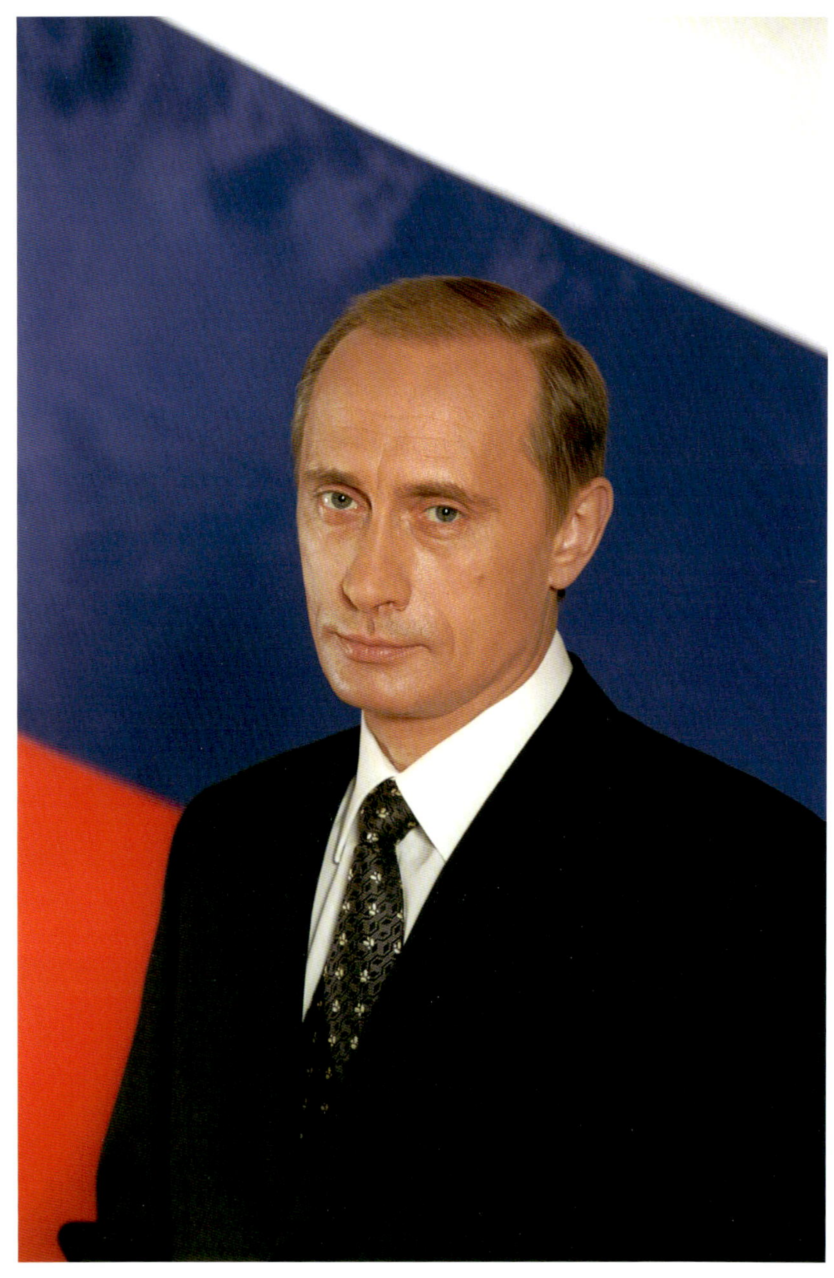

Russian Federation – President Vladimir Putin

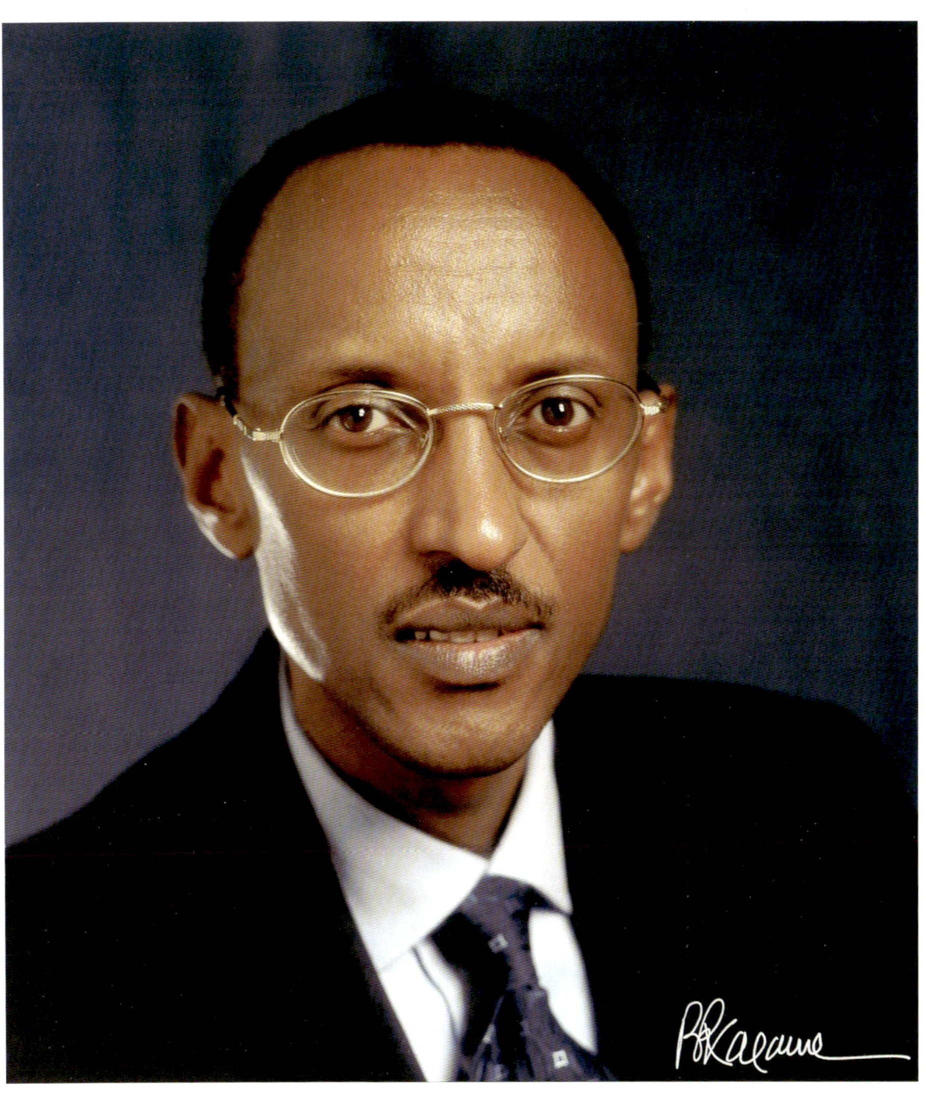

Republic of Rwandaa – President Paul Kagame

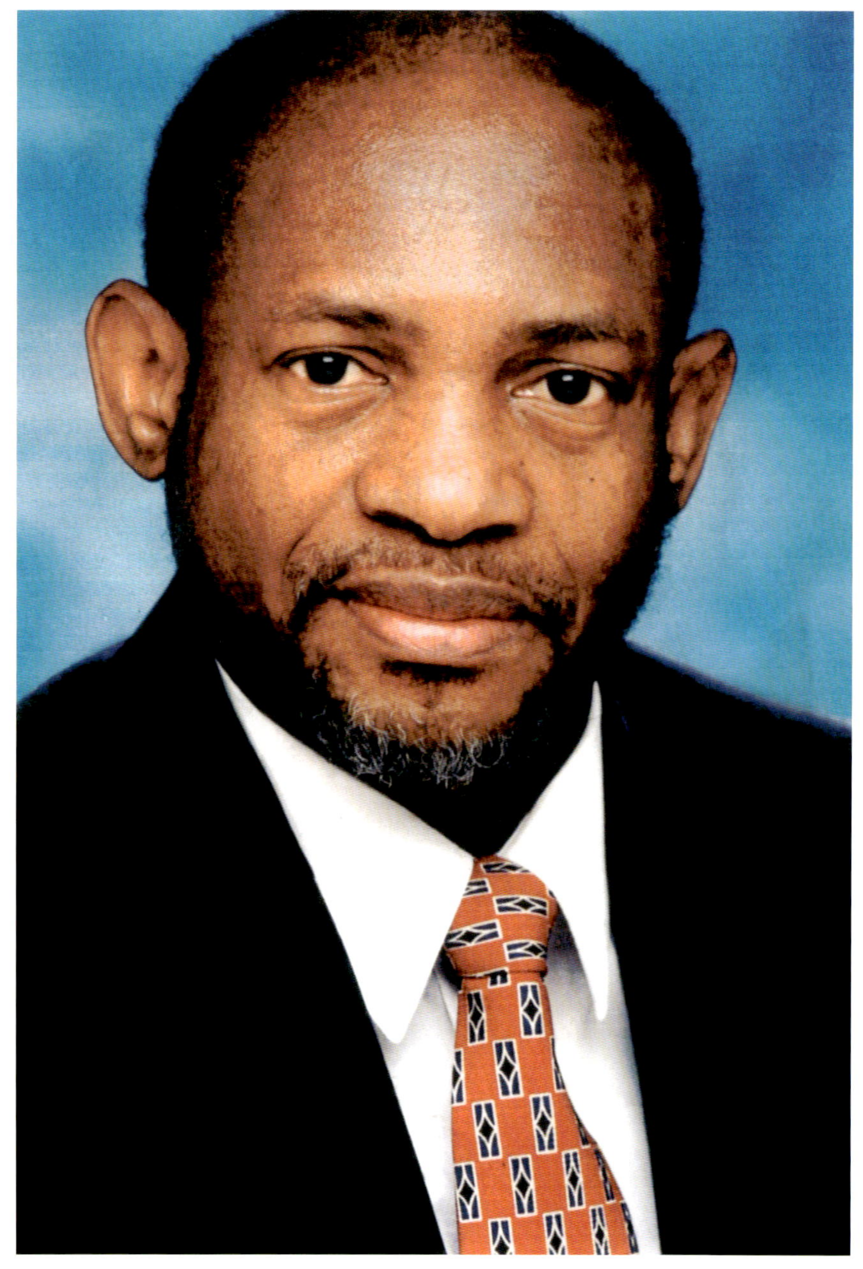

Federation of Saint Kitts & Nevis – Prime Minister Denzil L. Douglas

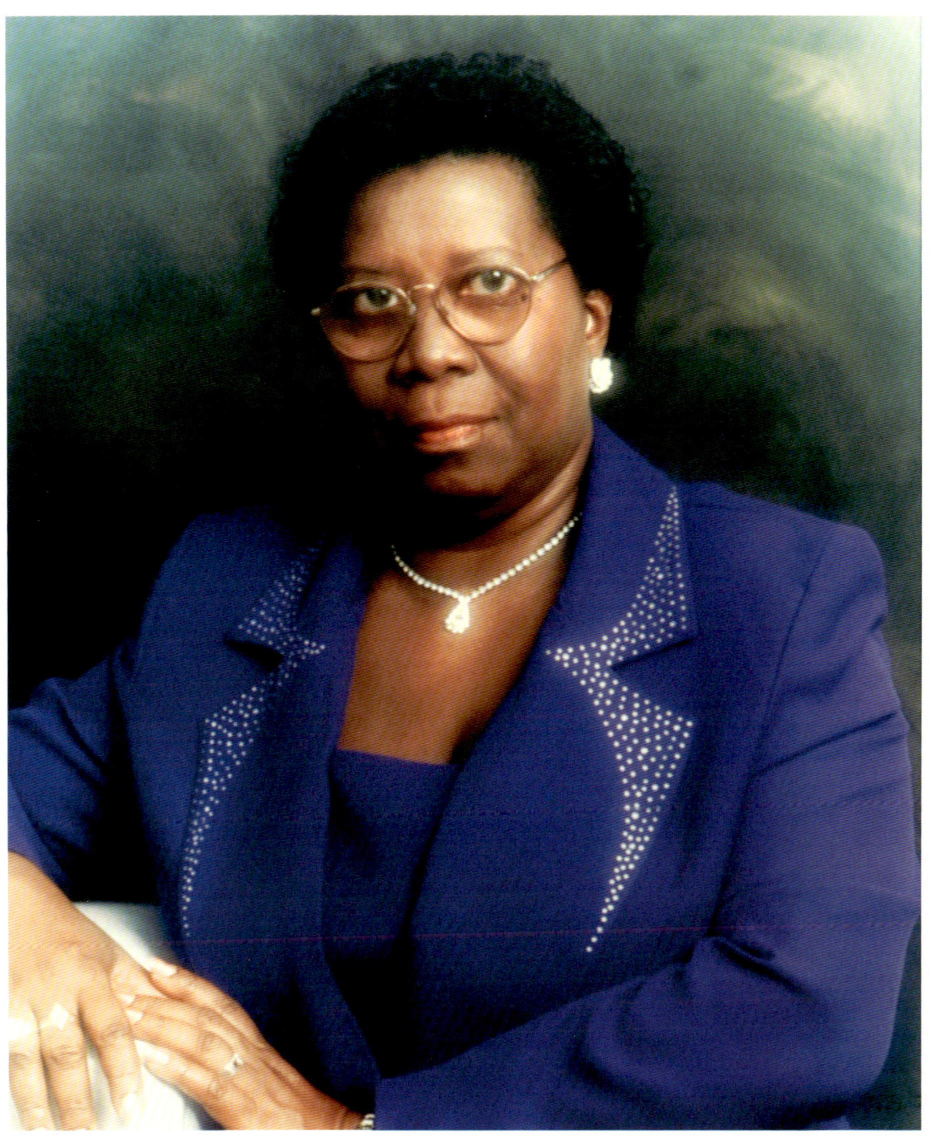

Saint Lucia – Governor General Dame Pearlette Louisy

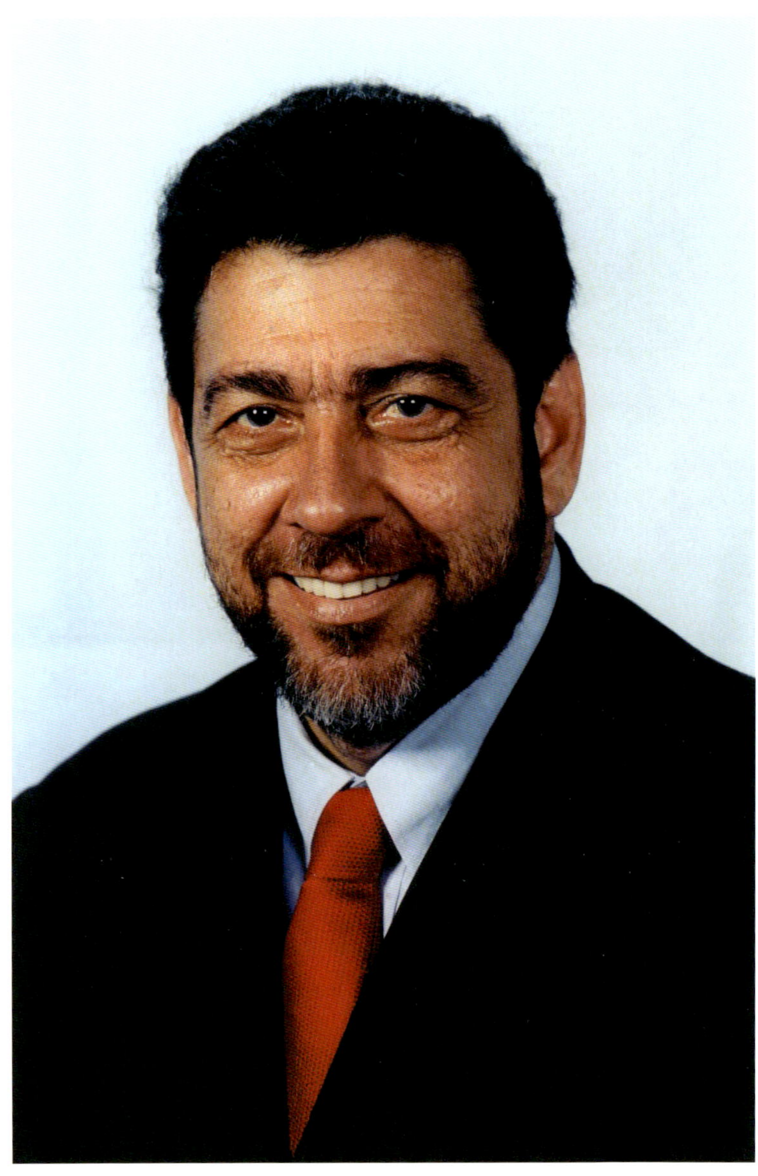

Saint Vincent & the Grenadines – Prime Minister Ralph Gonsalves

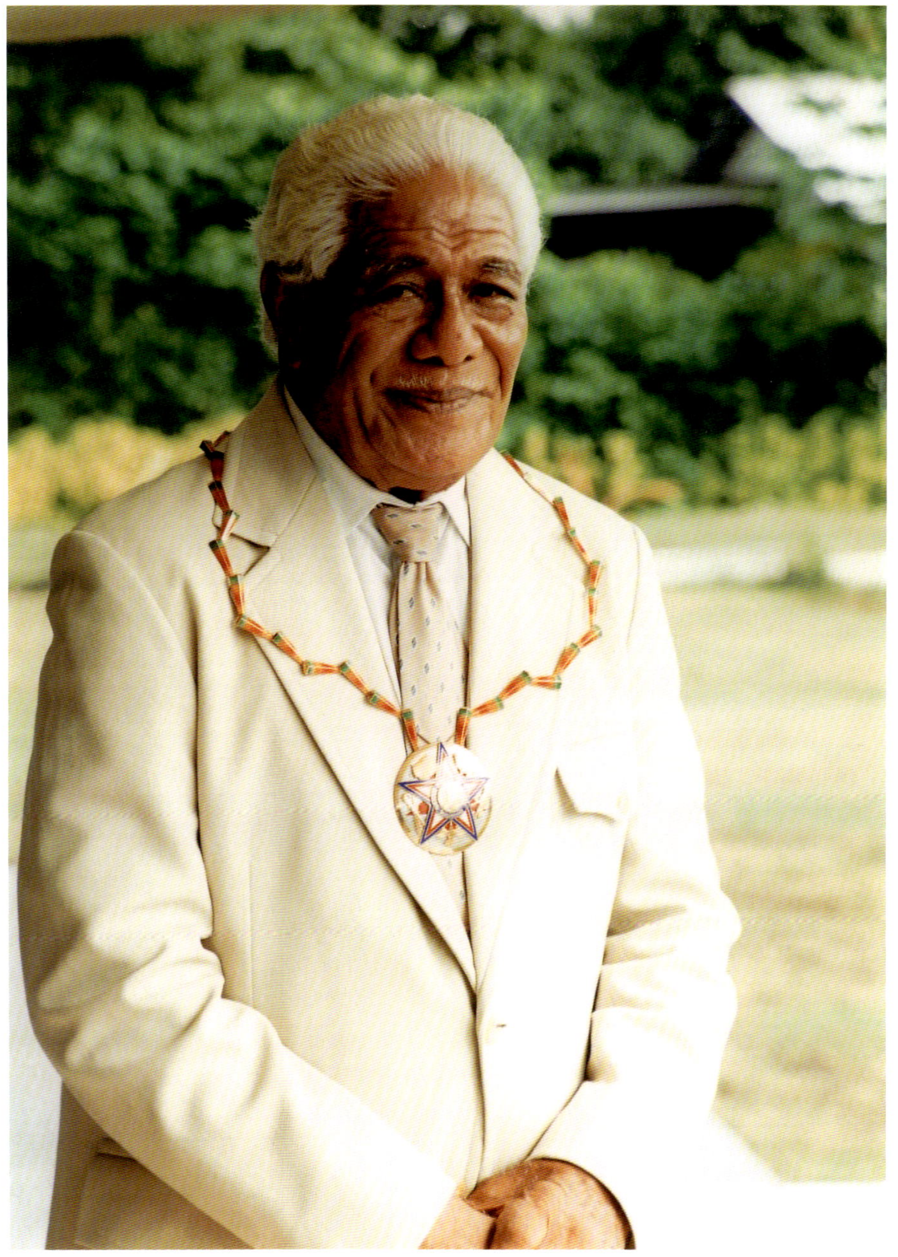

Independent State of Samoa – Chief Malietoa Tanumafili II

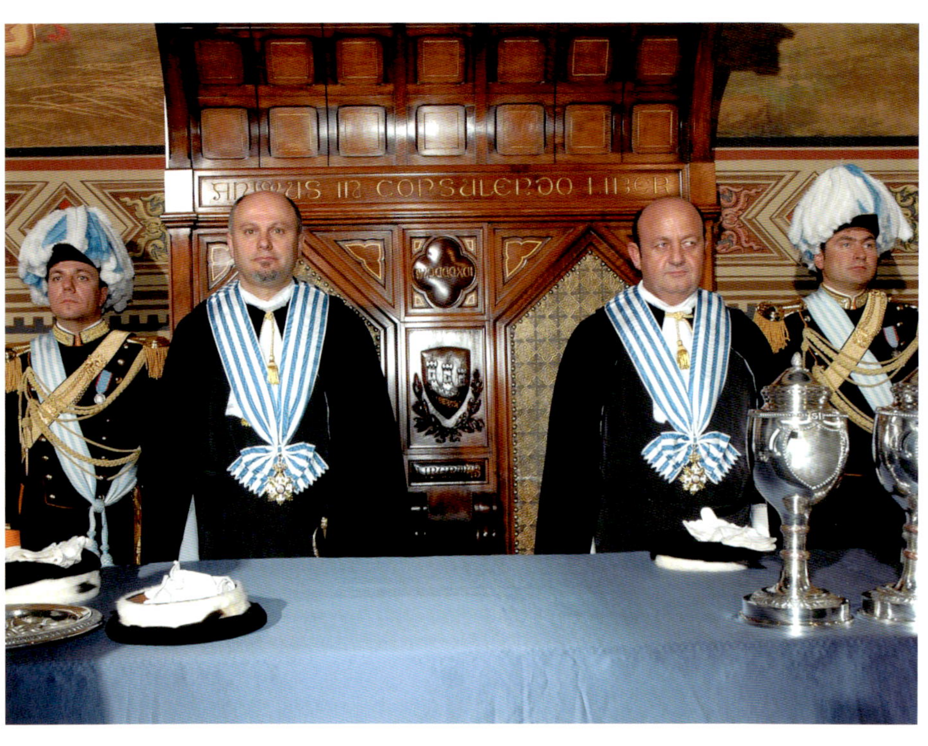

134

Republic of San Marino – Regent Captains Paolo Bollini and Marino Riccardi

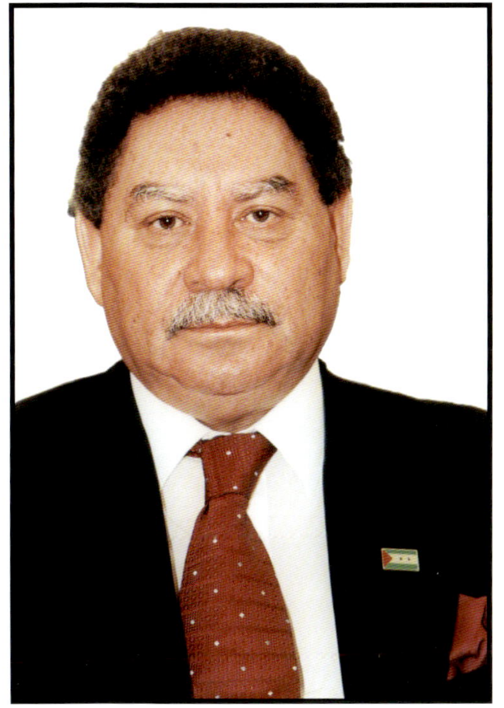

135

Democratic Republic of Sao Tome and Principe –
President Fradique Bandeira Melo de Menezes

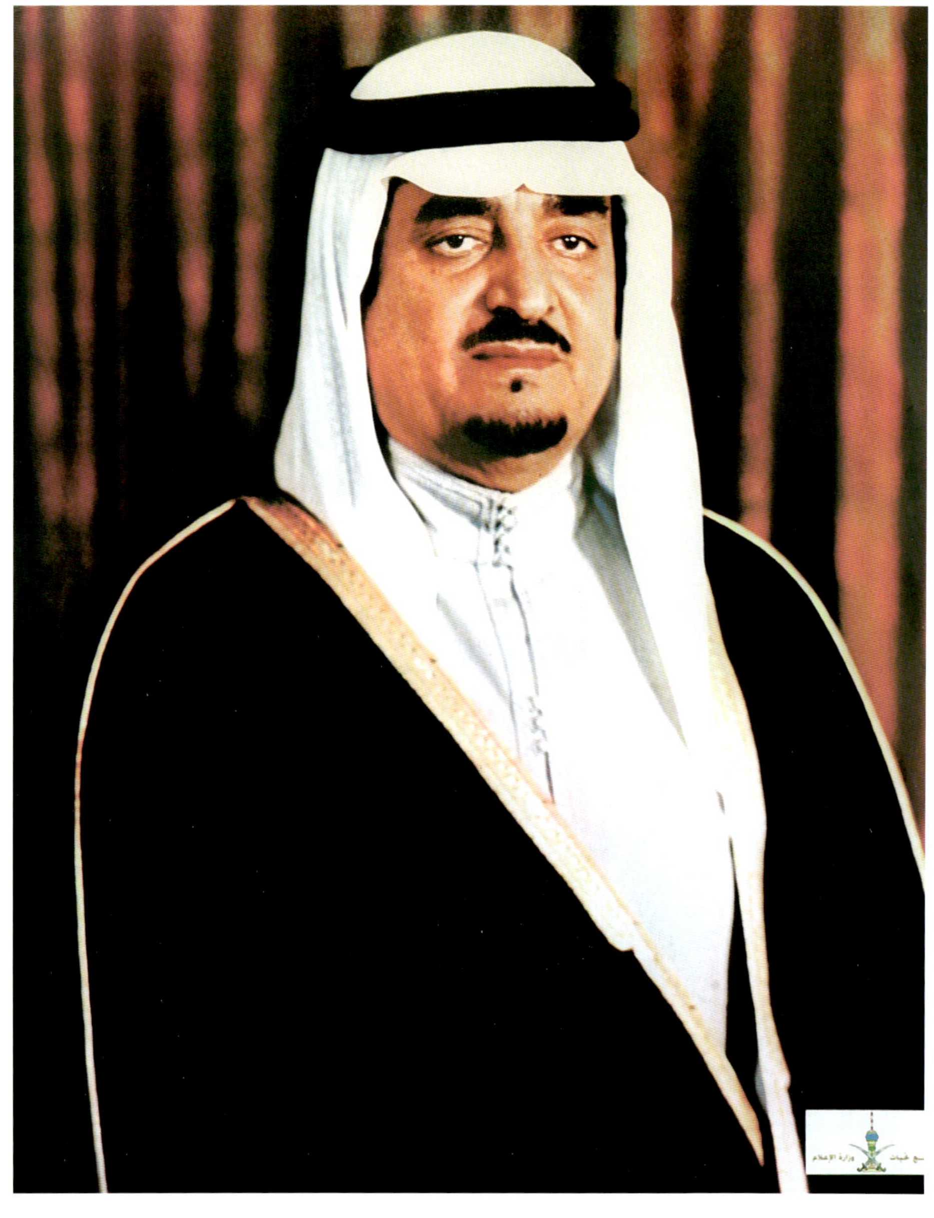

Kingdom of Saudi Arabia – Custodian of The Two Holy Mosques
King Fahd Bin Abdulaziz Al-Saud

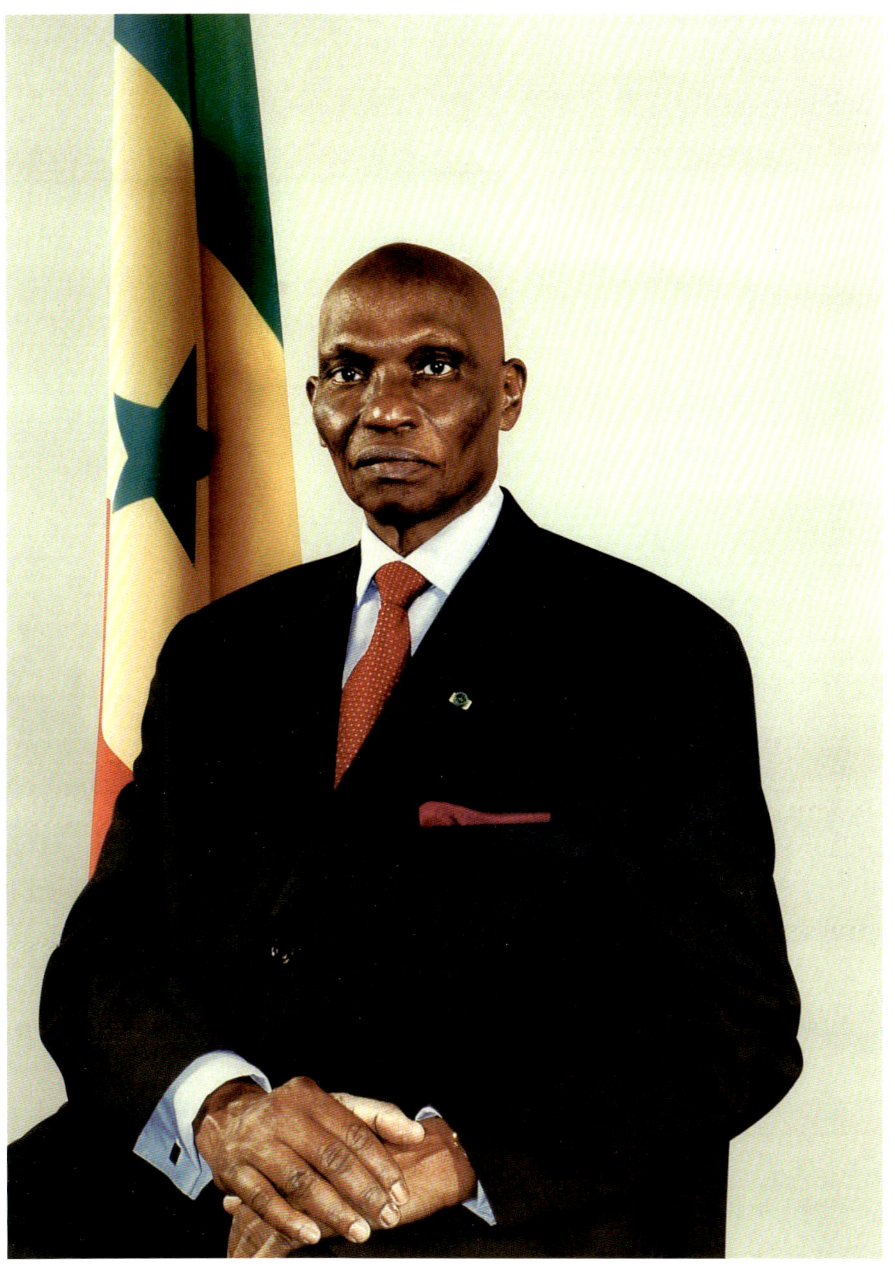

Republic of Senegal – President Abdoulaye Wade

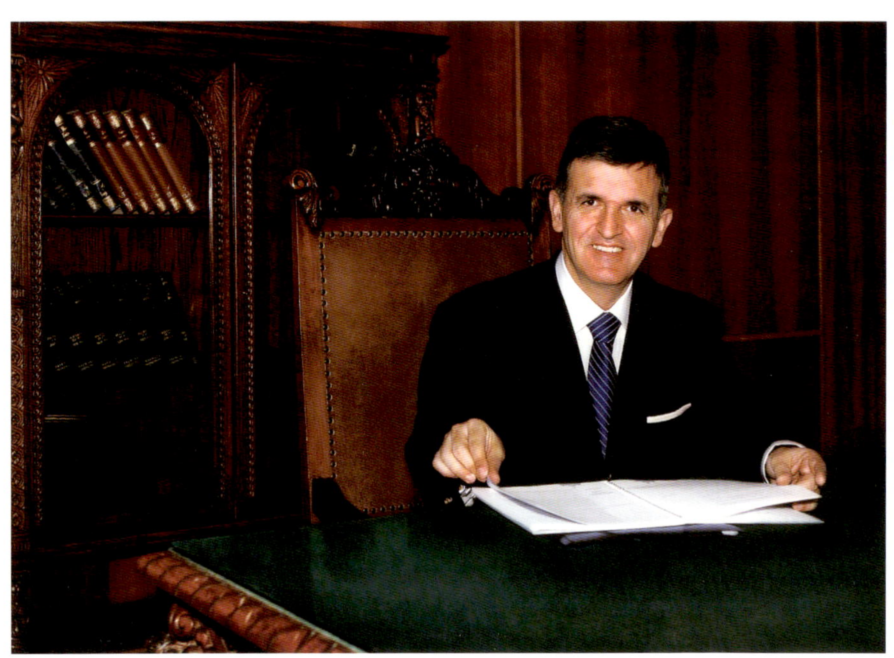

State Union of Serbia & Montenegro – President Svetozar Marovic

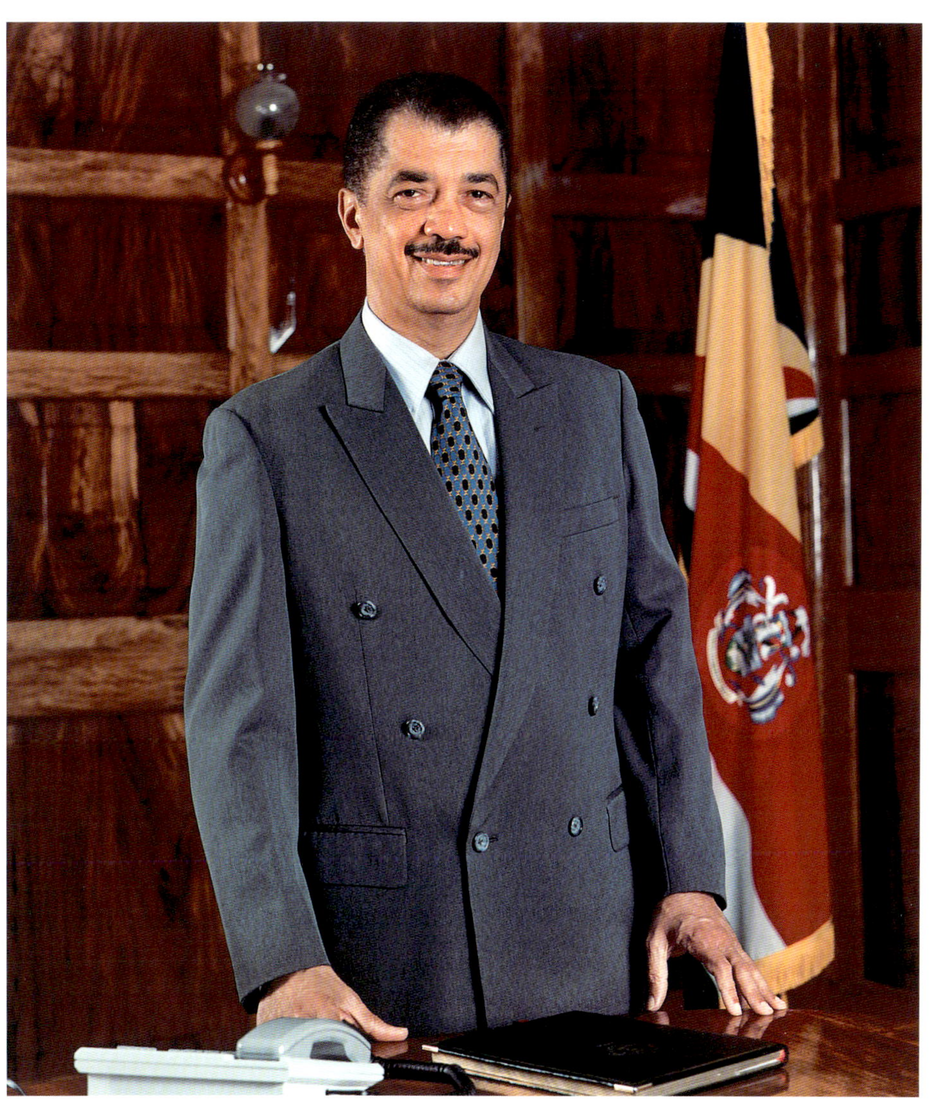

Republic of Seychelles – President James Michel

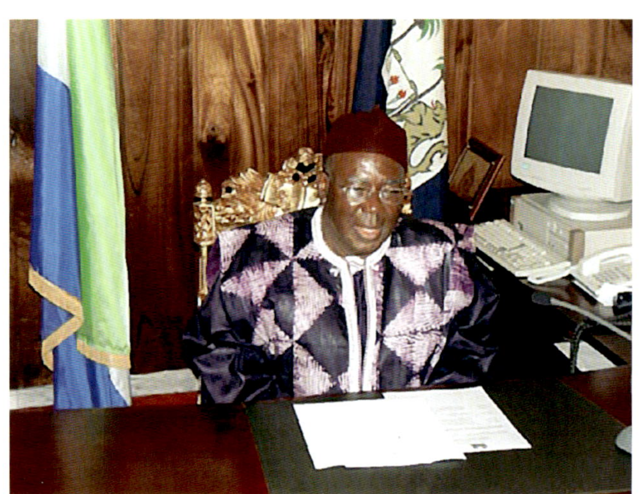

Republic of Sierra Leone – President Alhaji Ahmad Tejan Kabbah

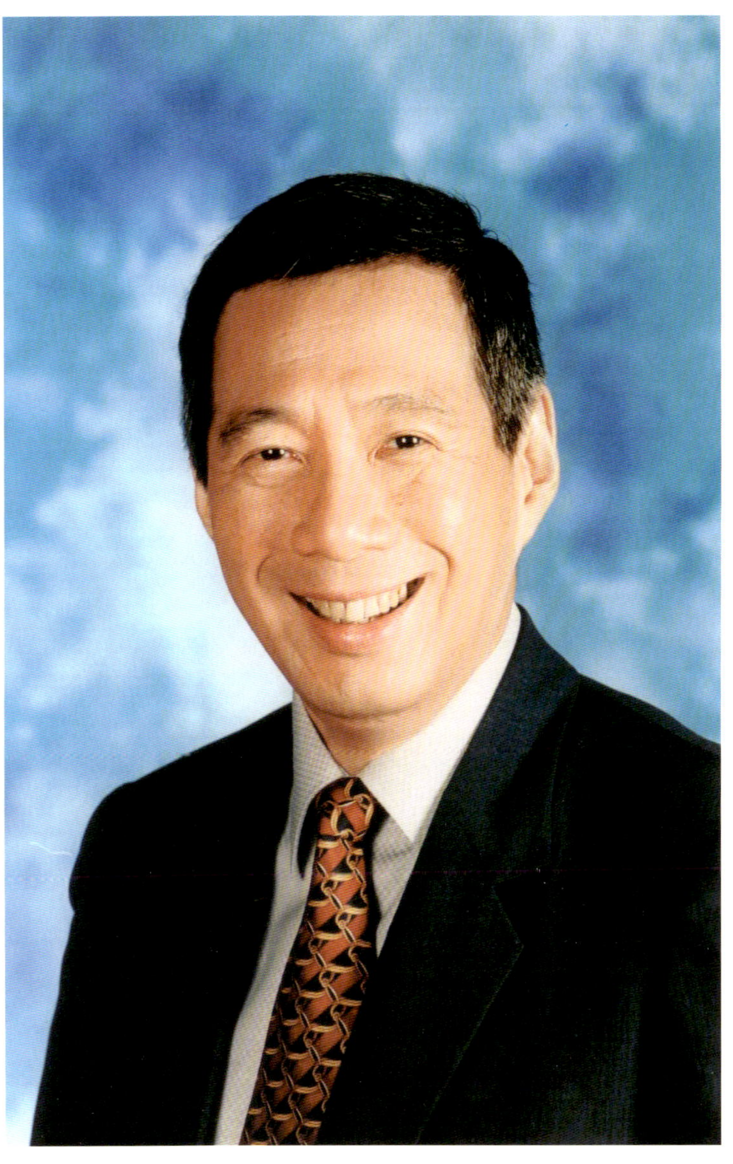

Republic of Singapore – Prime Minister Lee Hsien Loong

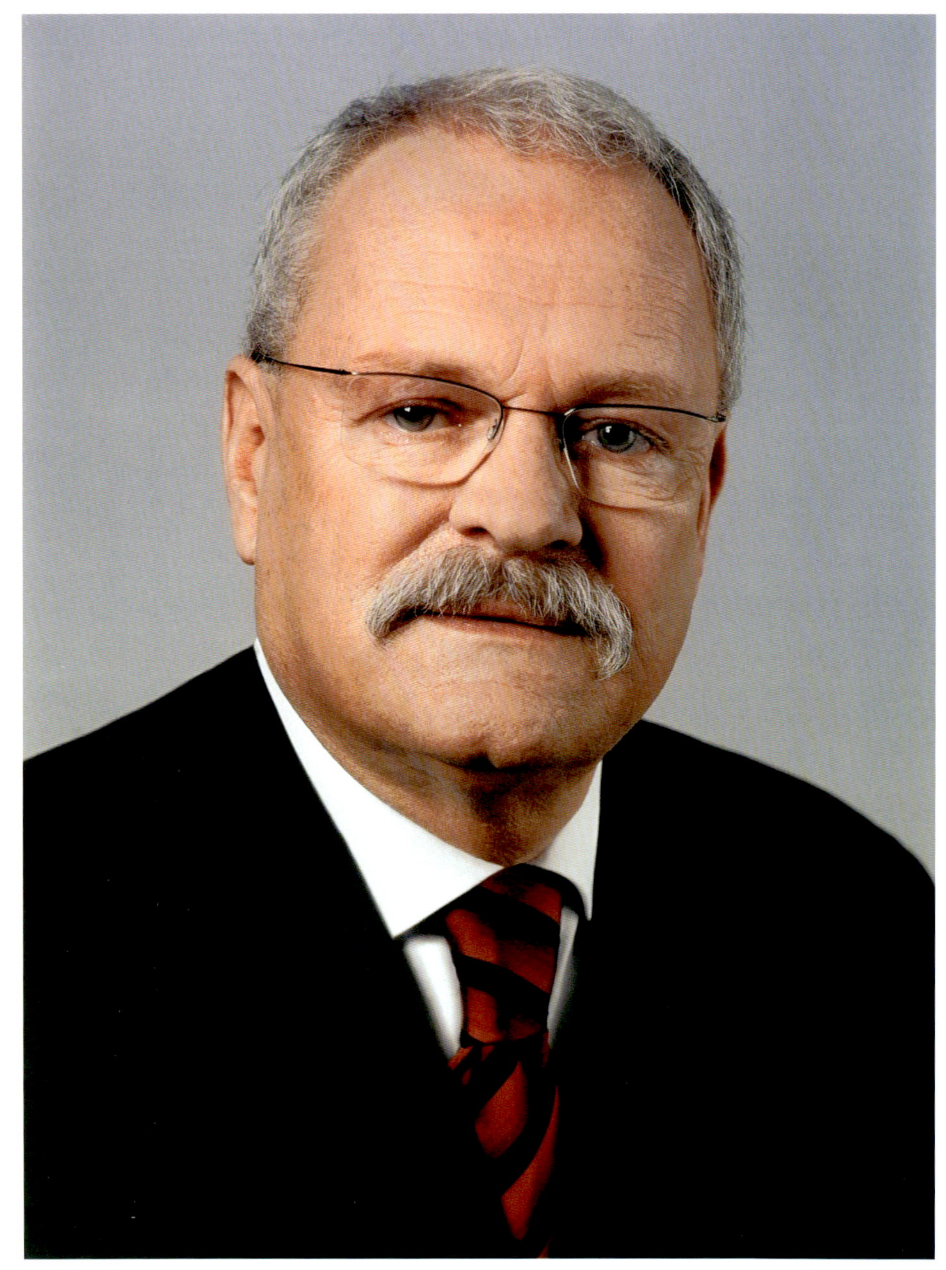

Republic of Slovakia – President Ivan Gasparovic

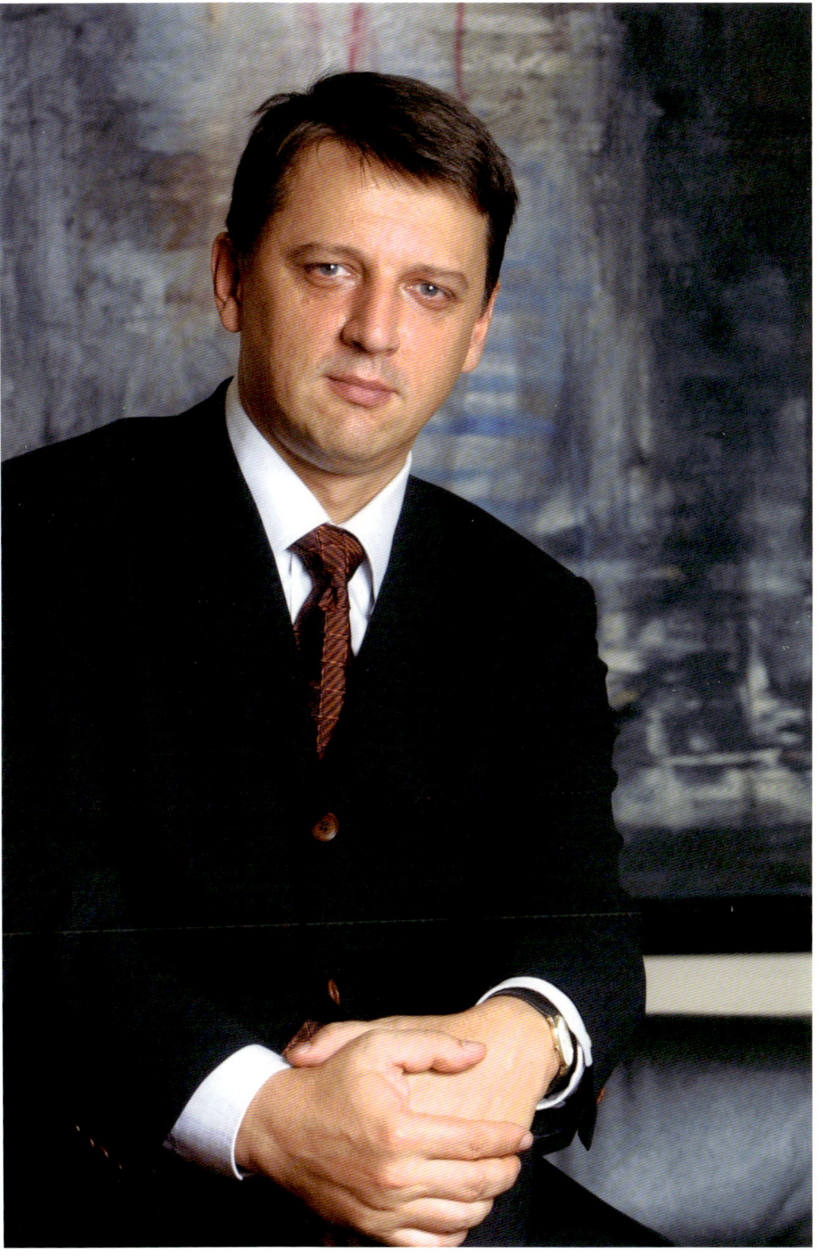

Slovenia – Prime Minister Anton Rop

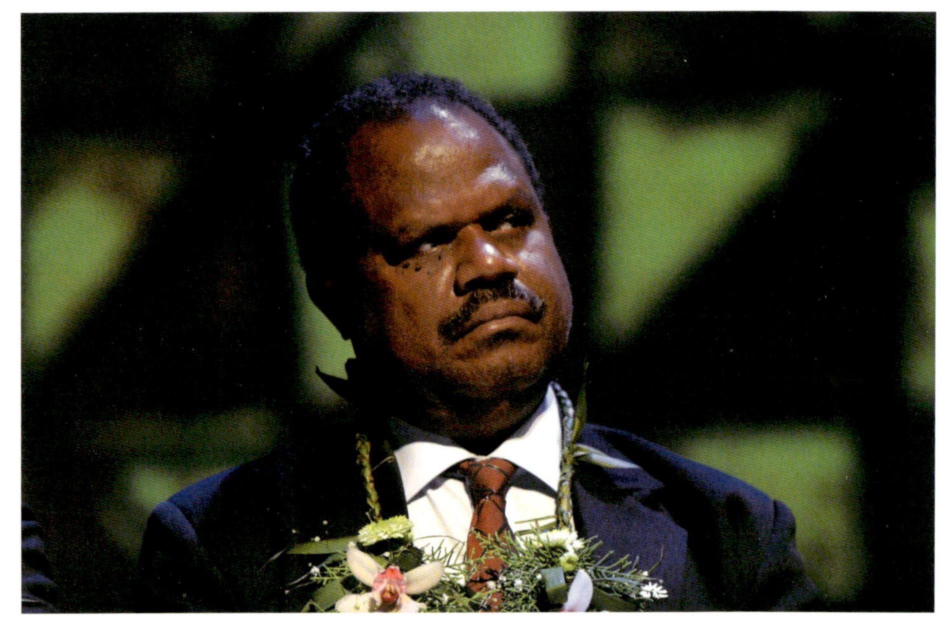

Solomon Islands – Prime Minister Sir Allan Kemakesa

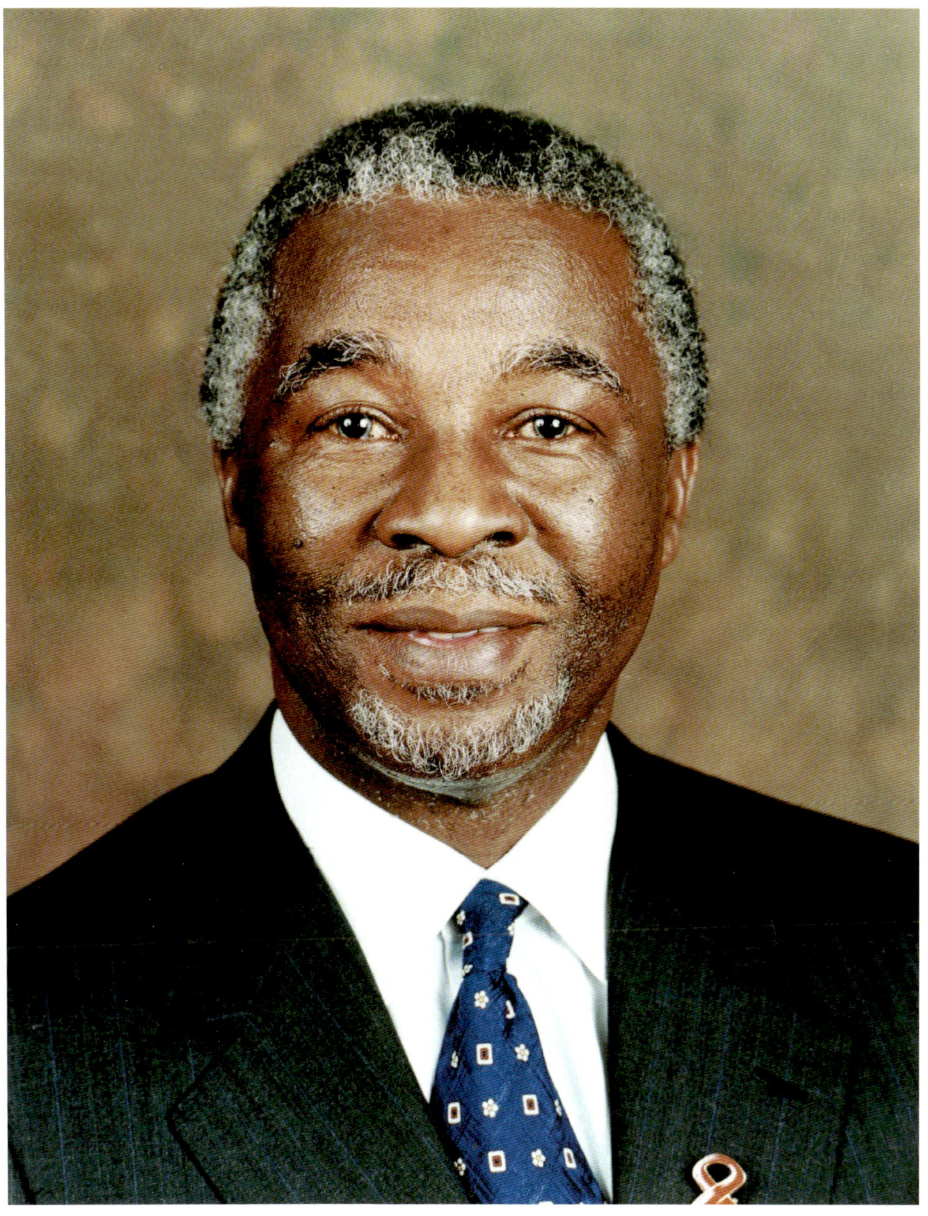

145

Republic of South Africa – President Thabo Mbeki

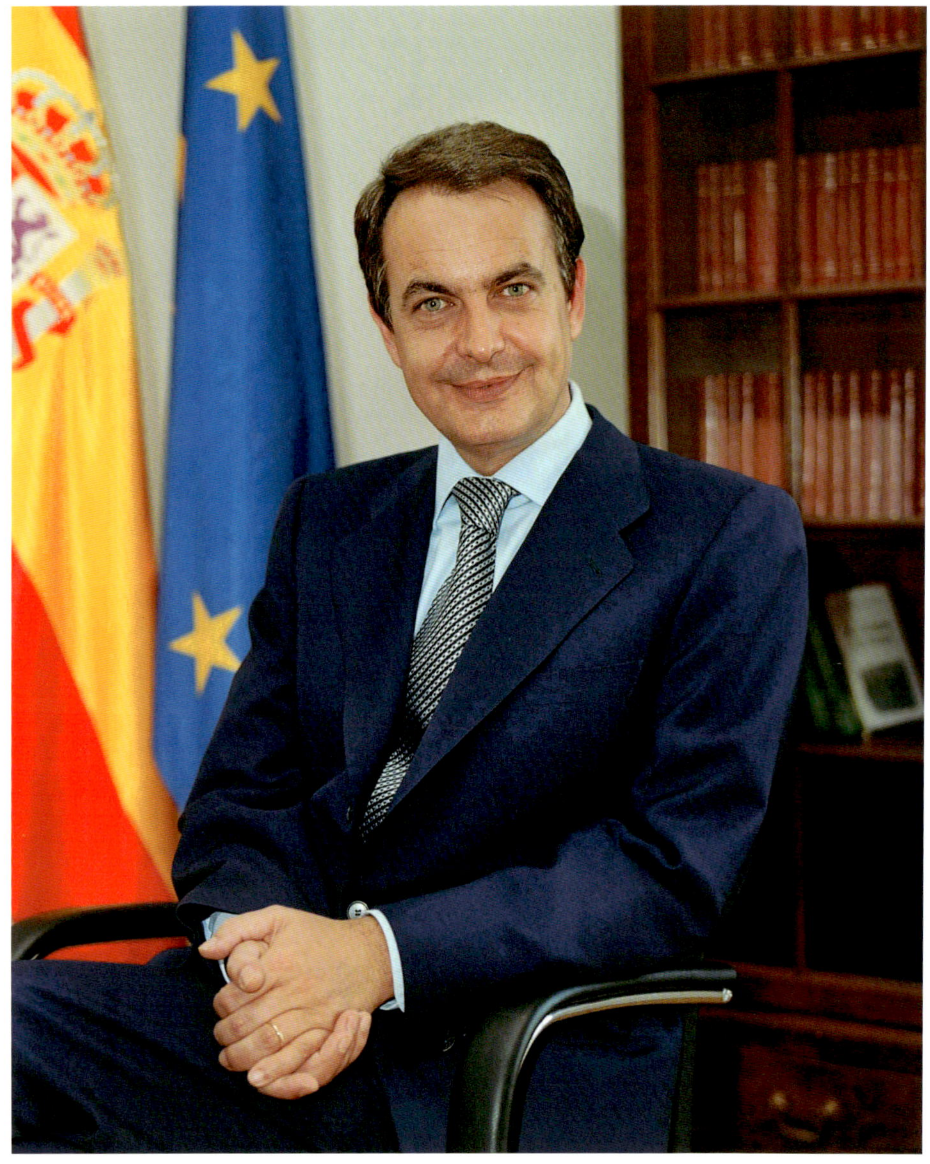

Kingdom of Spain – President José Luis Rodríguez Zapatero

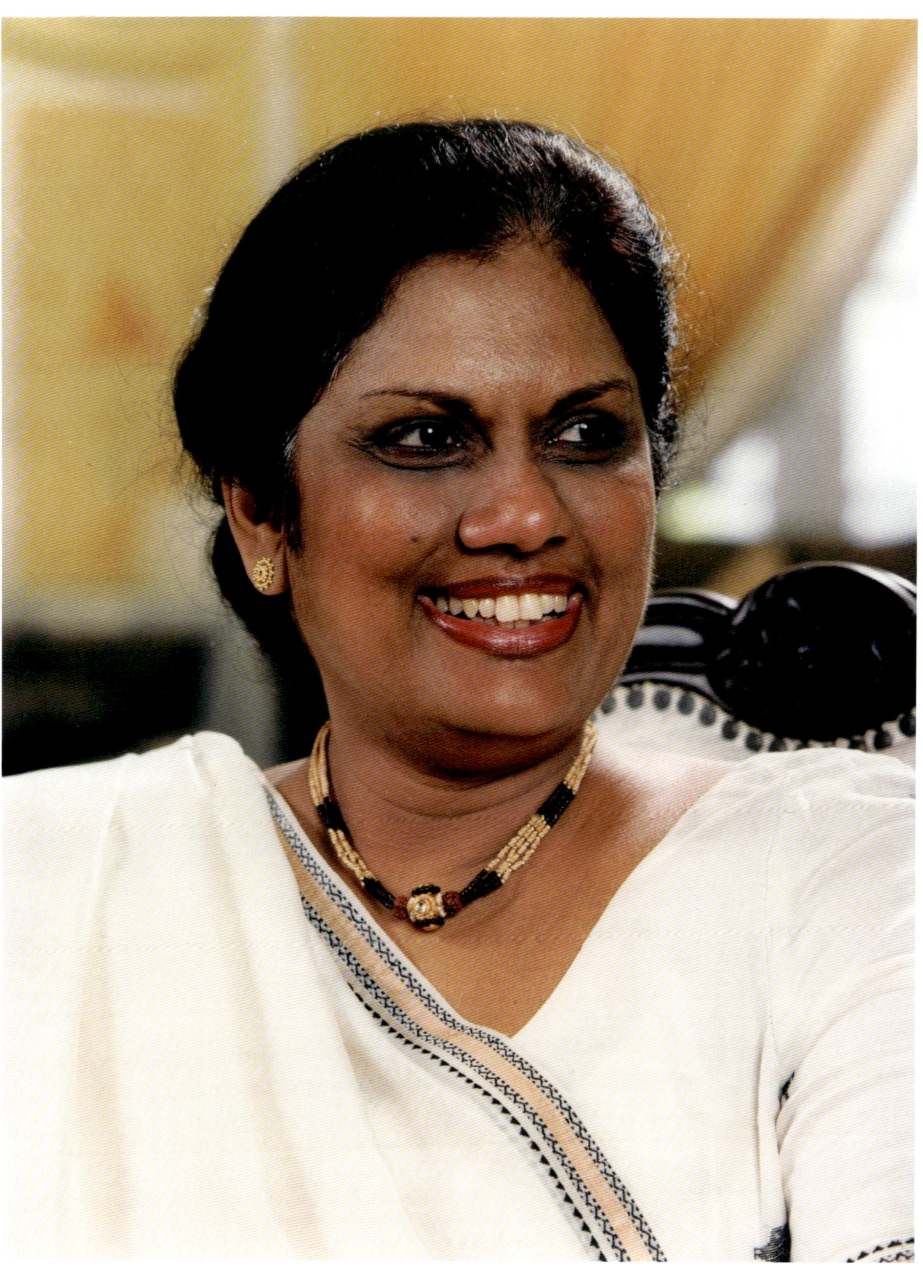

Democratic Socialist Republic of Sri Lanka –
President Chandrika Bandaranaike Kumaratunga

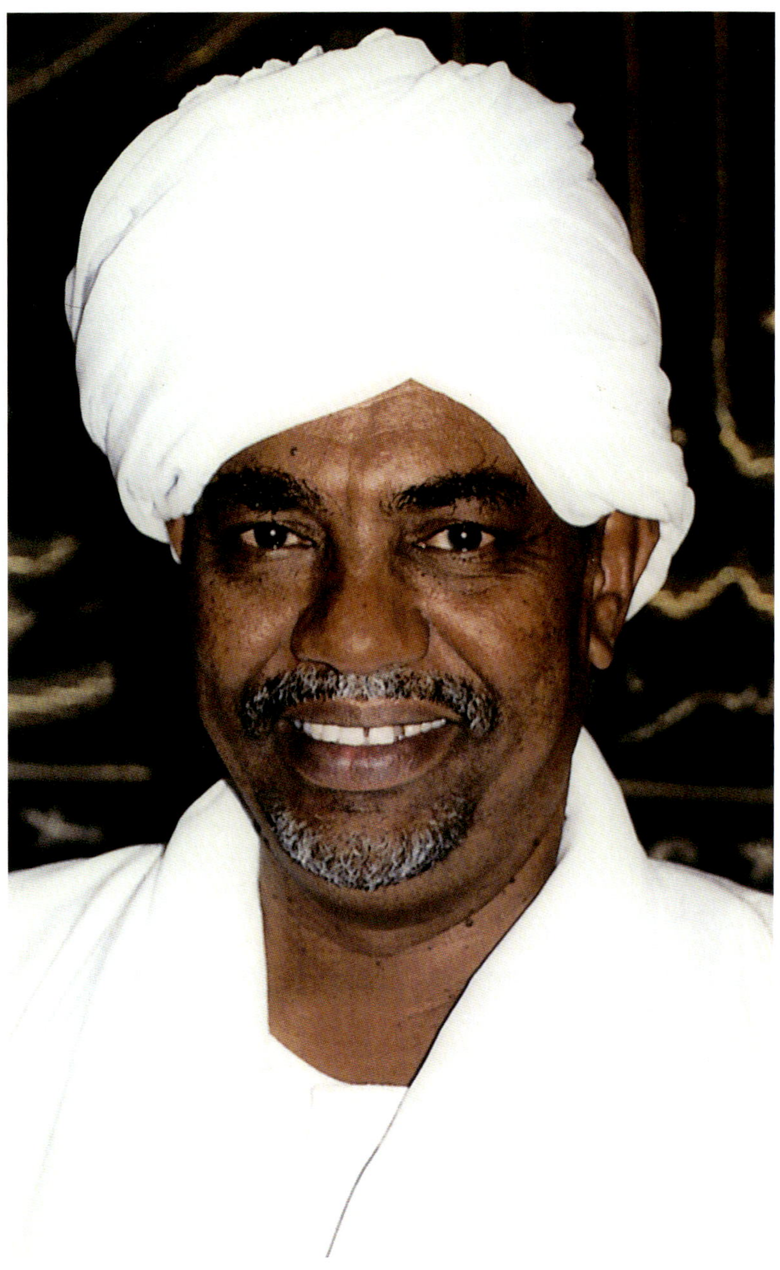

148

Republic of The Sudan – President Umar Hassan Ahmad Al-Bashir

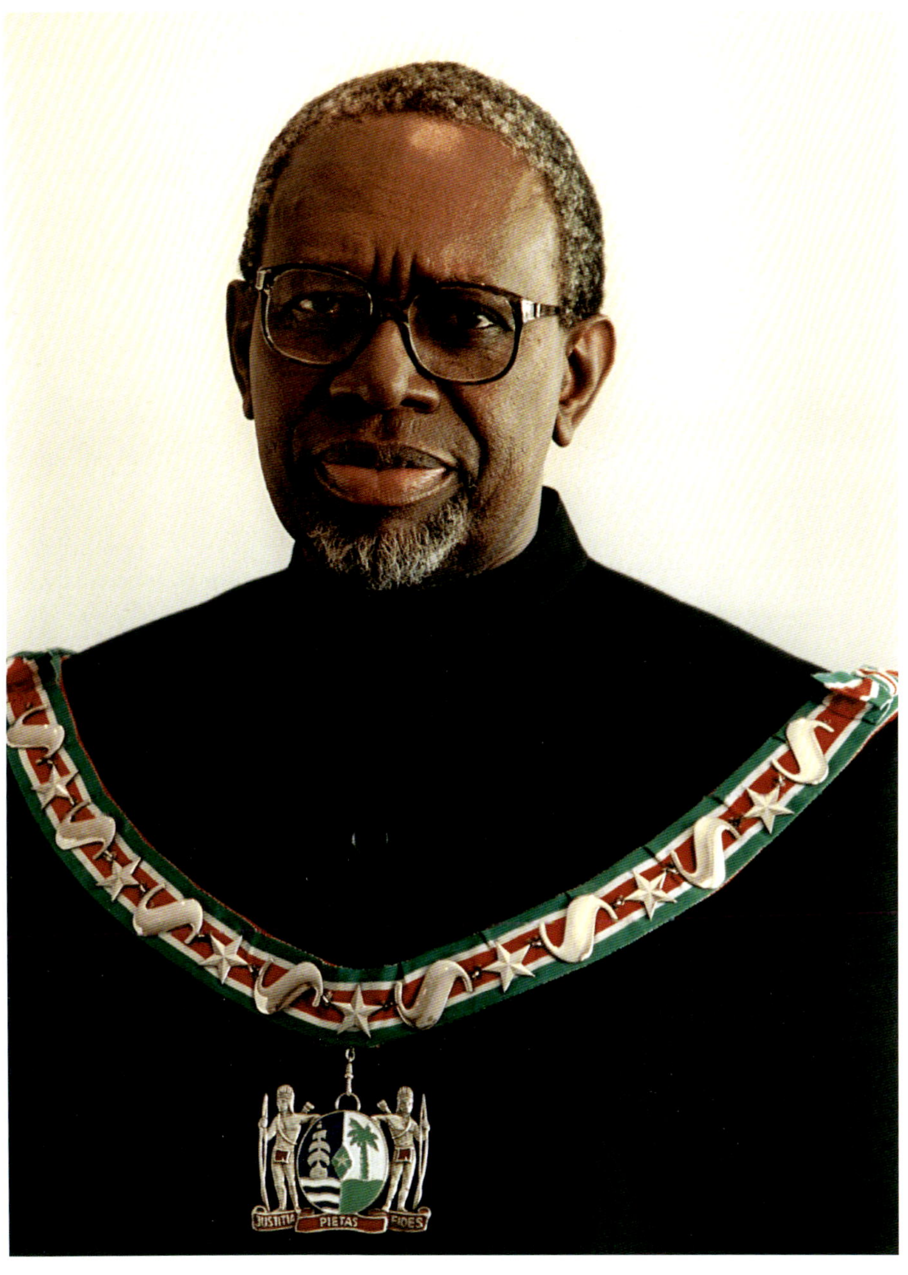

Republic of Suriname – President Runaldo Ronald Venetiaan

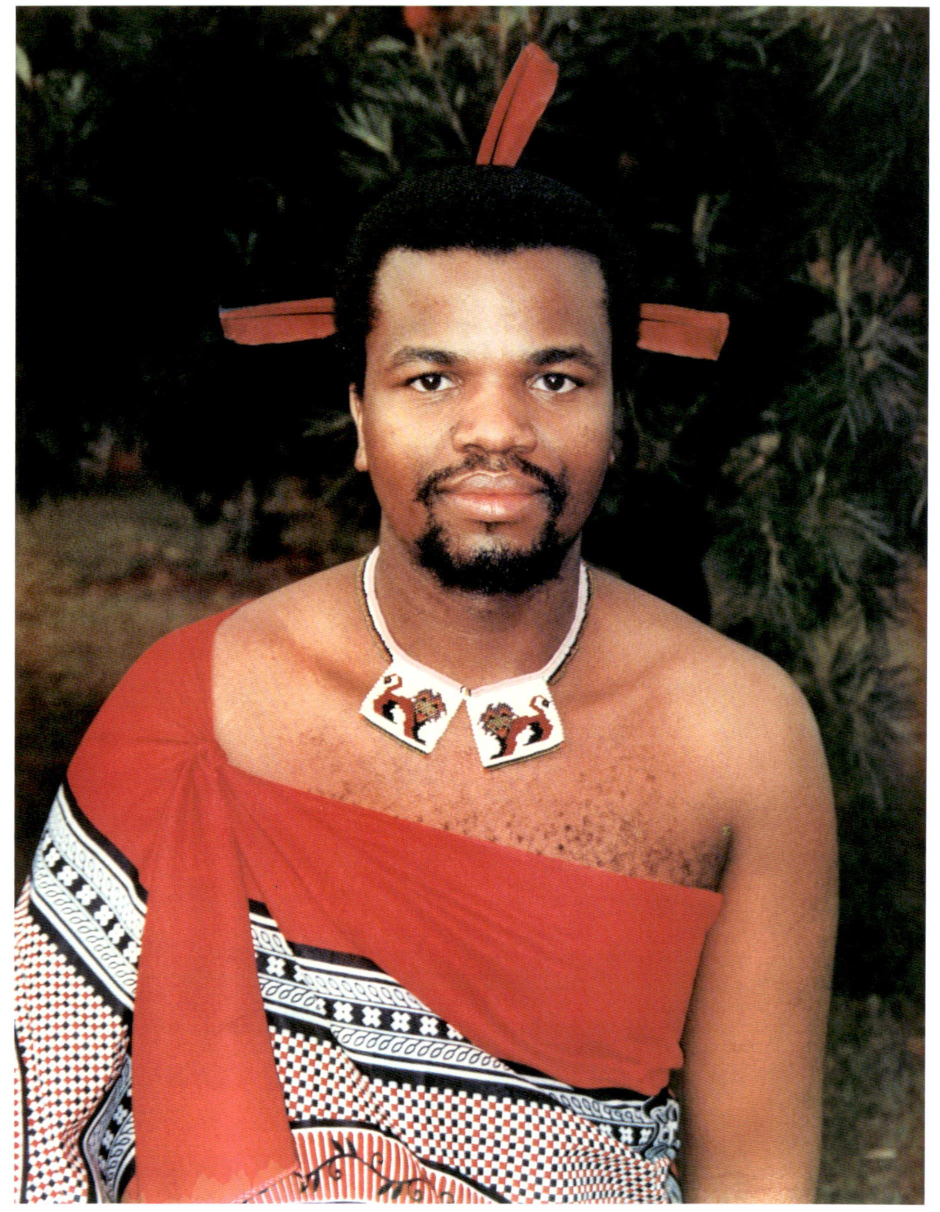

Kingdom of Swaziland – King Mswati III

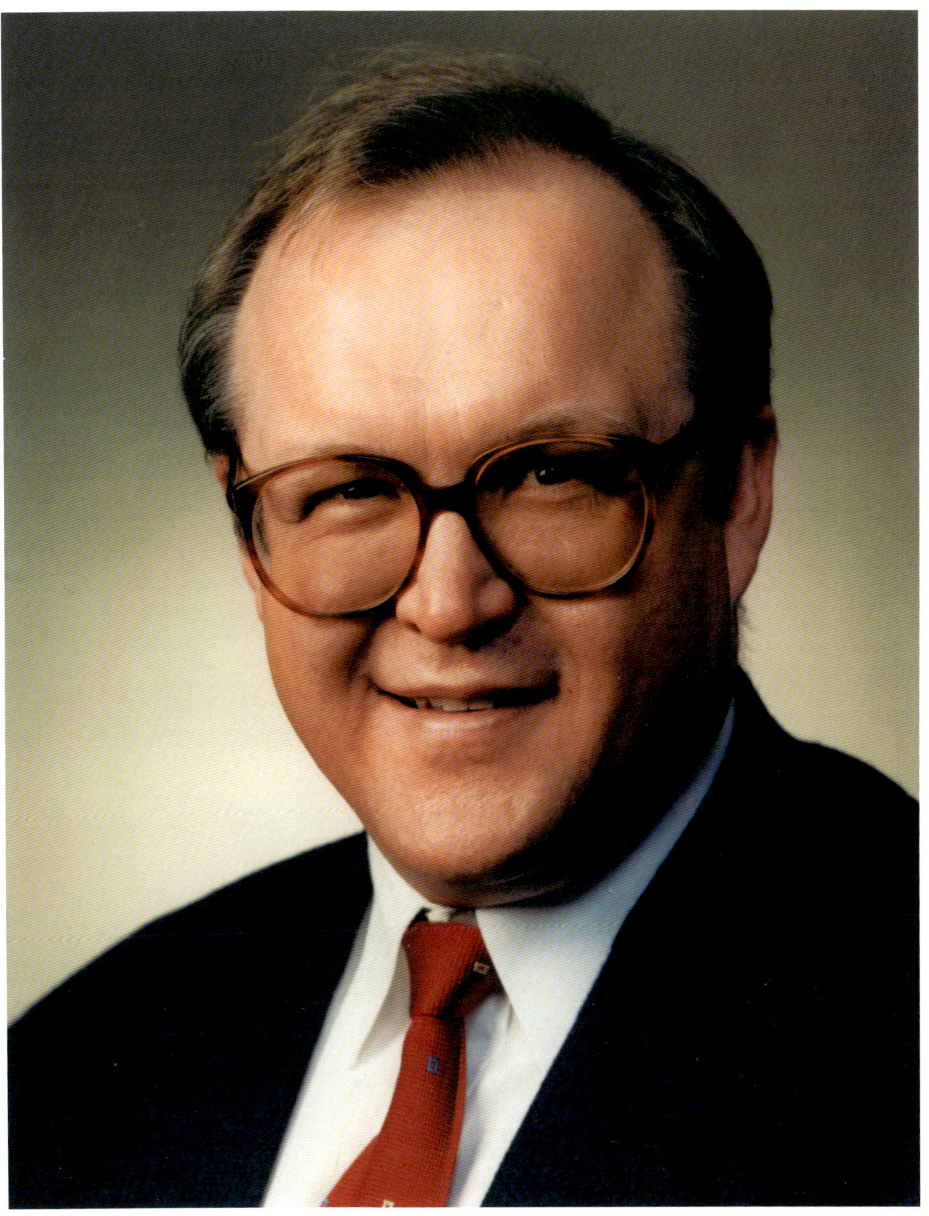

Kingdom of Sweden – Prime Minister Göran Persson

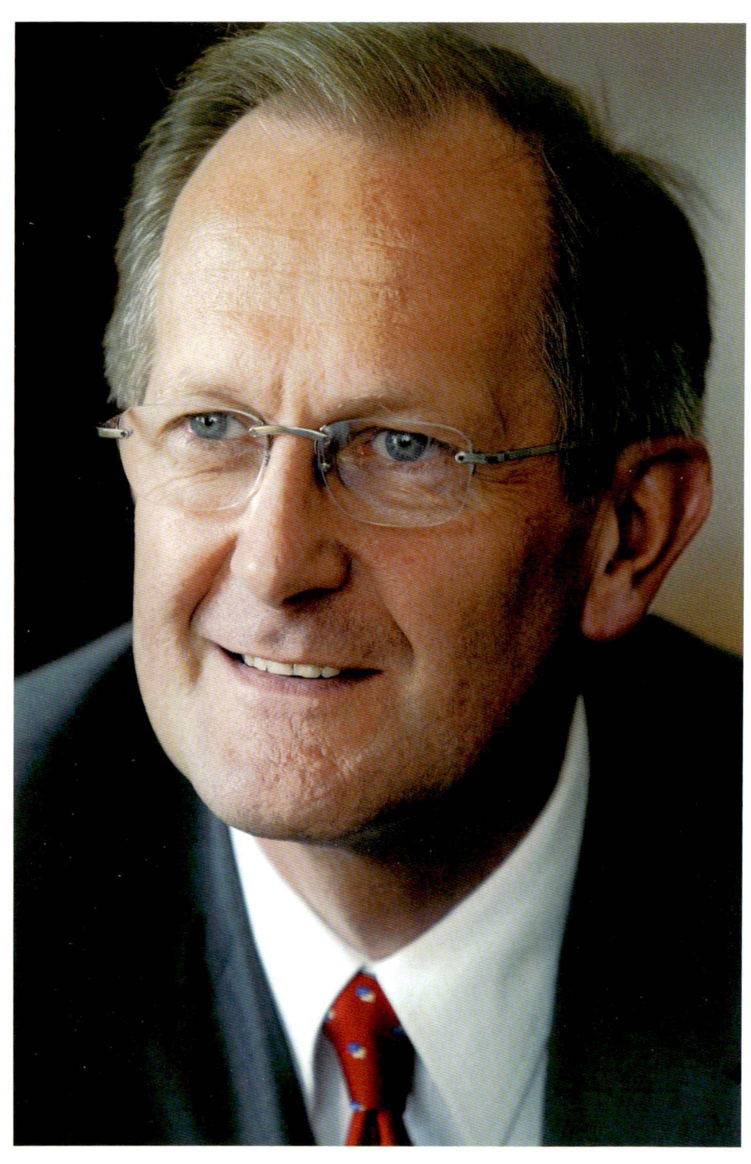

Swiss Confederation – President Joseph Deiss

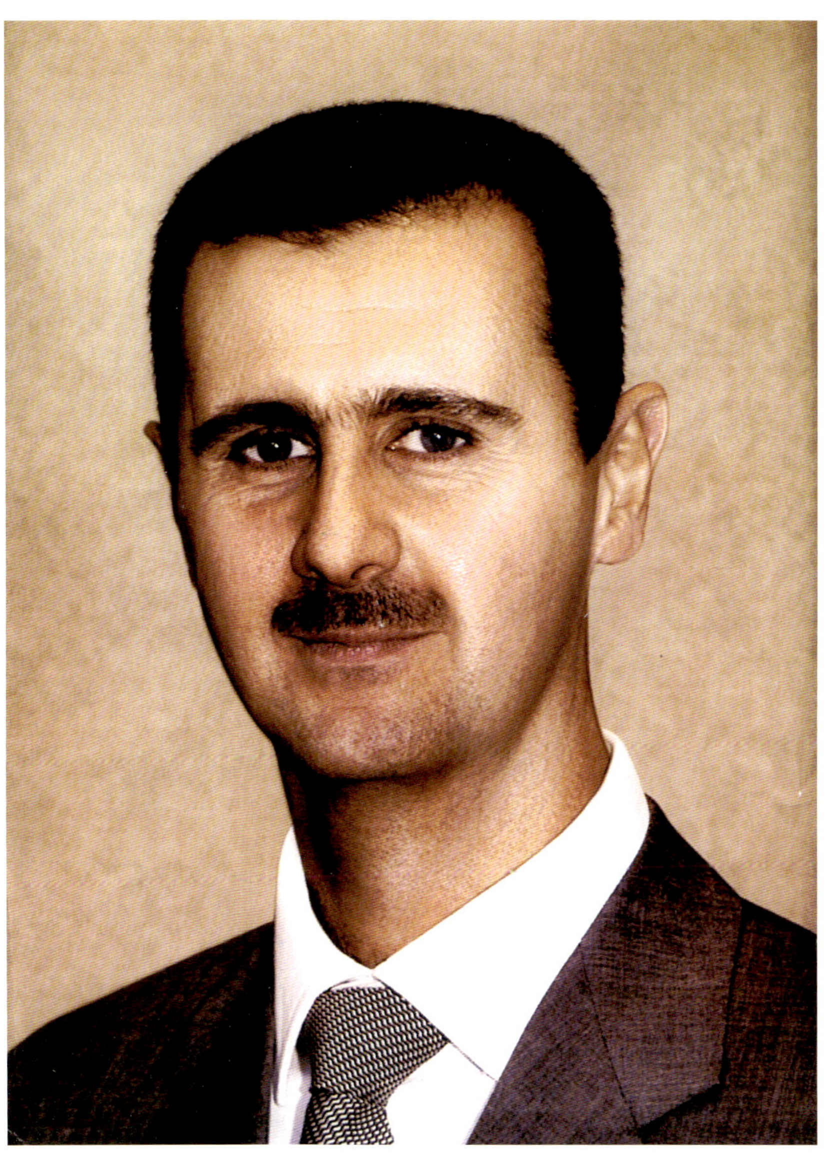

Syrian Arab Republic – President Bashar Al-Assad

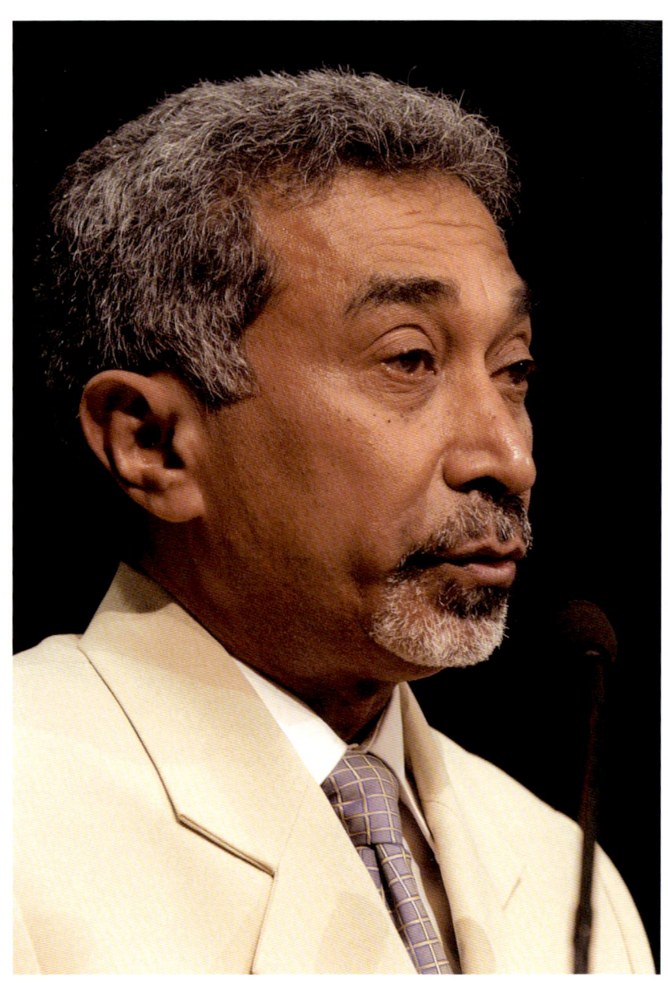

Timor-Leste – Prime Minister Mari Bin Amude Alkatiri

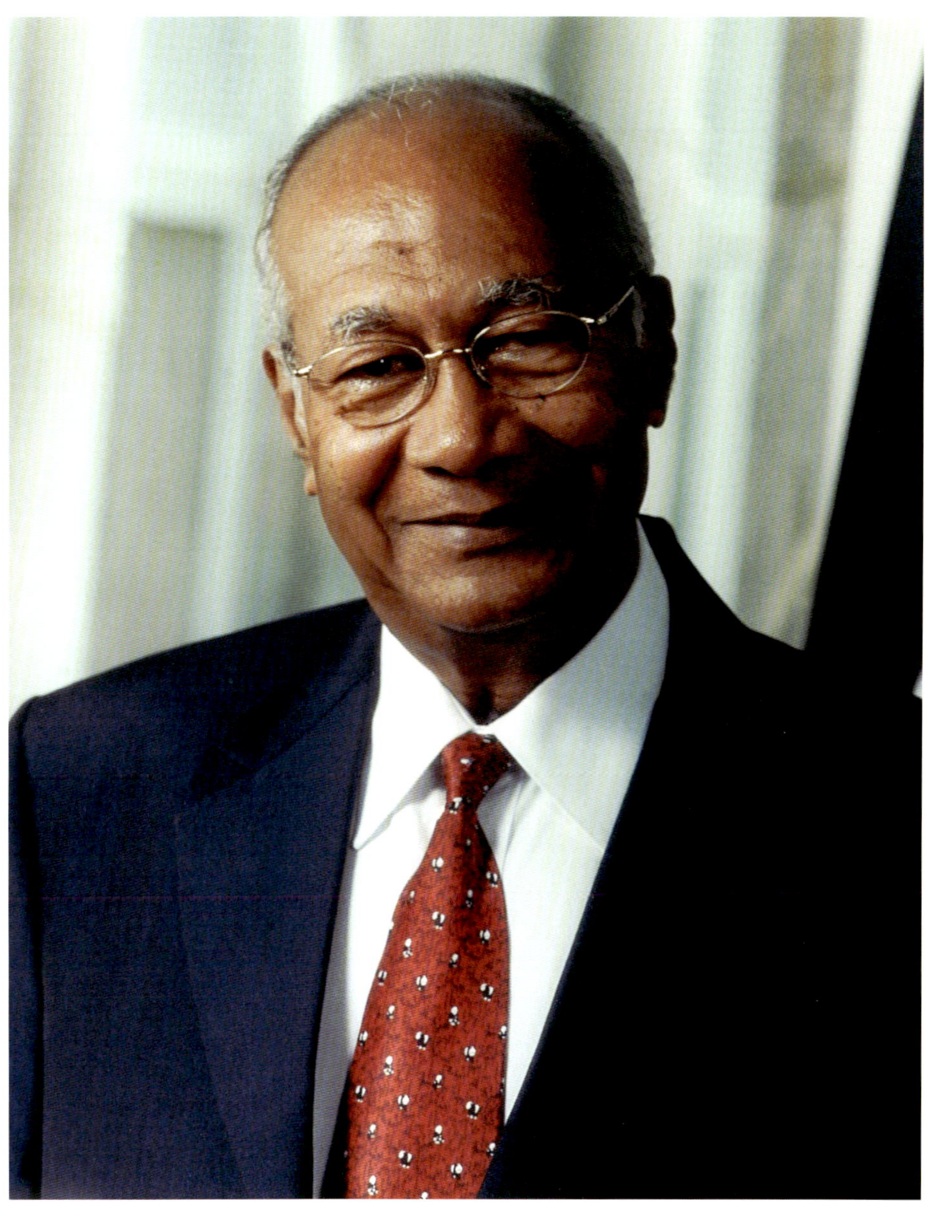

Republic of Trinidad and Tobago – President George Maxwell Richards

156

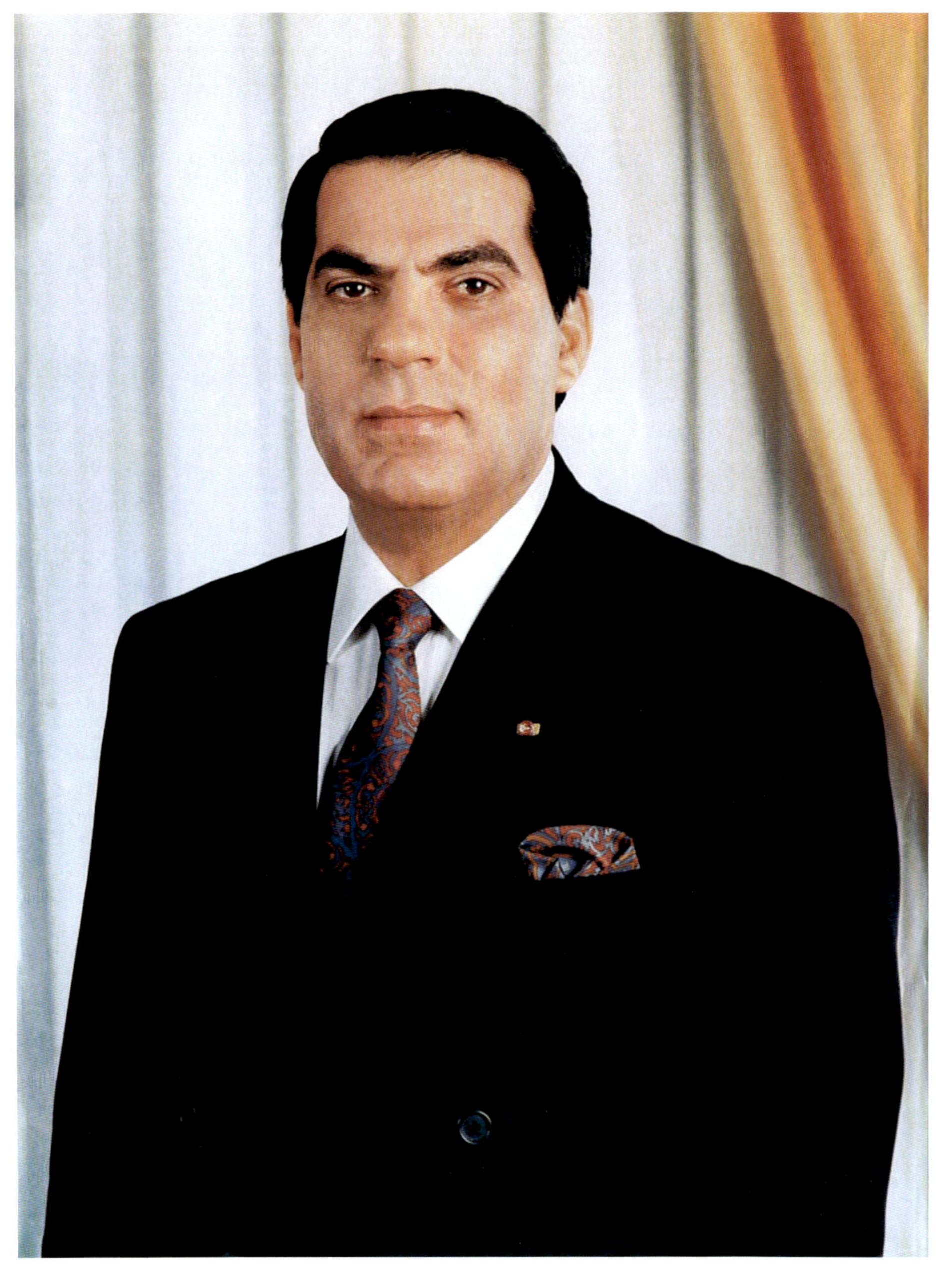

Republic of Tunisia – President Zine El Abidine Ben Ali

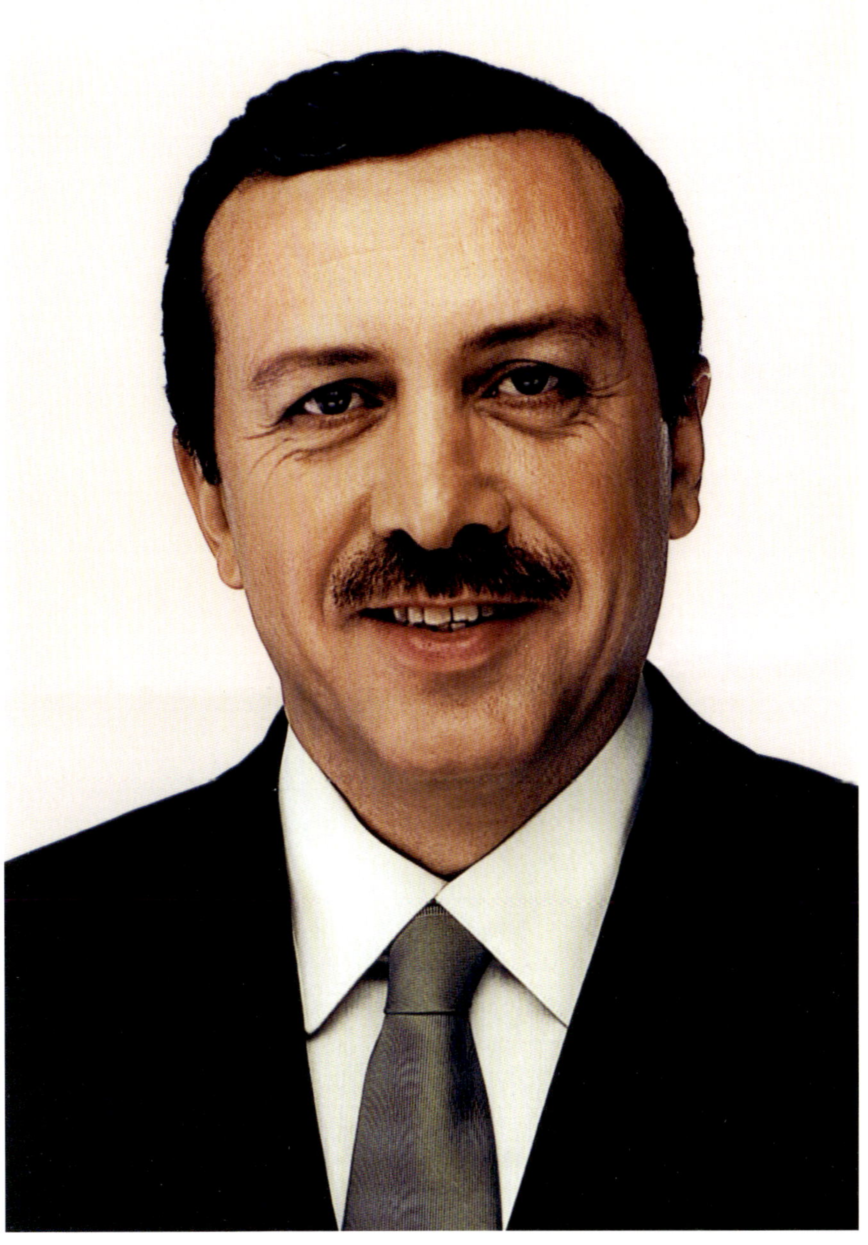

Republic of Turkey – Prime Minister Recep Tayyip Erdogan

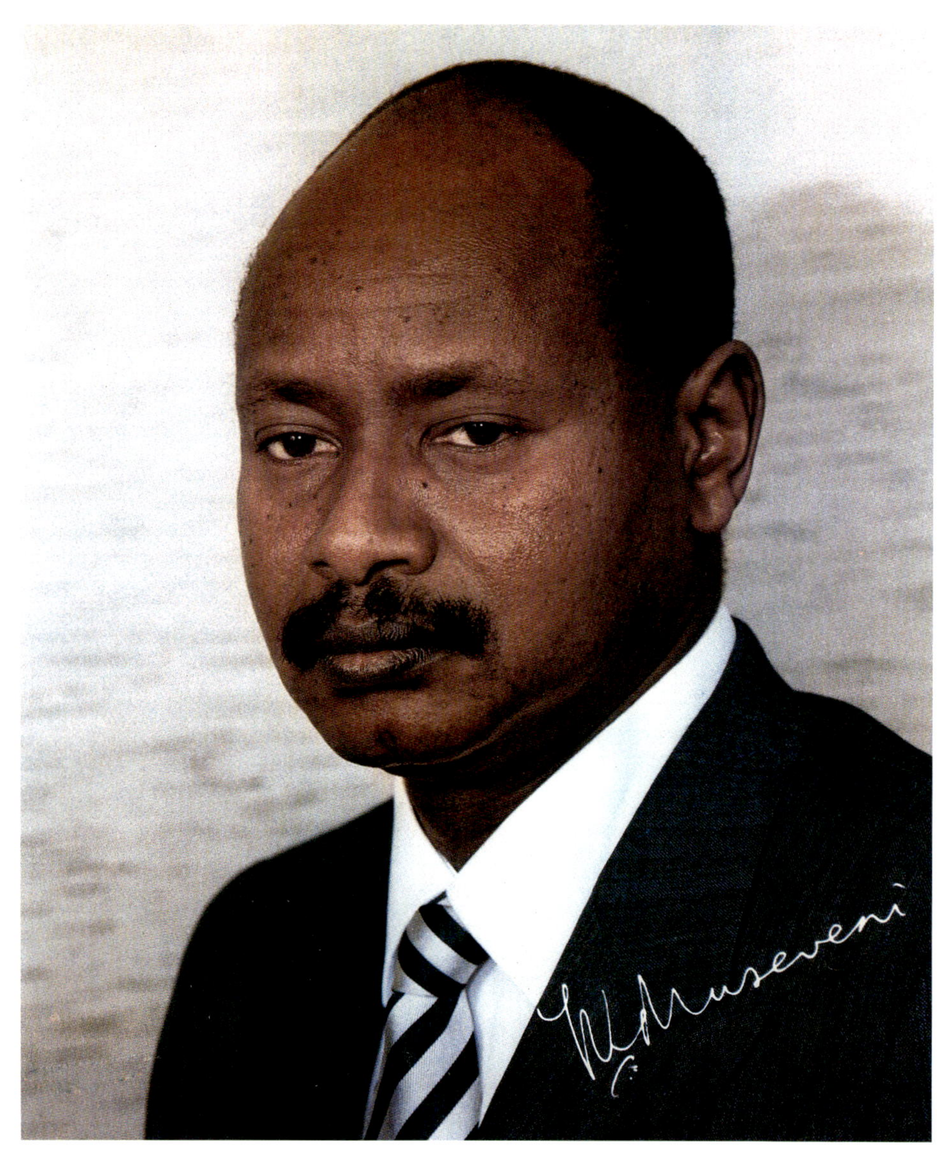

Republic of Uganda – President Yoweri Kaguta Museveni

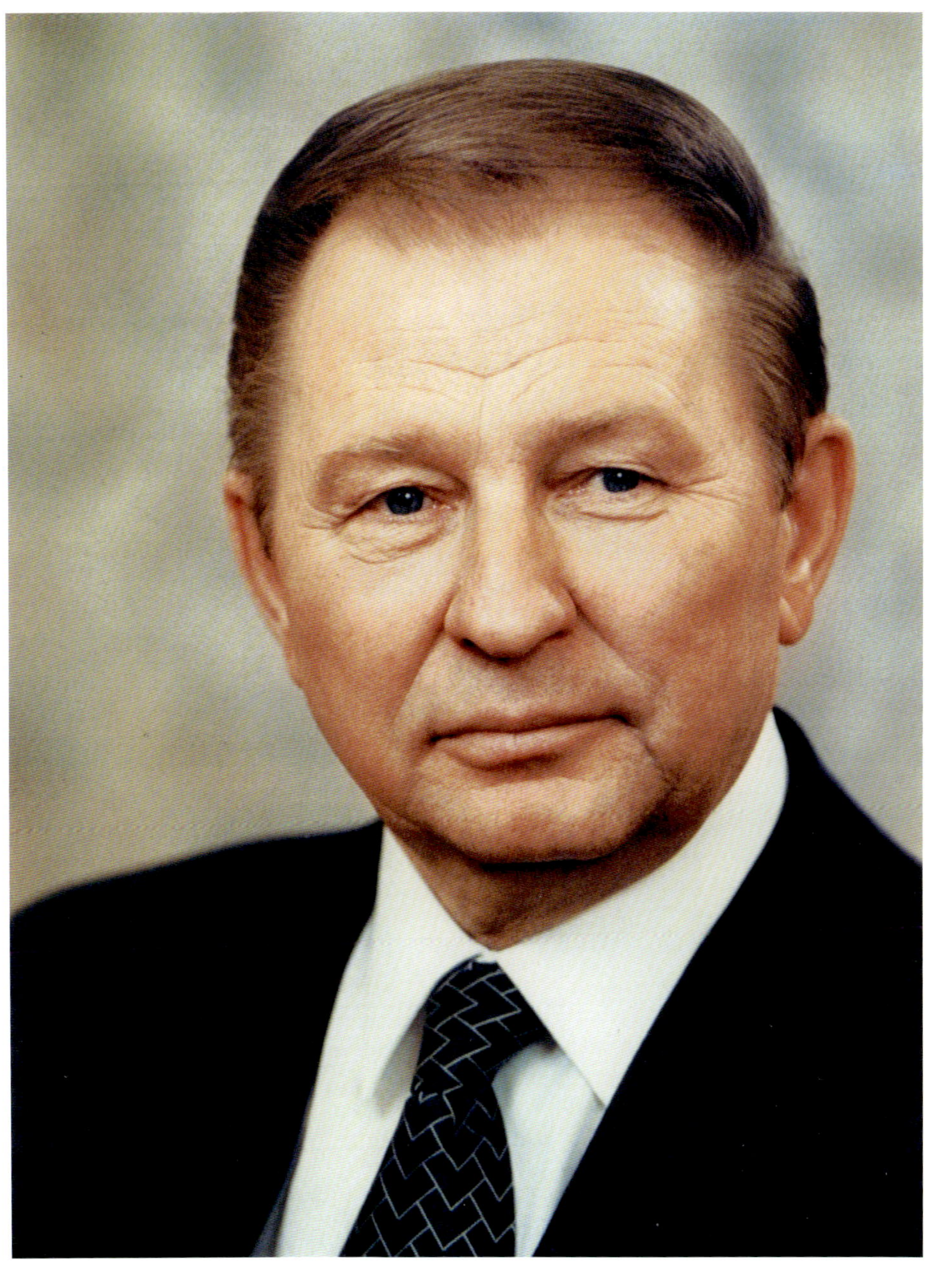

Ukraine – President M. Leonid Kuchma

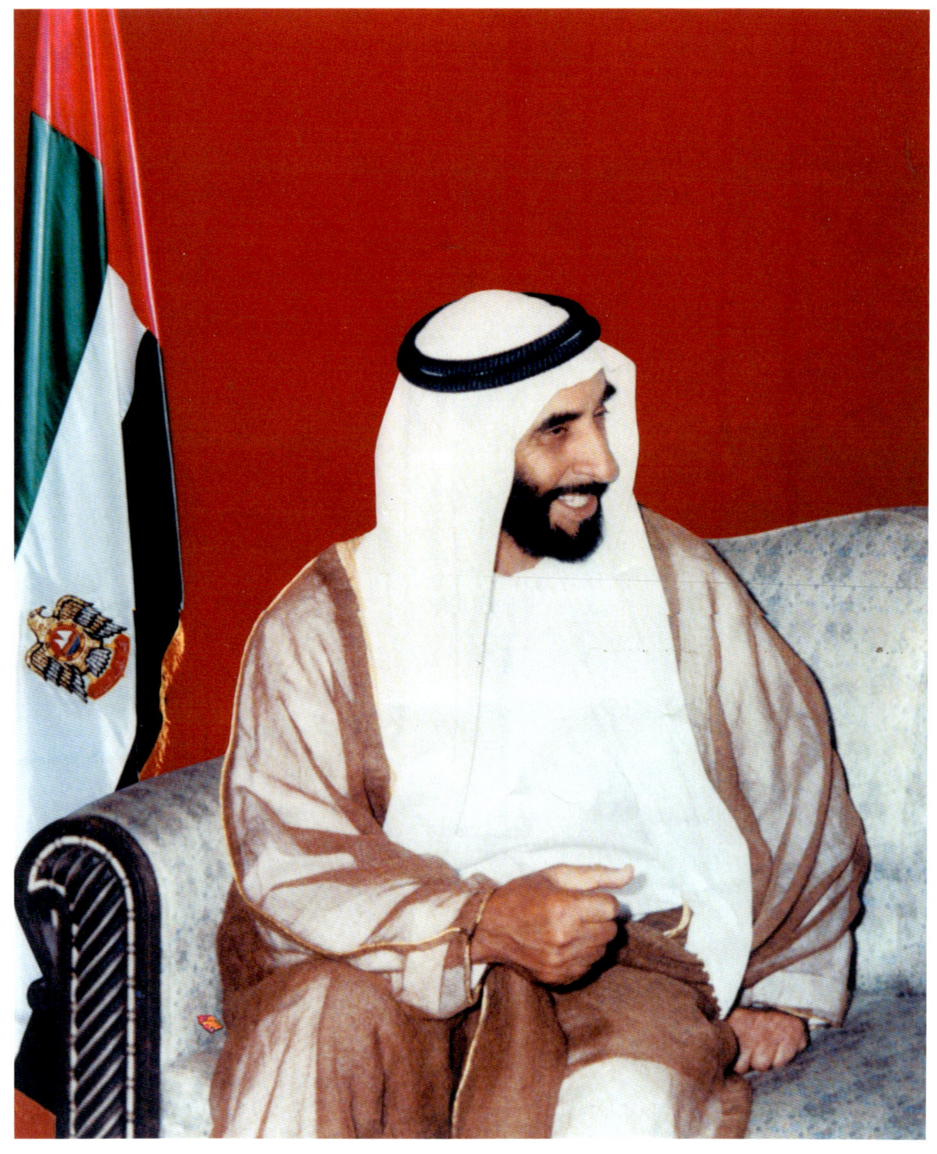

United Arab Emirates – President of the United Arab Emirates and Ruler of Abu Dhabi
Sheikh Zayed Bin Sultan Al-Nahyan

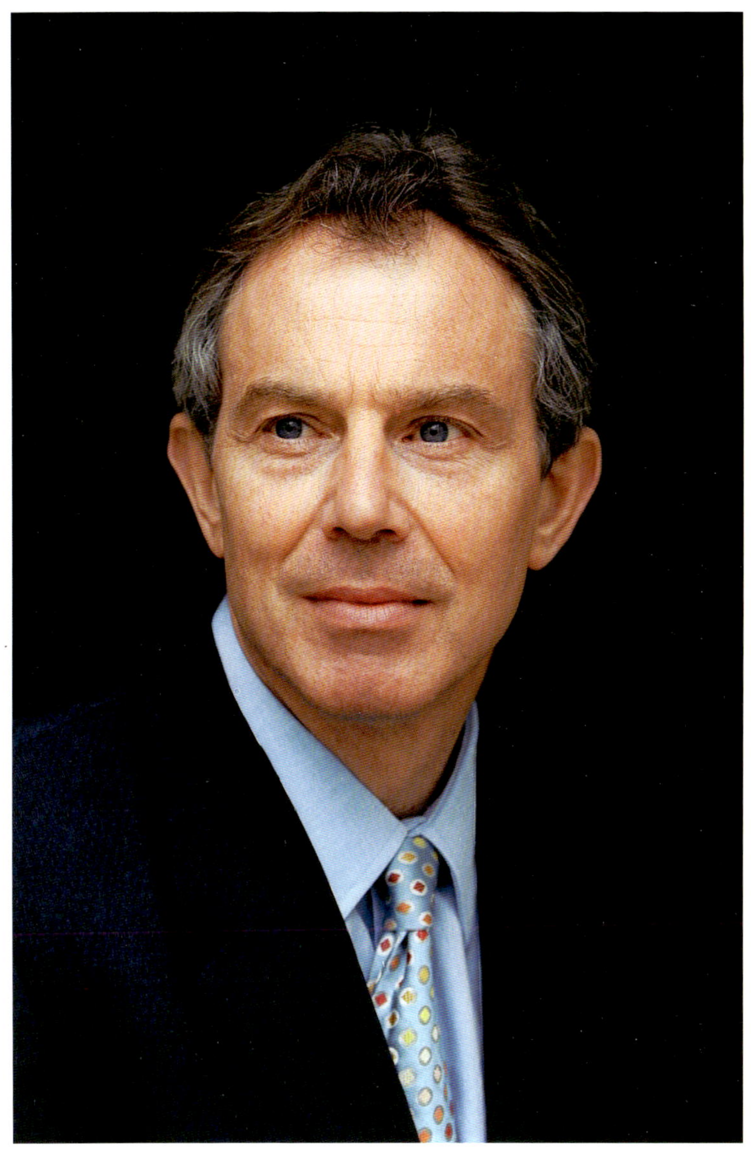

161

United Kingdom of Great Britain & Northern Ireland – Prime Minister Tony Blair

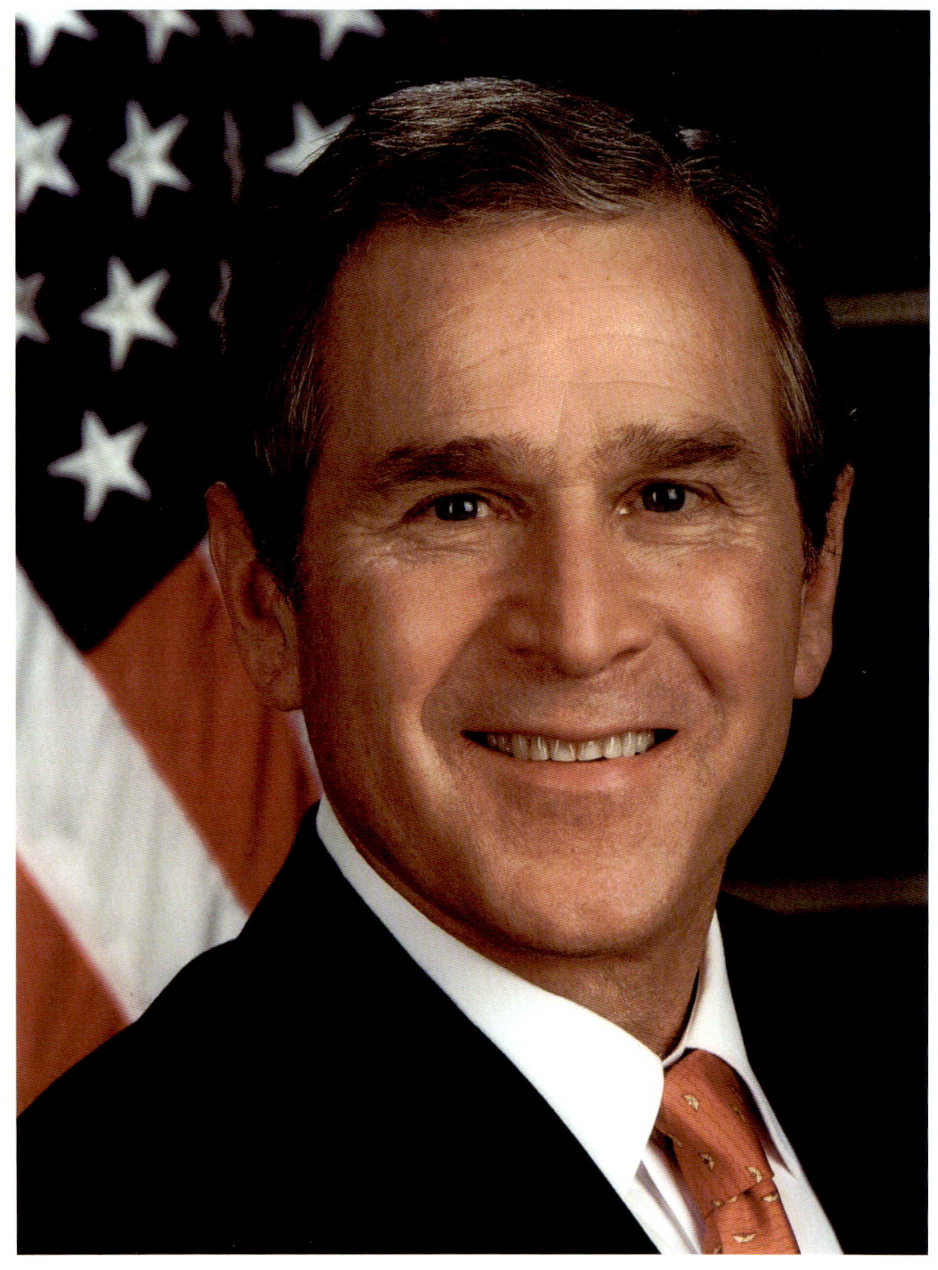

United States of America – President George W. Bush

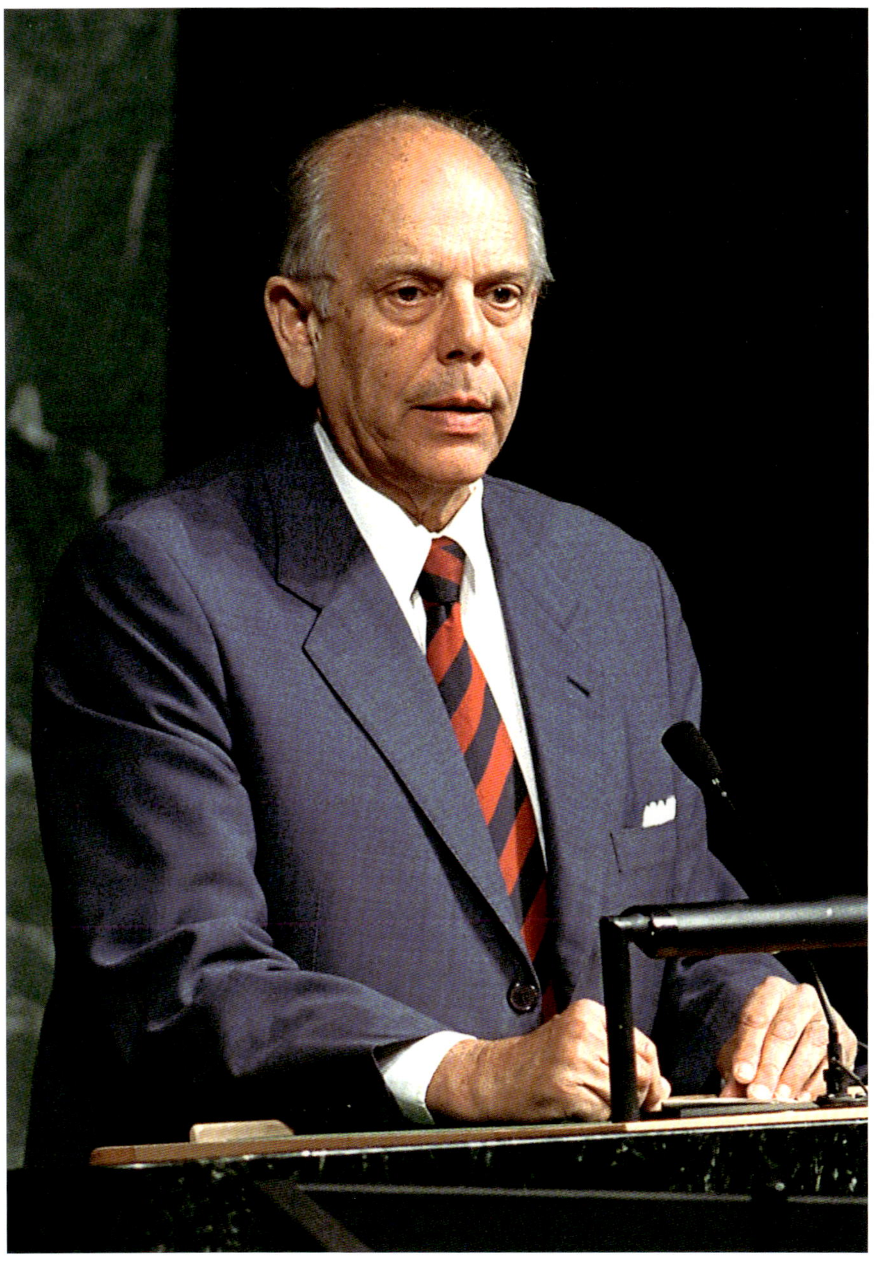

Oriental Republic of Uruguay – President Jorge Batlle Ibañez

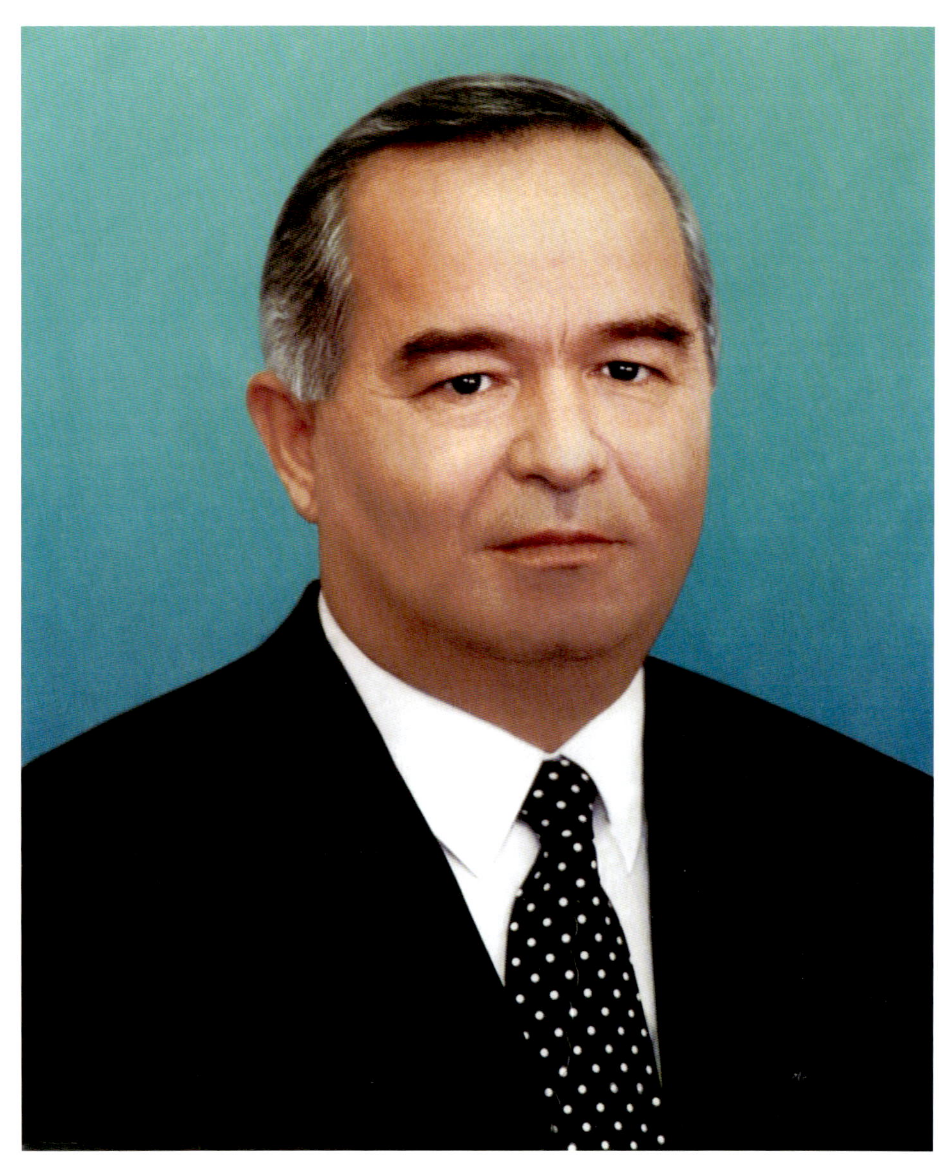

Republic of Uzbekistan – President Islom Karimov

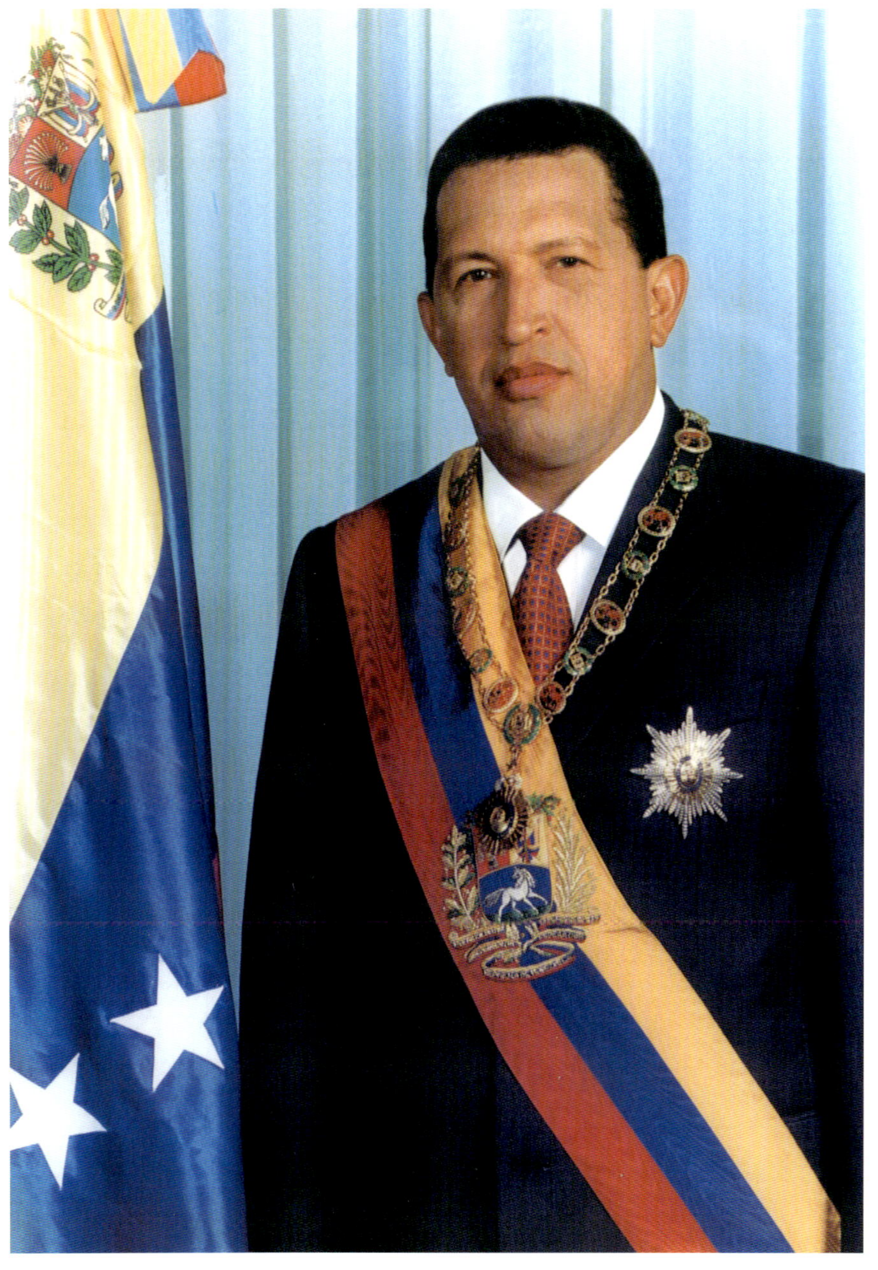

Bolivarian Republic of Venezuela – President Hugo Chavez

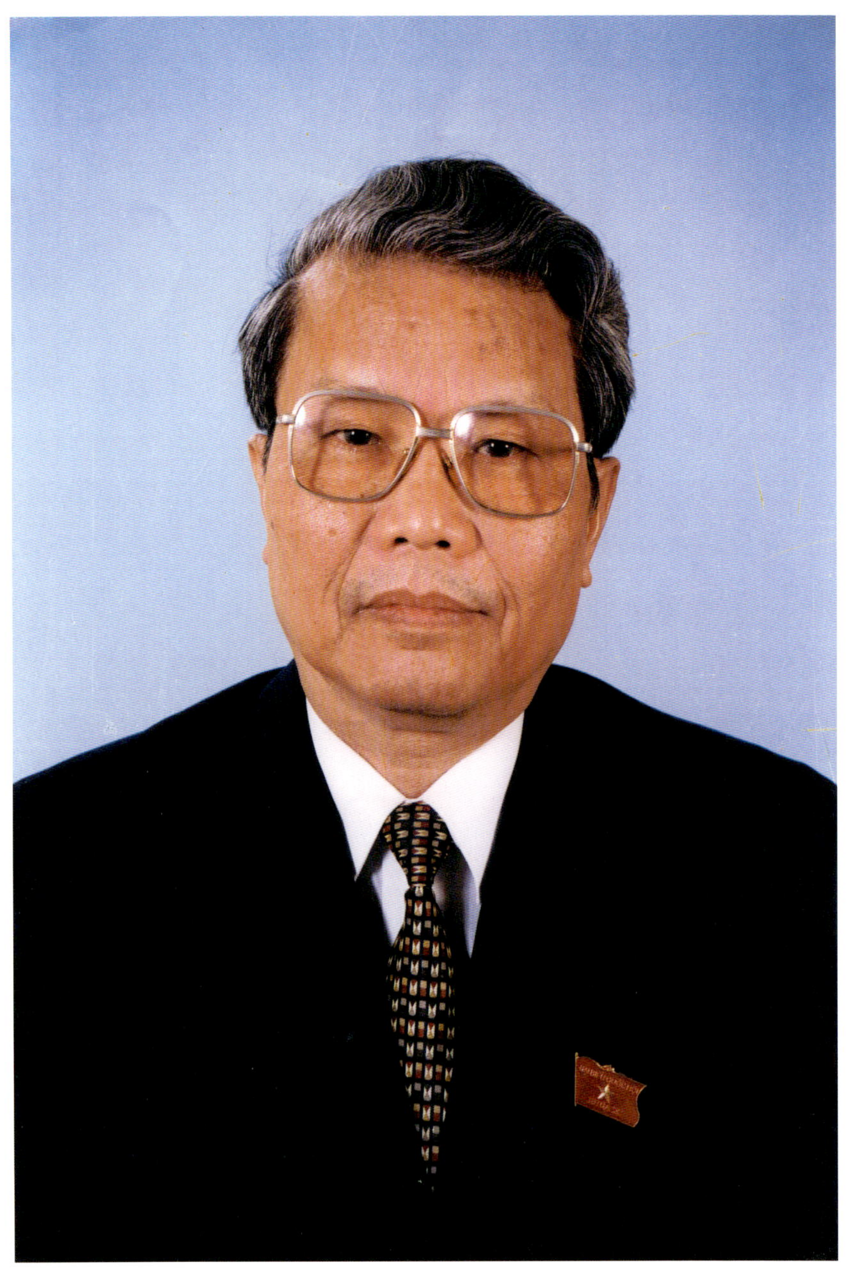

Socialist Republic of Vietnam – President Tran Duc Luong

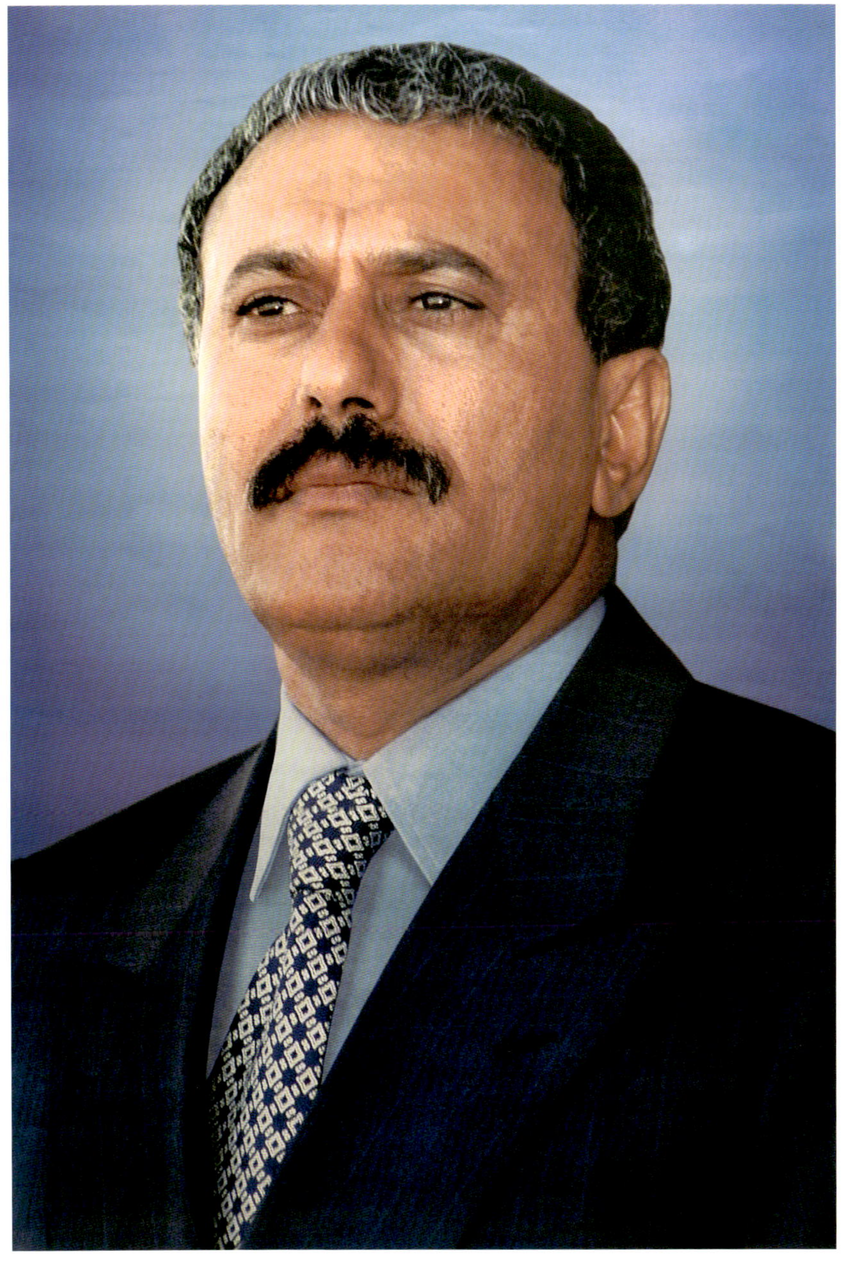

Republic of Yemen – President Ali Abdullah Saleh

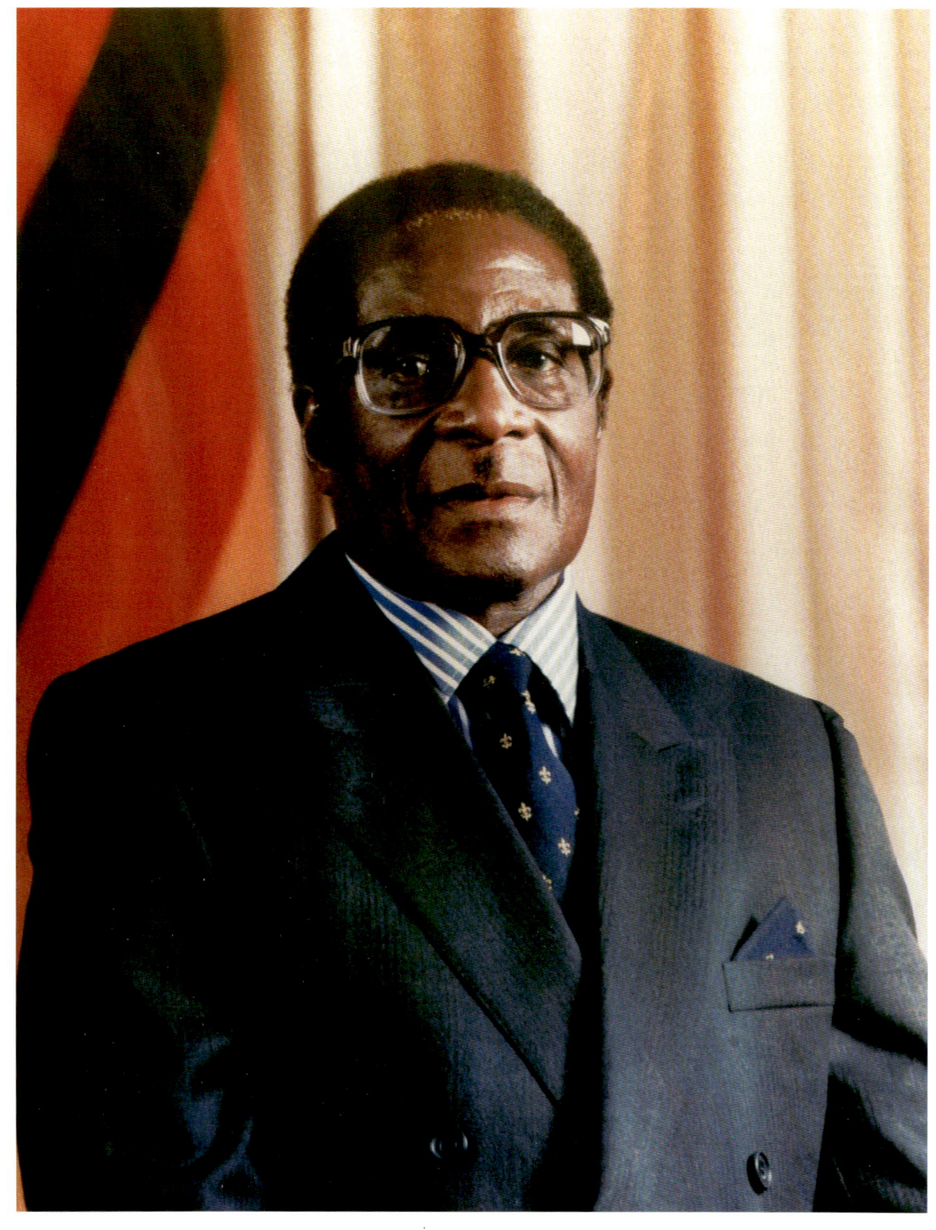

Republic of Zimbabwe – President Robert Gabriel Mugabe

The countries whose official portrait did not meet our print requirements
are in the following section

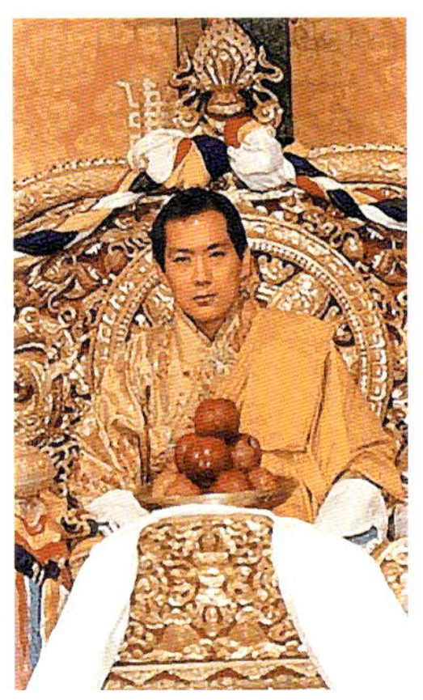

Kingdom of Bhutan
King Jigme Singye Wangchuck

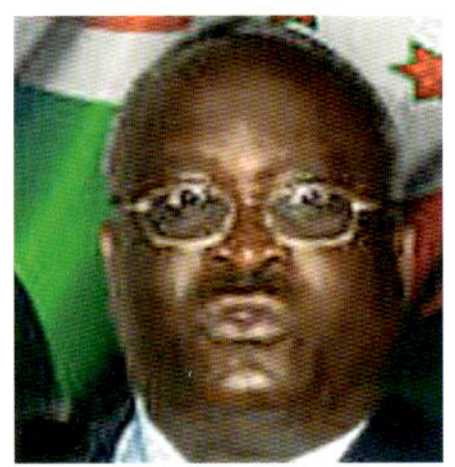

Republic of Burundi
President Domitien Ndayizeye

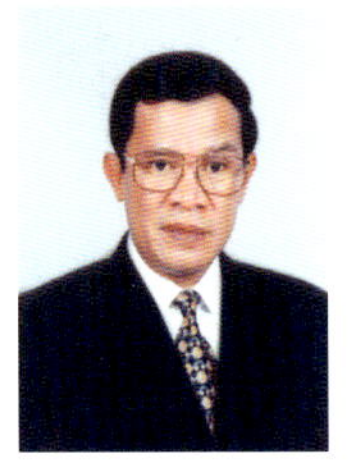

Kingdom of Cambodia
Prime Minister Samdech Hun Sen

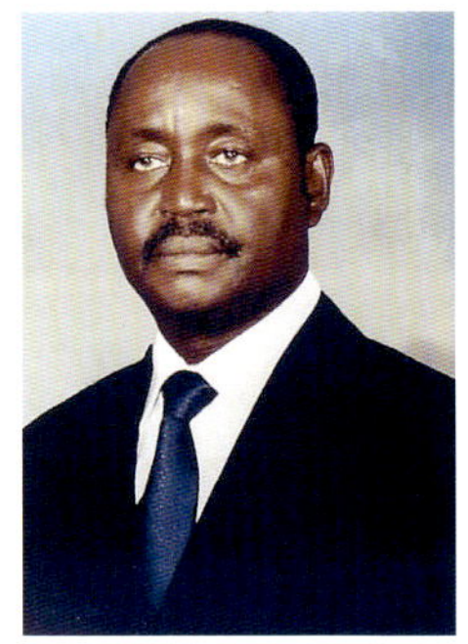

Central African Republic
President François Bozize

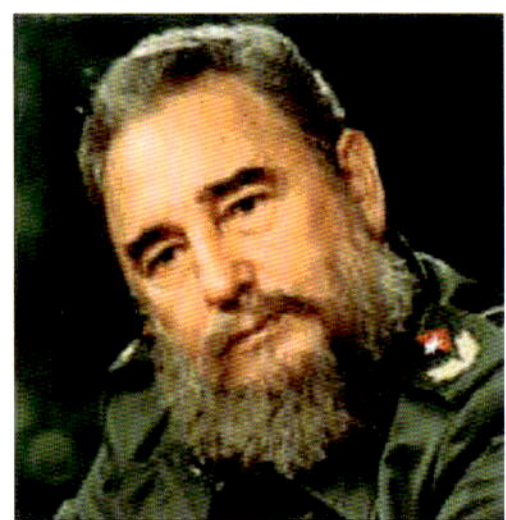

Republic of Cuba
President of the Council of State
Fidel Castro Ruz

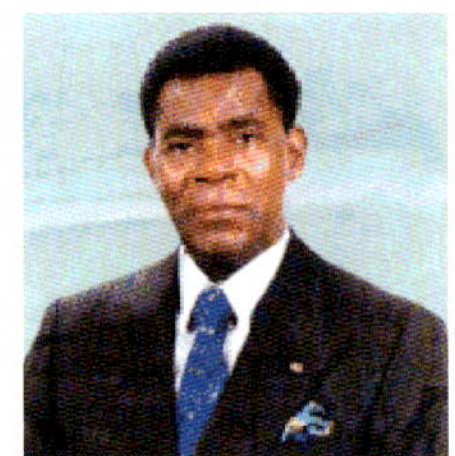

Republic of Equatorial Guinea
President Teodoro Obiang Nguema

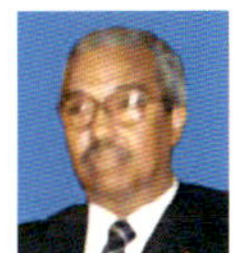

Guinea-Bissau
President Henrique Rosa

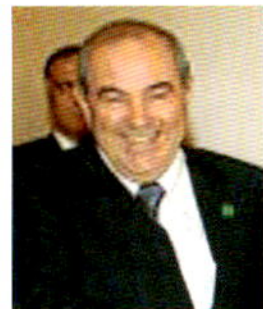

Republic of Iraq
Prime Minister of the Interim Government
Iyad Allawi

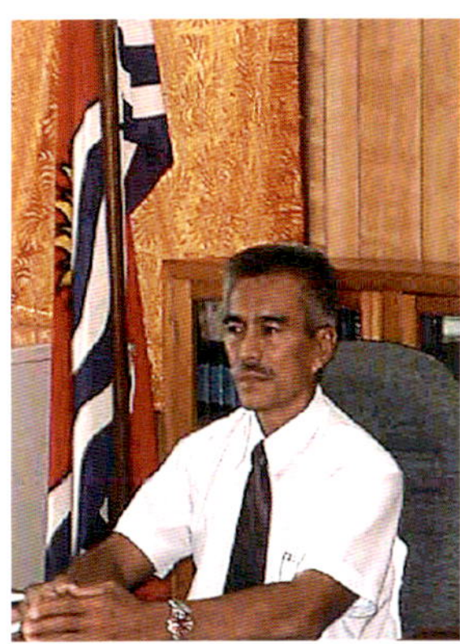

Republic of Kiribati
President Anote Tong

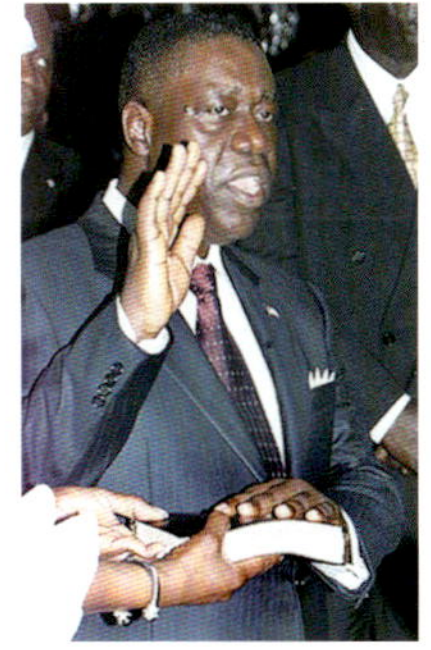

Republic of Liberia
Chairman Gyude Bryant

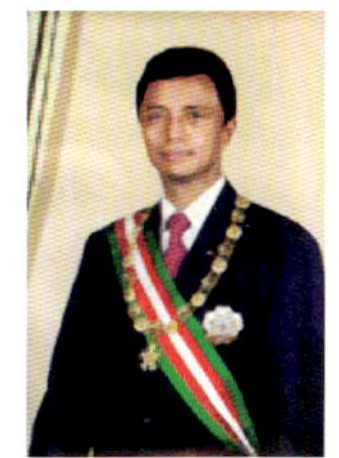

Republic of Madagascar
President Marc Ravalomanana

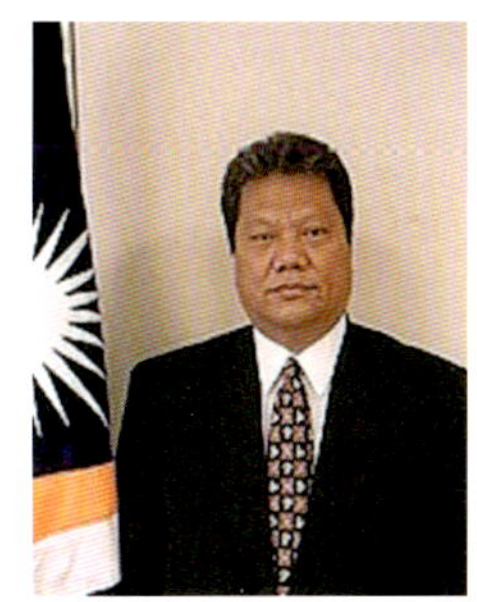

Republic of the Marshall Islands
President Kessai Hesa Note

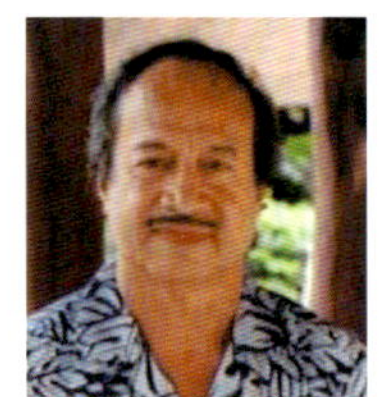

Republic of Nauru
President Ludwig Scotty

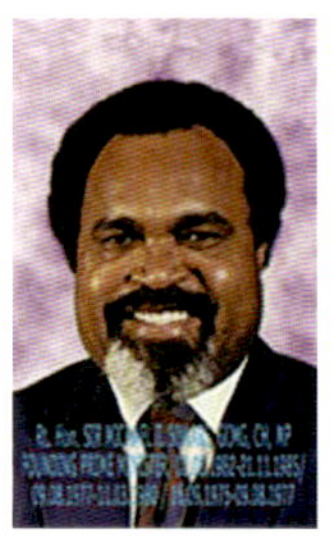

Independent State of Papua New Guinea
Prime Minister Sir Michael Somare

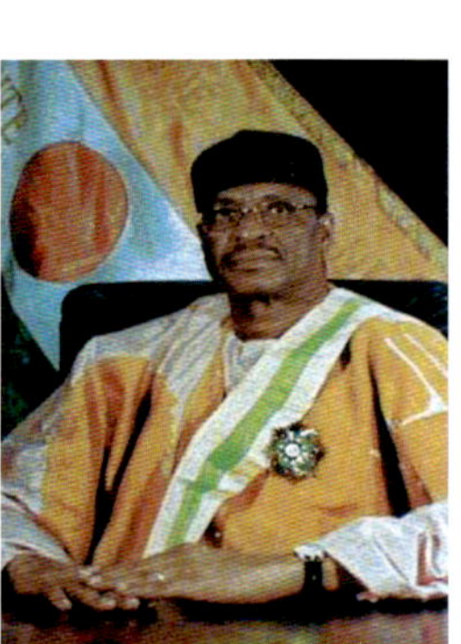

Republic of Niger
President Tandja Mamadou

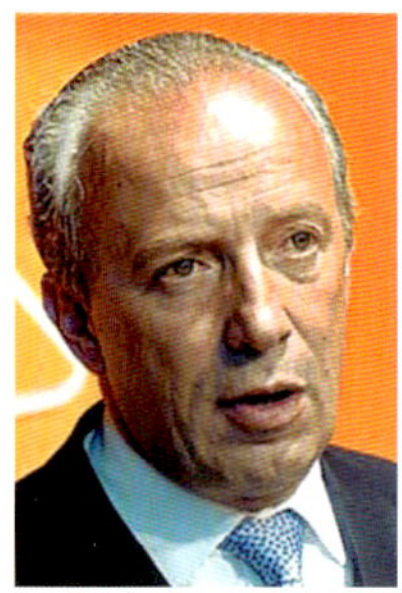

Republic of Portugal
Prime Minister Pedro Santana Lopes

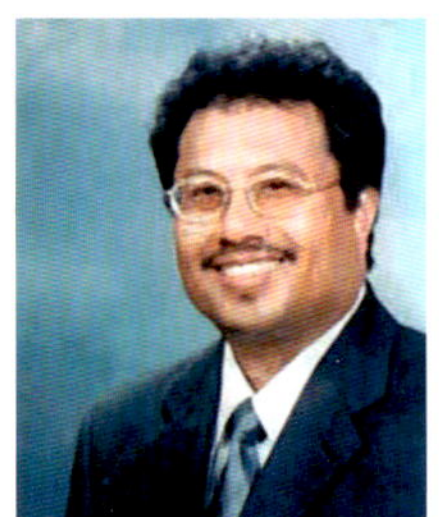

Republic of Palau
President Tommy Esang Remengesau, Jr.

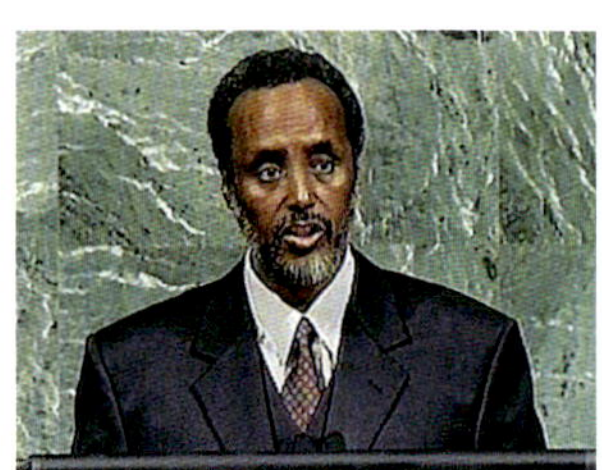

Somalia
President Salad Hassan Abdikassim

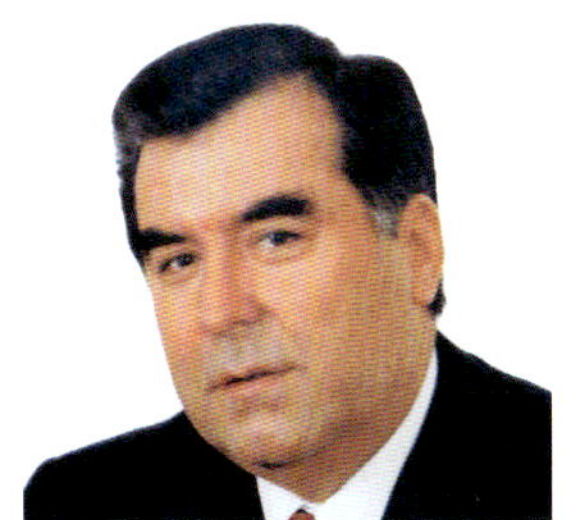

Tajikistan – President Emomali Rahmonov

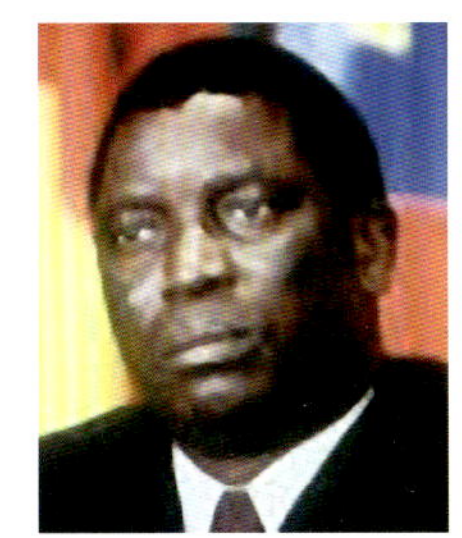

Republic of Togo
President Gnassingbe Eyadema

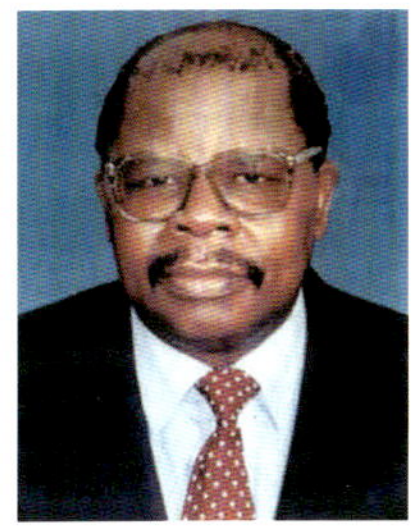

United Republic of Tanzania
President Benjamin William Mkapa

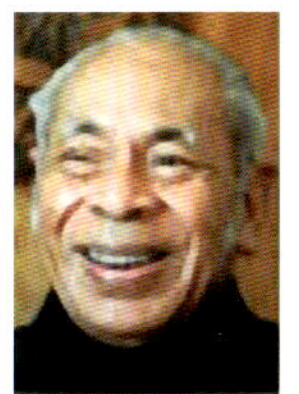

Kingdom of Tonga
King Taufa'Ahau Tupou IV

173

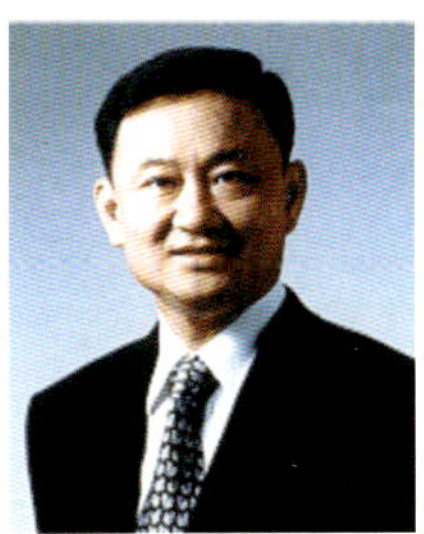

Kingdom of Thailand
Prime Minister Thaksin Chinnawat

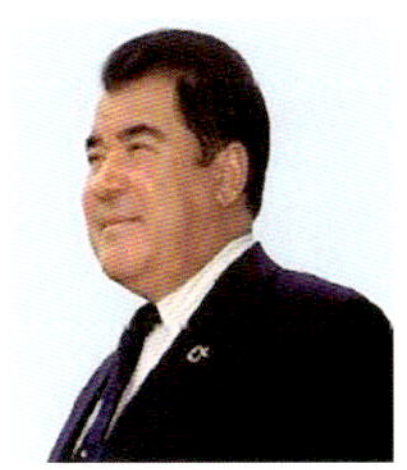

Turkmenistan
President Saparmurat Niyazov

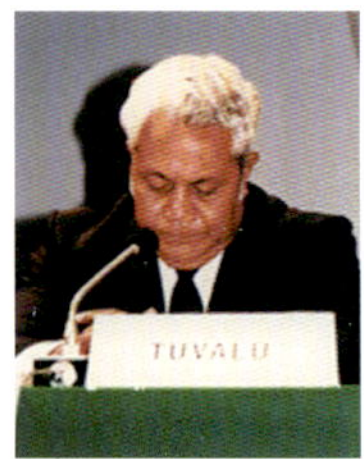

Tuvalu – Prime Minister Maatia Toafa

174

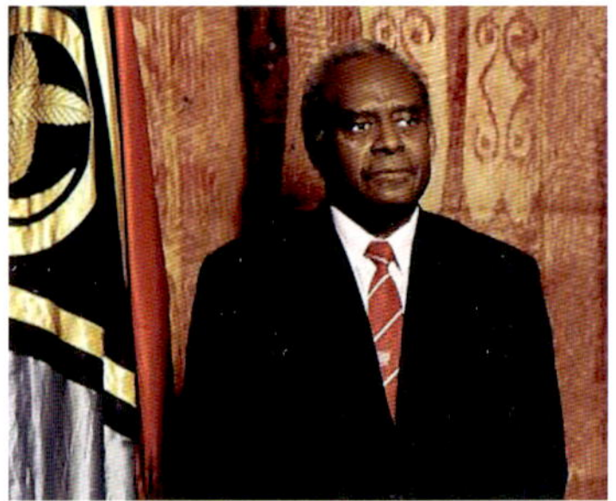

Republic of Vanuatu – President Kalkot Mataskelekele

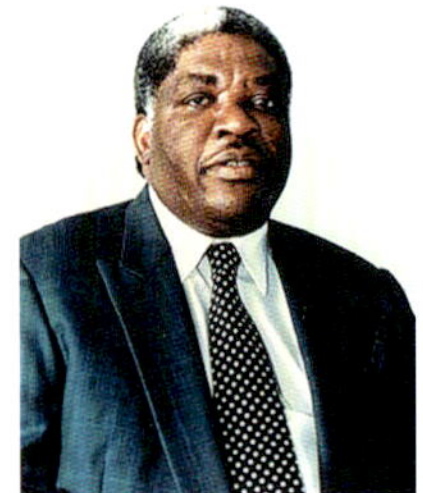

Republic of Zambia – President Levy P. Mwanawasa

INDEX

Imprint

Published by Trolley Ltd, 2004
www.trolleybooks.com

A Berlin Press publication
Licensed edition by Trolley
© Berlin Press

Editor:
Klaus Zwangsleitner

Project Management:
David Brown

Pepe Egger
Tamara Hurrell
Mathew Platt
Anna Schori
Lydia Tan .
Assistance:
Mahab Kazmi
Jennifer Kendall

Embassy Portrait Photography:
Klaus Madengruber

Design:
Iconic

Printed in Italy by Soso

Thank you to Isabelle Moffat

The following photographers
were explicitly credited
by the submitting state:

Azerbaijan: Rafig Bagirov
Bosnia & Herzegovina: Senad Kusevic
Bulgaria: Nikolay Nikolov
Haiti: Nesly Laude
Lithuania: Gunda Barysaite
Sierra Leone: Amadu Daramy
Sweden: Håkan Petterss
Israel: GPO